GREAT CRAFT PROJECTS FROM AROUND THE WORLD

written & illustrated
by
William Reid

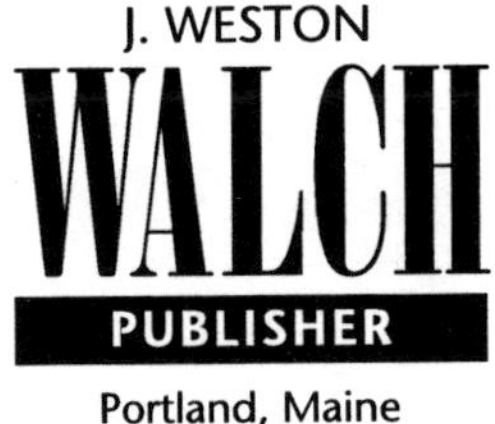

User's Guide
to
Walch Reproducible Books

As part of our general effort to provide educational materials that are as practical and economical as possible, we have designated this publication a "reproducible book." The designation means that purchase of the book includes purchase of the right to limited reproduction of all pages on which this symbol appears:

Here is the basic Walch policy: We grant to individual purchasers of this book the right to make sufficient copies of reproducible pages for use by all students of a single teacher. This permission is limited to a single teacher and does not apply to entire schools or school systems, so institutions purchasing the book should pass the permission on to a single teacher. Copying of the book or its parts for resale is prohibited.

Any questions regarding this policy or requests to purchase further reproduction rights should be addressed to:

Permissions Editor
J. Weston Walch, Publisher
321 Valley Street • P.O. Box 658
Portland, Maine 04104-0658

1 2 3 4 5 6 7 8 9 10

ISBN 0-8251-3851-5

Printed in the United States of America

Contents

To the Teacher

A craft is a technique for making something—sometimes for its usefulness, sometimes for its attractive appearance, yet always for the pleasure of making. To study crafts means to learn about the people who make them and the cultures in which these people have worked. The objects they have made help us understand their practical needs (e.g., drinking gourds, carpets), their beliefs (e.g., amulets, crosses), their sense of self (e.g., pendants, necklaces), and their sense of fun (e.g., kites, shadow puppets). To explore those purposes by shaping the objects is the intent of this book, designed so that all students, not just art students, might enjoy the search. Handing out photocopies of these craft projects is distributing the recipes of a culture's traditions.

Because of the complexity of the originals, many of the crafts given here are simulations of an actual process, adapted to make the craft suitable for classroom use. With the exception of Mexican tin-can art, which is so typical of that country, metal crafts are simulated with the use of metal foil. Aluminum soft drink cans are easily cut with ordinary shears (and do not cut careless fingers, as do normal cans) and so can provide the material for those projects that call for heavy foil.

A number of projects require clay. This must be clay that dries hard without a kiln. You can choose clay that air-dries, clay that can be cooked in a household oven, or even clay that hardens when immersed in water. Papier-mâché, called for in several projects, is most fully described in the first section, Basic Craft Techniques. This versatile material can substitute in some clay projects as well.

The projects are not strict in their directions. Therefore, you can make modifications to meet class needs—a simpler approach for a younger class, a more complicated one for older students. Some of the crafts are relatively simple and can be handled by individual students. Others are more complex and you may prefer to assign groups of students to work together.

The illustrations provide examples of a culture's typical designs. Students can find more in those books that supplement their study of a culture, or you can encourage them to design their own motifs as inspired by those of a particular culture. The small maps scattered throughout indicate the areas where particular crafts are practiced.

As art ideas, these projects can stand on their own. However, their primary strength is to give a special dimension to the study of a culture region through hands-on learning. It is hands on paper, cloth, paste, paint, dripping wax, and sticky glue—messy, perhaps, but a lasting learning experience.

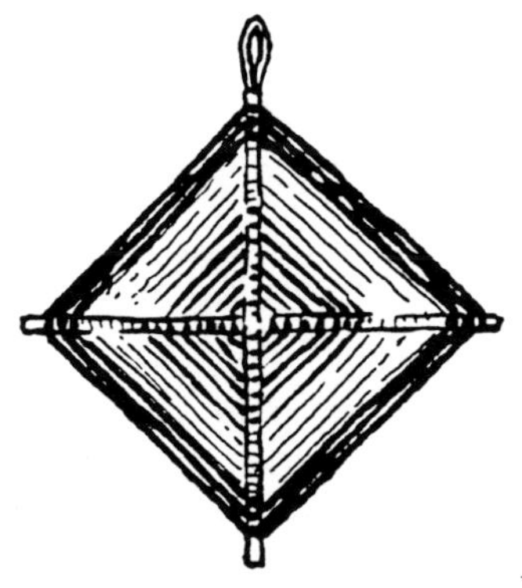

Part I:

Basic Craft Techniques

I. Basic Craft Techniques

Some craft techniques seem to have developed in one region only and are associated primarily with that area. Other techniques are found in one form or another in many parts of the world. The essential technique of weaving, for example, can be found worldwide. However, the specific way the technique is handled by a culture—ikat weavings of Guatemala, or African kente cloth—can make that variation unique.

This section offers reproducible directions for several basic techniques that are handled in different ways by different cultures. You can use these activities in many ways to supplement the study of the crafts of a region. One approach would be to gather photographs and examples of the crafts and design motifs of an area. Have students examine these motifs to determine what makes them distinctive and recognizable. Then have students create their own interpretations of these motifs and apply them to a craft item, such as a clay pot or a weaving.

This section also offers expanded directions for making papier-mâché. Several projects in this book call for papier-mâché. If your students do not have prior experience with this medium, you may wish to supplement the project directions with this handout.

Name ______________________ Date ______________

Project 1: Coiled Pottery

Materials
For this activity you will need: • clay

The craft of pottery is found all around the world. Virtually every culture has produced its own distinctively colored and decorated pottery. This tells us much about the people who created it. Many people of ancient history are only known to us by their broken pieces of pottery, found by archaeologists. Illustrated here are a vase made about 5000 B.C. in the area later known as Czechoslovakia and another made about 3000 B.C. in China.

Although mass-produced dishes and plates are available, many people still make pottery by hand. Their handcrafted vases, cups, and plates are often much more distinctive and appealing than machine-made dishware. Many people learn pottery for the creative pleasure it gives them.

Potters particularly enjoy creating the shapes of vases. Perhaps you have only noticed the decoration of vases and never thought about their shapes. Coiled pottery lets you experiment with vase shapes. Coiling is one of the oldest potting techniques. It has been practiced for thousands of years.

You can use any clay for making coiled pottery. If it is self-drying clay, you will be able to preserve your favorite vase shape. If your school art department has a kiln, you can fire your pottery when it is finished.

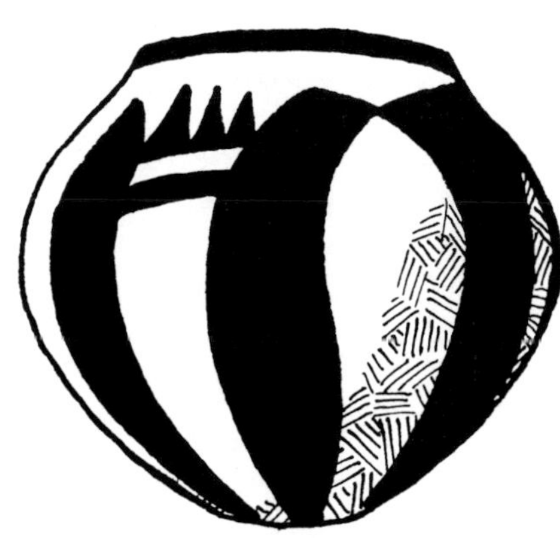

Czechoslovakian vase, about 5000 B.C.

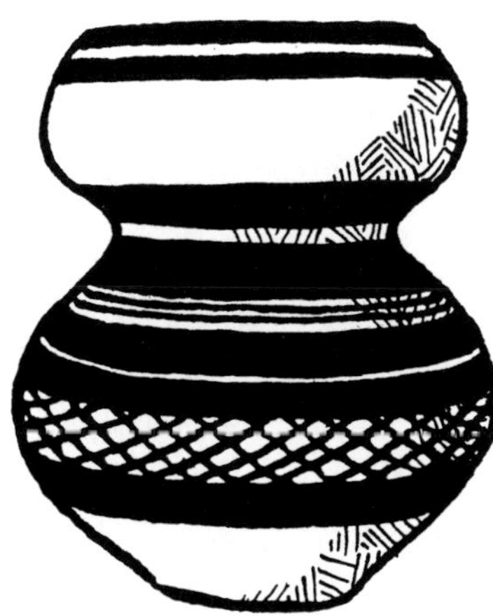

Chinese vase, about 3000 B.C.

(continued)

Name ______________________ Date ______________

Project 1: Coiled Pottery *(continued)*

1. Roll up a ball of clay. Then flatten it out like a pancake.
2. Roll out more clay into a long snake.

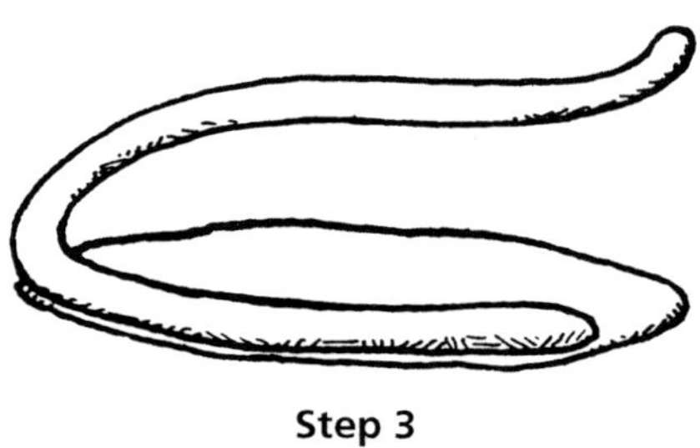

Step 3

3. Lay the snaked clay around the rim of the pancake shape. Pinch the snake where it meets the pancake shape to make the snake and pancake stick together *(Step 3)*.

4. Coil the snake around, adding one coil on top of another as you build up the vase shape. Pinch the circles of coil together to make them stick *(Step 4)*.

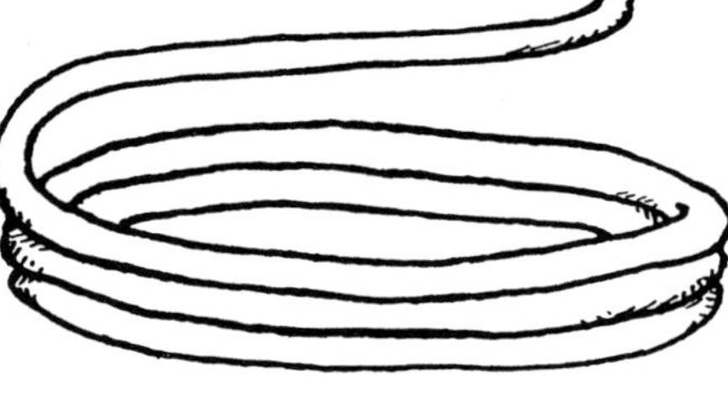

Step 4

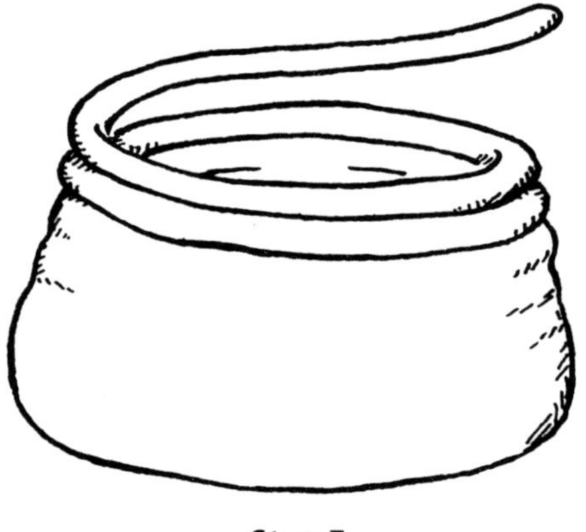

Step 5

5. As you coil, pinch the clay to flatten it out to form the side of the vase *(Step 5)*.

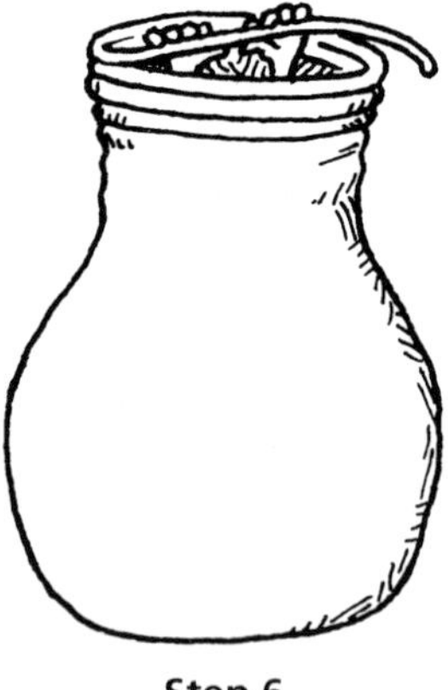

Step 6

6. Develop the shape of the vase with the coiling *(Step 6)*. You can make it tall and narrow or short and fat. You can swell it out, then in, then out again. Create a shape **you** like. It is this creation that attracts many to the potter's craft.

7. When you have finished, let the clay dry. If it can be fired and there is a kiln available, you can preserve the shape as a fired vase. Dried or fired, you have a vase of an interesting and maybe beautiful shape.

Name ______________________________ Date ______________

Project 2: Single-Heddle Weaving

Materials	
For this activity you will need:	
• wood or heavy cardboard	• heavy-gauge colored thread

Weaving has been practiced by virtually every culture since history began. Ancient Greeks and Romans wove cloth of wool, cotton, and linen. They even had silk, which came from China along the famous silk route that wound through Asia into Europe. Vase paintings and painted statues show that Roman and Greek clothes were brightly colored and decorated. Amazingly, a few pieces of ancient cloth from both Greece and Rome have survived. The illustration at right is of a fragment of cloth found in excavations of an ancient Greek colony in the Russian Crimea.

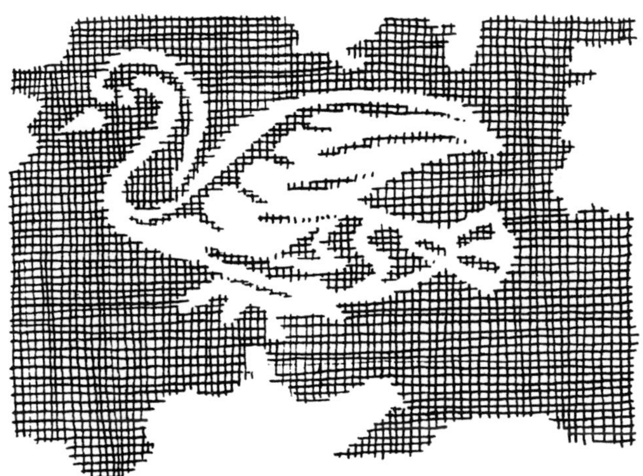

Cloth fragment from ancient Greek colony

A loom is required to weave cloth. This hand-operated machine raises alternate strands of threads so that another thread can be "woven" through the network. A loom can be mechanically involved and very large. There are small hobby looms available for you to try the craft on your own. Here is a project using the simplest loom and technique of all—single-heddle weaving.

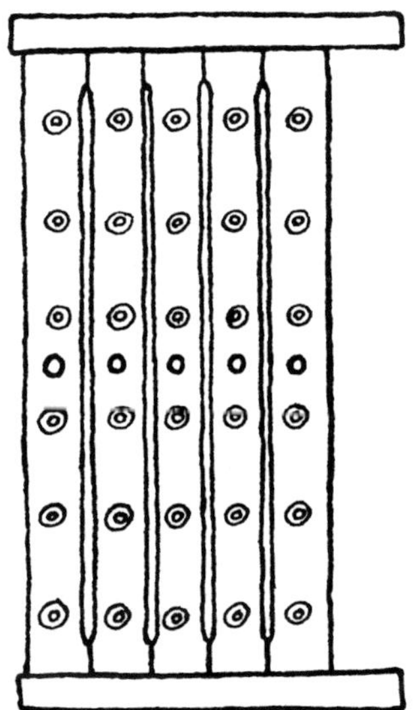

Ancient Roman single heddle

A **heddle** is the apparatus that raises and lowers alternate rows of thread in the weaving process. In single-heddle weaving, thread is woven with only a heddle. This technique was developed a long time ago. Although ancient weavers used complicated hand looms, they also used single-heddle weaving for creating decorative bands for costume borders. The illustration here is of an ancient Roman single heddle found in England. A weaver used it to create a decorative ribbon several thousand years ago when Roman soldiers occupied part of the British Isles. It is made of bone. The double circles are mere decoration. The single circles and the slots are the working parts of the heddle.

You can make a similar heddle and practice weaving in this way.

(continued)

Name ______________________________ Date ______________

Project 2: Single-Heddle Weaving *(continued)*

1. Copy the pattern at right on a piece of thin wood or heavy cardboard and cut out the holes and slots *(Step 1)*.
2. Tie one end of nine long strands of heavy thread together. Then tie those ends to something fixed—a doorknob, a wall hook, or other stationary object. These are your **warp** threads.
3. Thread the strands through the heddle, the first strand through a hole, the second through a slot, the third through a hole, and so on.

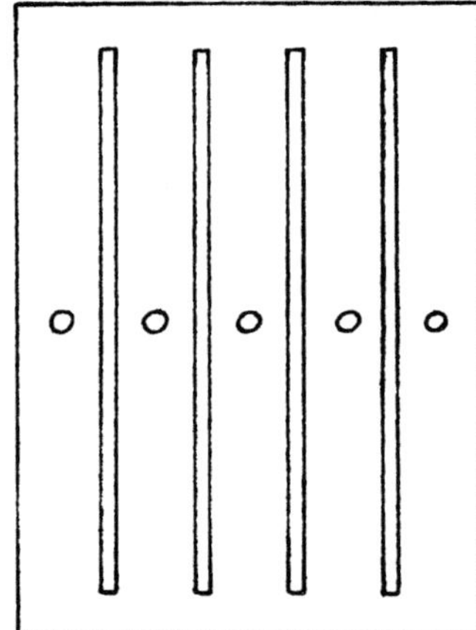

Step 1

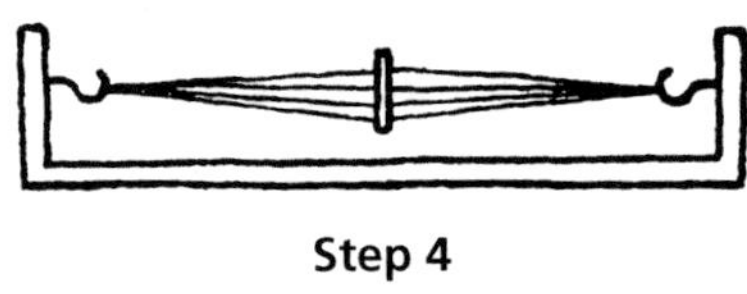

Step 4

4. Tie the free ends together and hook them to another fixed object, such as a chair or table. If you plan to weave frequently with the heddle, you can make a simple loom. It is a frame consisting of a base and two end pieces of wood with hooks as illustrated *(Step 4)*.
5. Tie a long piece of colored thread to one of the warp threads. This is called the **woof** or **weft** thread.
6. Attach the free end of this thread to a heavy needle, a nail, or a piece of wood or cardboard to make it easy to handle the thread. This is the **shuttle**.
7. To operate the single-heddle loom, lift the heddle. This will lift alternate strings. Using the shuttle, pass the weft thread through the space between the warp threads *(Step 7)*.

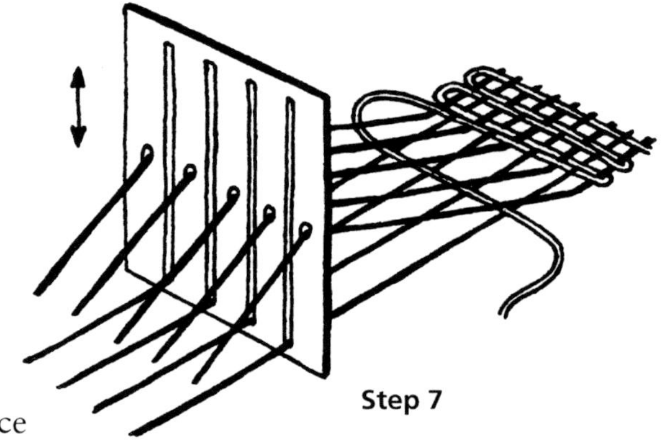

Step 7

8. Now drop the heddle, dropping the alternate warp threads. Pass the weft thread back through the opening.

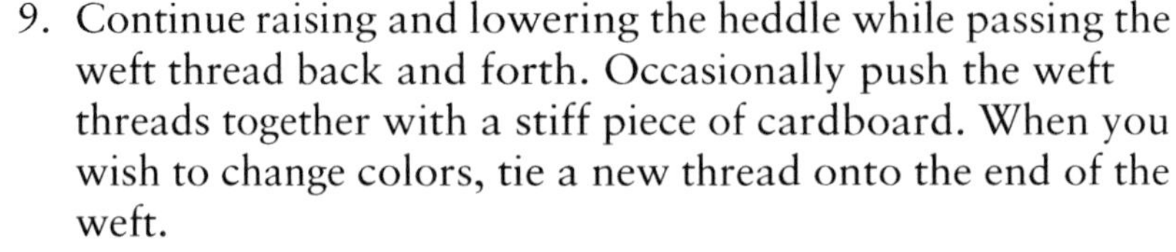

9. Continue raising and lowering the heddle while passing the weft thread back and forth. Occasionally push the weft threads together with a stiff piece of cardboard. When you wish to change colors, tie a new thread onto the end of the weft.
10. At the end, tie the weft thread to the ends of the warp. Remove the woven band from the hooks. Let the loose ends hang as fringe *(Step 10)*.

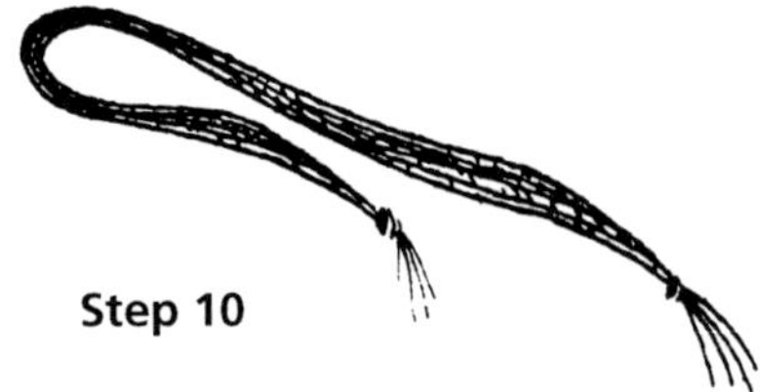

Step 10

Name ______________________ Date ______________

Project 3: Papermaking

Materials	
For this activity you will need: • paper scraps • basin (larger than the mold) • pieces of felt (larger than the mold) • two drawing boards • kitchen blender	For 6" × 8" papermaking mold and deckel: • 4 pieces of wood, 1" × 2" × 6" • 4 pieces of wood, 1" × 2" × 8" • heavy-duty stapler and staples • window screening fabric

Many crafts call for one of the most ordinary of materials, paper. Many projects use papier-mâché, cardboard, or poster board. For most of the projects you first sketch your ideas on paper. These pages are made of paper. What would we do without paper?

Paper was invented by a Chinese named Tsai Lun in A.D. 105. The date—and his name—are still honored in China. For seven centuries his invention remained in China. It was not until the twelfth century that it reached Europe, when the Moors set up a paper-making industry in Toledo, Spain. In another century it had spread through most of Europe. Even so, it was 1490 before the English began producing their own paper.

For all of those centuries and for many afterward, paper was made by hand. It was such a special craft that papermakers stamped their papers with identifying seals. Only in 1799 was a papermaking machine invented. Now most paper is machine-made. However, some paper continues to be made by hand for high-quality stationery, fine books, and other special purposes. When done by hand, papermaking is a craft.

The Chinese first made paper from plant fibers. For centuries, cotton, flax, and hemp were the main materials used for paper. High-quality papers today are made from these plant fibers or else from rags, which in turn are made from cotton or linen. About the time the first papermaking machines were developed, wood pulp began to be used for paper fiber. It was cheaper and available in great quantity. Heavy use of paper by booming populations has led to an awareness of the environmental impact of paper waste. As a result, discarded paper is now often recycled into new paper.

Making recycled paper is a good way to learn the craft of papermaking. Recycling eliminates some of the initial processing of reducing plant fibers, rags, or wood chips to pulp. Once the pulp has been made, the rest of the process is the same.

(continued)

Name ________________________________ Date ________________

Project 3: Papermaking *(continued)*

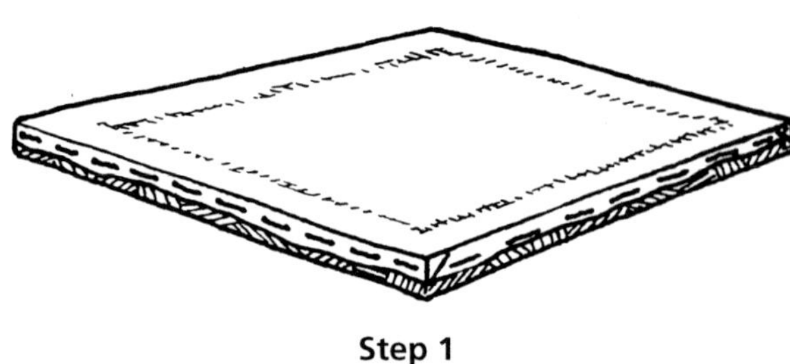

Step 1

1. Build a wooden frame to be the mold. Attach the frame pieces with the heavy-duty staples. When the frame is finished, stretch a piece of window screening across the opening *(Step 1)*. Staple the wire mesh to the wooden frame.
2. Construct another frame the same size as the mold. This is the deckel. You will lay it on the window screening to keep the paper pulp from flowing away.
3. Tear scrap paper into small pieces. Avoid cheap paper such as newsprint. Better-quality scraps make better-quality paper and are easier to work with.
4. Make pulp by adding water to the scraps and thoroughly pulverizing them in an electric blender.
5. Select a basin large enough to hold the mold. This is your dipping vat. Fill it with warm water to within several inches of the top. Using a spoon to transfer it from the blender, add the prepared pulp, mixing well with your hands. The solution should be neither watery nor thick like papier-mâché pulp. It should be about the consistency of heavy cream. Experience will give you a better idea of the proper thickness for the pulp in the vat.
6. Lay a piece of felt, larger than the mold, on a drawing board beside the vat.
7. When you think the pulp is well mixed and of the proper consistency, grasp the mold, screen side up. Lay the deckel on the screen and hold it in place with your thumbs. Dip the mold below the surface of the pulp. Move it smoothly from side to side and back to front. Lift the mold out of the pulp solution and let it drain into the vat *(Step 7)*. The pulp should lie about a sixteenth of an inch thick on the screen.

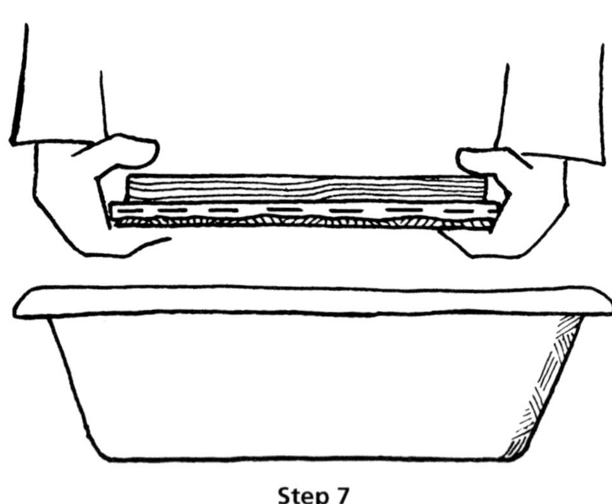

Step 7

8. Carefully remove the deckel from the mold. Lay the felt across the top of the mold and then flip the mold over. Place the mold and felt on the table.
9. Press down on the screen with your fingers to transfer the pulp to the felt. Carefully lift away the mold, leaving the thin sheet of pulp on the felt. Lay another piece of felt on top of the wet pulp.

(continued)

Name ________________________ Date ______________

Project 3: Papermaking *(continued)*

10. Stir the pulp in the vat. Lay the deckel on top of the mold and again dip it into the vat. Again slowly and smoothly agitate the mold. Lift from the vat, let drain, and transfer the pulp to the felt.

11. Lift the mold away. Lay another piece of felt on top of the fresh sheet of pulp and repeat the mold process. Add another piece of felt on top of each sheet of pulp.

12. As you continue the paper molding process, keep the pulp well stirred. Because you are draining water back into the vat, the pulp will gradually get thinner. Add more pulp to the solution after every few dips of the mold, checking to see that the consistency remains the same.

13. Continue molding paper until you have used all the pulp solution or have run out of pieces of felt. Lay another drawing board on top of the last piece of felt. Now apply a lot of pressure to remove all the excess water from the paper sheets. You could even sit or stand on the top drawing board to squeeze out water in the paper sandwiched between the felt pieces.

14. Cover a work table with an old sheet for drying the paper.

15. Remove the top drawing board. Carefully lift away the top felt piece. Then carefully lift off the top sheet of paper and lay it on the sheet to dry. Remove all of the felt pieces and sheets of paper from the pile just as carefully. Spread the paper sheets on the sheet-covered table to dry.

16. When the paper has almost dried, lay flat boards on top of each sheet so that they will dry flat and not become wrinkled.

17. When the material is completely dry, you have made recycled paper.

18. Experiment with ways to decorate your handmade paper. Dried leaves and flowers, sequins, bits of tinsel, and scraps of colored paper can be added to the pulp, either while it is in the basin or when you have a layer of pulp on the mold.

Name ______________________________ Date ______________________

Project 4: Papier-Mâché

Papier-mâché is a mixture of paper and paste that can be used in any number of different ways. Although the word comes from French (it means "mashed paper"), the process of papier-mâché actually developed in Asia centuries ago. It was first used in France during the 1700s. It soon became popular in Europe. Papier-mâché was used to make toys, trays, picture frames—even furniture!

The strength and texture of papier-mâché can be varied by using different papers and different binding materials, but there are just two basic processes for making papier-mâché: the strip method and the pulp method. Use the strip method to build a shape on a form or mold. The pulp method is best for use as a modeling material.

Strip Method

Materials	
For this activity you will need: • old newspapers • wheat paste	• shallow basin • water • wire, crushed paper, or balloon

To use this method, you should begin with an armature—a form to build the papier-mâché onto. This can be made of wire, crushed paper, a balloon, or some other object.

1. Tear the newspaper into long strips. Tear with the grain, not against the grain; this way your strips will be straight and even.

2. Half-fill the basin with water. Pour a small amount of the wheat paste into your hand. Let the paste granules sift between your fingers into the water. Mix the water with the wheat paste until it is smooth and creamy.

3. Dip a strip of newspaper into the paste mixture, and pull it back out. Hold the paper strip at the top with one hand. Gently squeeze the strip between the first and second fingers of your other hand. Slide that hand down the strip from top to bottom to remove any extra paste from the paper.

4. Place the strip on your armature. Repeat to build up layers of paper.

(continued)

Name ______________________________ Date ____________

Project 4: Papier-Mâché *(continued)*

Pulp Method

Materials	
For this activity you will need:	
• old newspapers	• wheat paste
• bucket	• water
• basin	• *optional:* chlorine bleach

1. Tear the newspaper into strips. Soak the strips in a bucket of water overnight.

2. The next day, remove excess water from the pail. Squeeze the paper to get rid of any remaining water. This is your paper mash.

3. In the basin, mix wheat paste with water. Pour a small amount of the wheat paste into your hand. Let the paste granules sift between your fingers into the water. Mix the water with the wheat paste until it is smooth and creamy.

4. Once the paste water is smooth, pour it into the bucket of wet paper mash. Mix the paste and mash thoroughly until you can model it like clay. If you wish, add a tablespoon of bleach to the mixture to keep mold from forming.

5. Use the mixture to model toys, puppets, plates, etc. Let air-dry.

6. When the pulp has hardened completely, it can be carved or sanded, then painted.

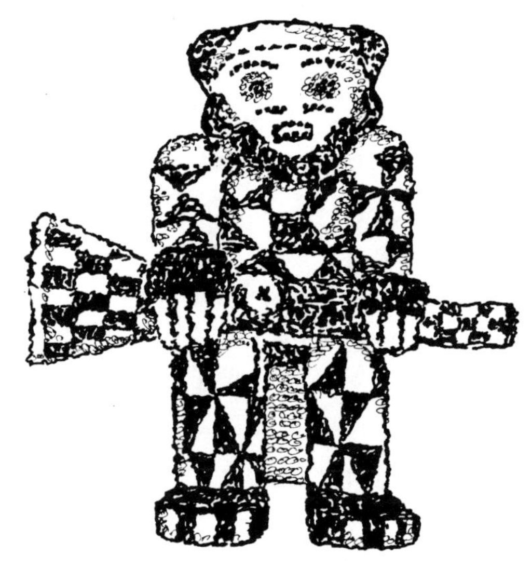

PART II:

Sub-Saharan Africa

II. The Arts and Crafts of Sub-Saharan Africa

Africa is huge in size and complex in geological features, with Mount Kilimanjaro rising over 19,000 feet and the Danakil Depression dropping to 383 feet below sea level. Lake Victoria is the second-largest freshwater lake in the world, while the Sahara makes other deserts seem to be sand boxes.

As varied as the environment are African cultures, the products of tribal traditions and native beliefs mixed with Islamic and Christian creeds. Cultural borders are not always political, as many of Africa's political borders were drawn without regard to the cultures within an area.

A clearer picture of Africa may be found by looking at geographic and climatic regions: north or south of the Sahara, West Africa, East Africa, Central Africa, and Southern Africa. Different cultures—and decorative styles—developed in the desert and in the rain forest, in wooded areas and in the grasslands, in the mountains and on the plateaus.

Name ____________________ Date ____________

Project 5: Africa: Bead Work

Shell Beads

Materials	
For this activity you will need:	
• shells	• file
• cord for stringing	• hand drill
• hobby knife	• pliers

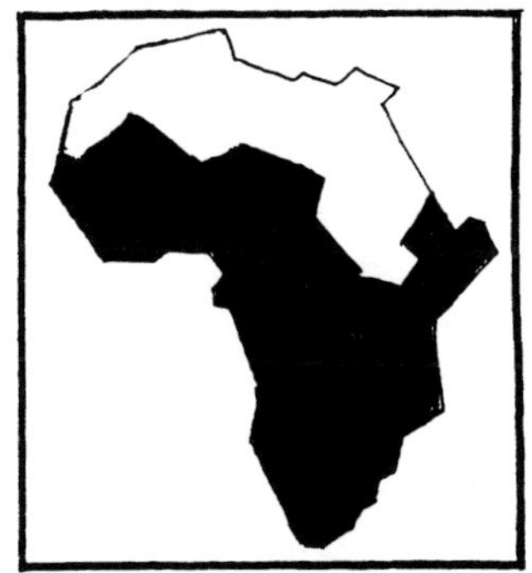

Throughout Africa, bead craft provides decorative adornment. African beads are of amber, glass, ostrich egg shells, or sea shells. Strung, they are made into necklaces, head pieces, and bands for arms and legs. Create your own beaded jewelry from shell disks or paper beads that you make or purchase.

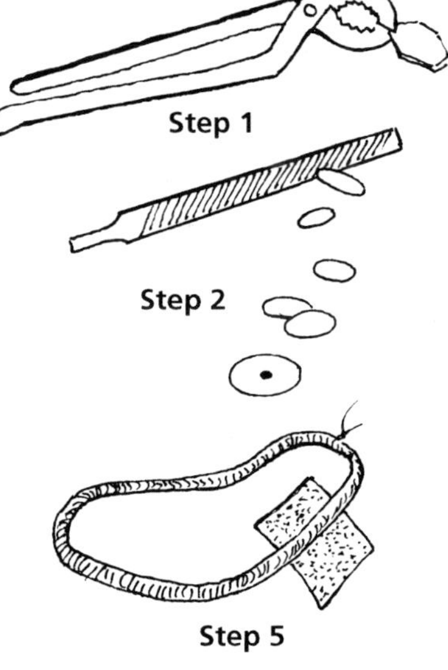

1. Break up pieces of shell into roughly rounded shapes by breaking corners with pliers and cutting with a hobby knife *(Step 1)*.
2. Round the shape of a shell disk with a metal file *(Step 2)*.
3. Drill a hole in the center of each shell disk with the small bit of a hand drill. Do not force the drill. Let the spin of the drill wear away the hole without pushing.
4. String the beads on a cord the length you need for decoration.
5. Rub the strung beads with sandpaper to give the strand a uniform shape *(Step 5)*.

Paper Beads

Materials	
For this activity you will need: • newspaper strips	• paste • scissors

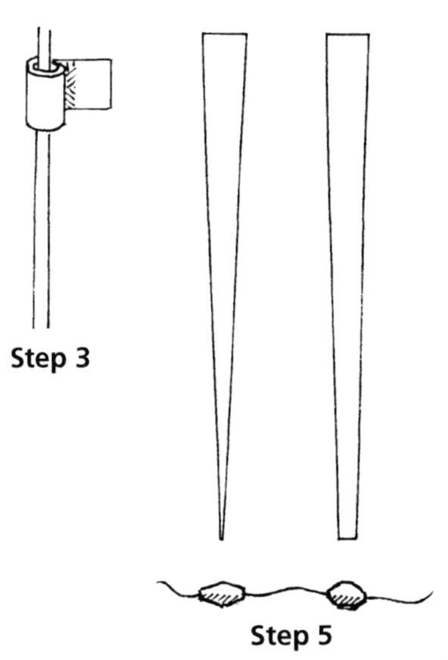

1. Cut newspaper strips one foot long and $\frac{1}{4}$ inch wide.
2. Spread paste along one side within a half inch of the end.
3. Wrap the paper strip, the paste-free end first, around a thick nail or knitting needle *(Step 3)*.
4. When it is dry, remove the paper bead from the nail and paint it.
5. Variously shaped paper strips make different shaped beads *(Step 5)*.

Name ______________________________ Date ______________

Project 6: Cameroon: Beaded Figure

Materials
For this activity you will need: • clay • different colored beads

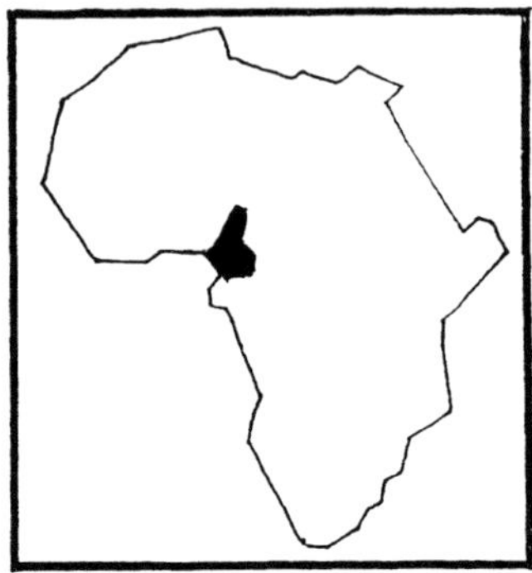

Beads are used for more than only costume adornment in African crafts. The musician below is part of a chief's beaded throne from Cameroon. A tribal leader's authority was expressed by the richness of his home and ceremonial furniture, just as royalty or a nation's president express theirs by living in a large official house or palace. This figure was first carved in wood then decorated with beads. You can make a similar figure by modeling it with clay and then covering it with beads, bringing out details and costume decoration. If your figure is small, use tiny seed beads in order to make interesting details.

1. Plan your figure on paper, including the details and decoration.
2. Model the figure in clay.
3. Following your plan, decorate the figure, pushing beads into the soft clay.

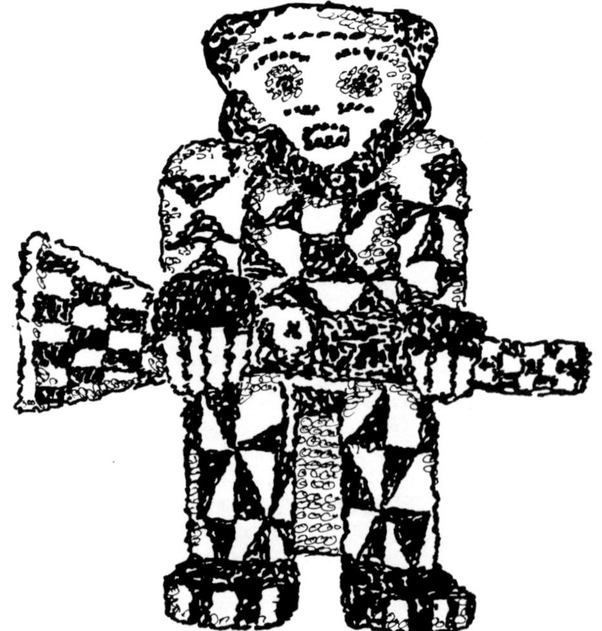

Cameroonian beaded musician

Name ______________________ Date ______________

Project 7: Central Africa: Inadan Necklace

Materials	
For this activity you will need:	
• metal foil	• beads
• poster board	• heavy cord
• glue	• wire

On the southern edge of the Sahara lie landlocked Chad, Niger, and Mali. Here live the nomadic Tuareg people who farm and operate camel caravans. For manufactured products, they depend upon their neighbors, the settled Inadan, who make and sell them pots, pans, other utensils, and costume jewelry. Recent droughts have brought poverty, starvation, and death to the southern Sahara. Yet, even as Sahara sands crept southward, Inadan artisans worked at their age-old crafts, using scrap metal, such as coins and tin-can metal, when precious metals were no longer available. Use scrap metal or foil to make the Inadan necklace illustrated here.

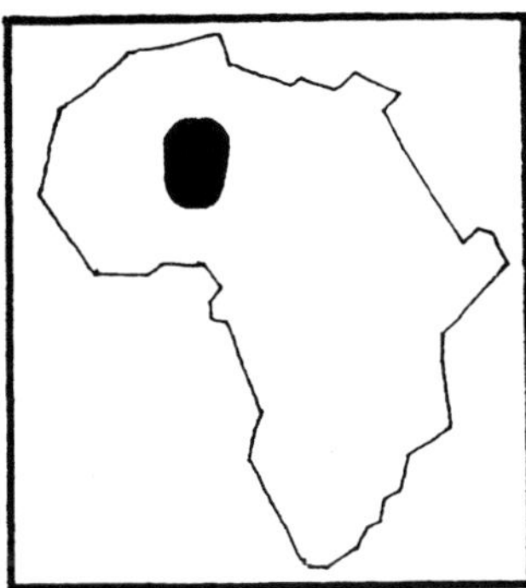

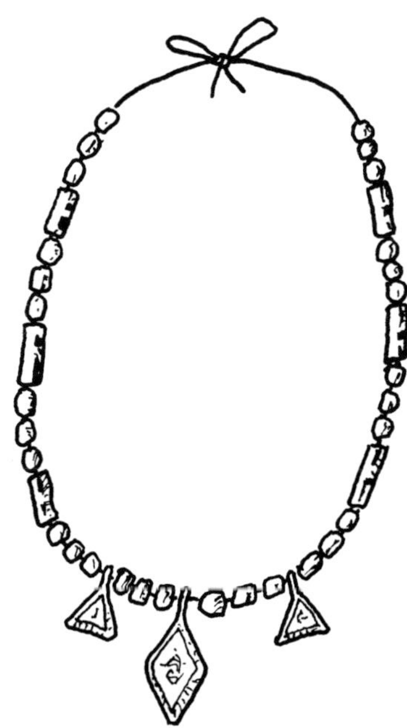

Inadan necklace

(continued)

Name ______________________________ Date ______________________

Project 7: Central Africa: Inadan Necklace *(continued)*

1. Cut poster board into the triangle or diamond shapes shown *(Step 1)*.
2. Pierce the top with a small loop of wire, bending the ends to hold the circle shape.
3. Wrap the ornament tightly with metal foil, gluing in the back.
4. Draw designs on the foil with a blunt point *(Step 4)*.
5. Make silver tubes by doubling a rectangle of foil into a square and then wrapping the square foil around a pencil *(Step 5)*.
6. String beads, tubes, and ornaments on a heavy cord to complete an Inadan necklace.

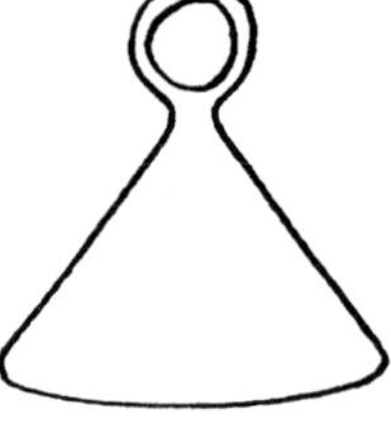

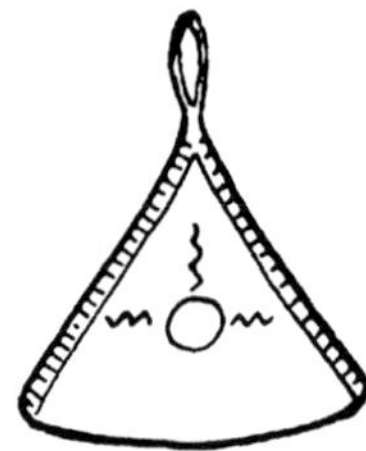

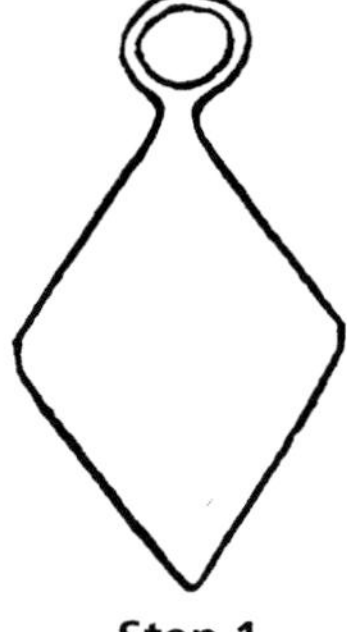

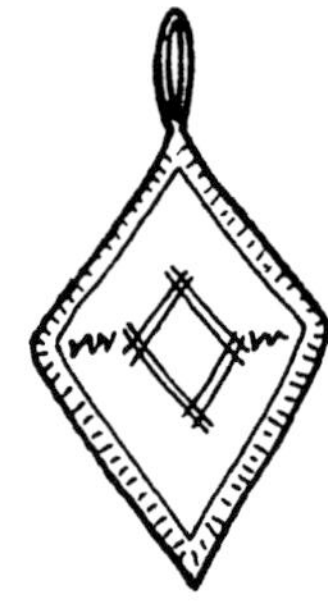

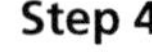

Step 1 Step 4

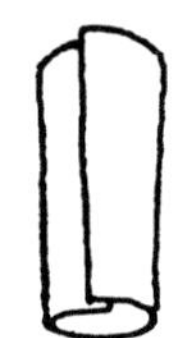

Step 5

Name ______________________________ Date ______________

Project 8: Ethiopia: Coptic Cross

Materials	
For this activity you will need: • heavy poster board or plywood	• silver wrapping foil • glue

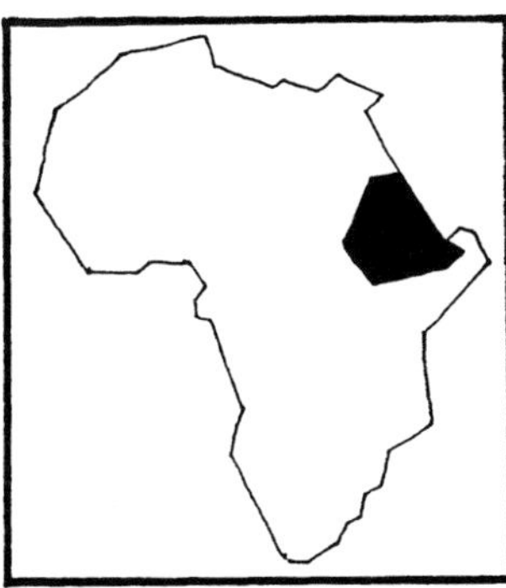

Christianity, which appeared in Ethiopia in the middle of the fourth century, is practiced there as the Coptic Christian faith. The country also has a large Muslim population and a special group of Ethiopians known as the *Falasha*, the so-called Black Jews. Yet, it is the Coptic Church that has remained the dominant religion of the country. Tradition claims the country was founded by the son of the Bible's King Solomon and the Queen of Sheba. Ethiopian arts and crafts are as unique as its historical traditions, with artists making ornate silver crosses and brightly colored paintings of Biblical stories.

1. Cut poster board or thin plywood in the shape of an ornate cross copied from the examples below or from your own design.
2. Wrap carefully with pieces of silver foil, smoothing the foil as you glue it to the cross shape.

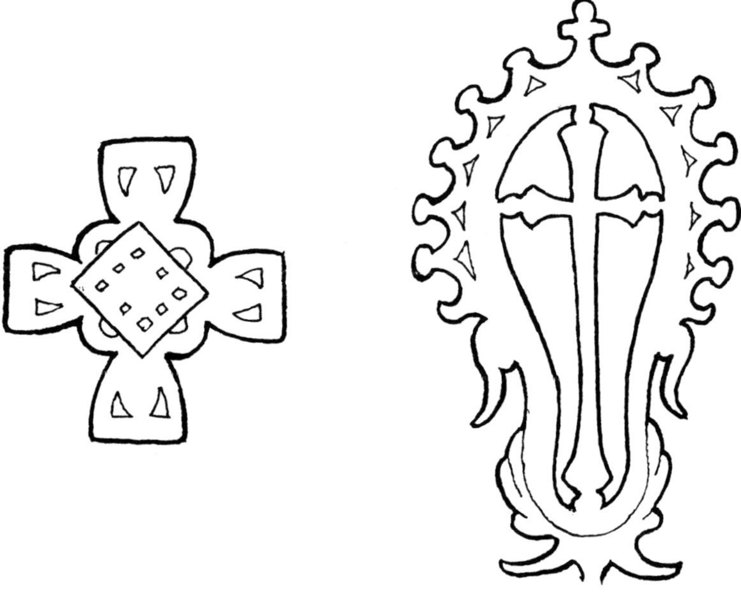

Ethiopian Coptic crosses

Name ______________________________ Date ____________________

Project 9: Nigeria: Metal Plaque

Materials	
For this activity you will need: • kitchen foil • poster board	• glue • collection of flat objects for rubbing

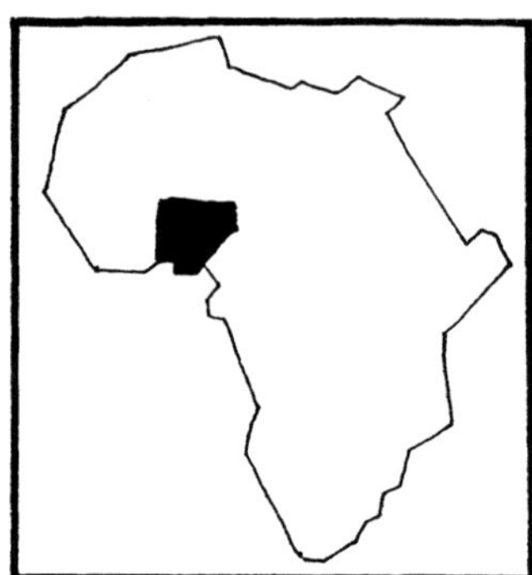

Great museums of the world display the thirteenth-century metal art of the Yoruba of Nigeria and metal plaques that adorned the sixteenth- and seventeenth-century palace of Benin City. A Benin plaque is illustrated on the next page. Today, as in other African countries, contemporary artists in Nigeria have turned traditional art into modern crafts. Asiru Olatunde was a Yoruba metalsmith who began as a maker of jewelry for tourists. Then he turned to picturing folk themes on large sheets of metal, as in the drawing of his aluminum panel entitled *Friends* below. Collect flat objects to rub with kitchen foil and make your own plaque.

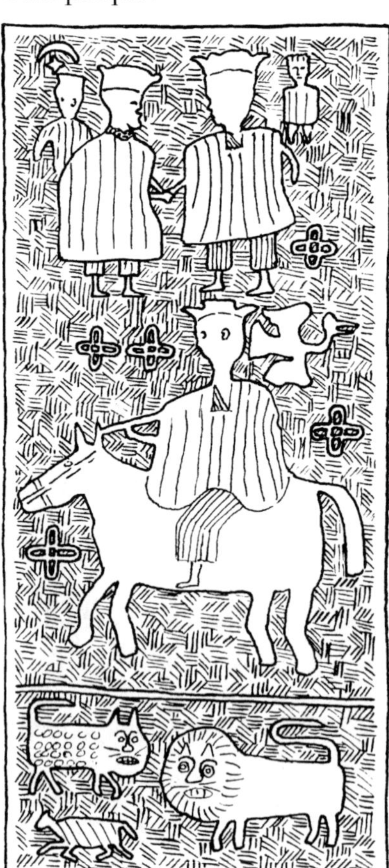

***Friends*, by Asiru Olatunde**

(continued)

Name ______________________________ Date ______________

Project 9: Nigeria: Metal Plaque *(continued)*

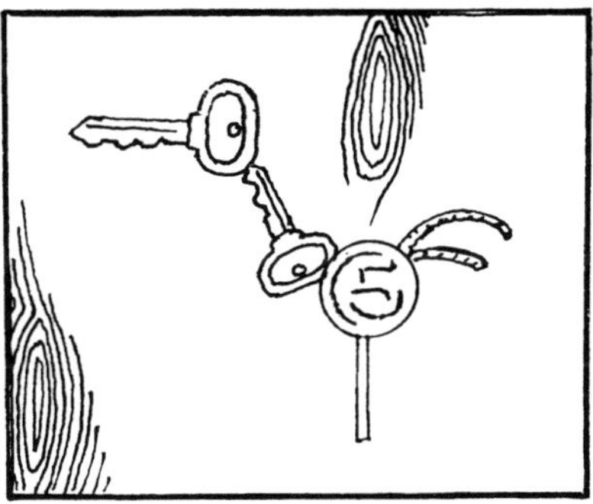

Step 2

1. Collect small flat objects such as coins, old keys, buttons, match sticks, paper clips, or string.
2. Arrange the objects on poster board, moving them about until they suggest a picture idea *(Step 2)*.
3. Glue the objects in place. Develop the picture idea by adding putty or clay.
4. Cut a piece of kitchen foil larger than the poster board.
5. Spread glue over the poster board but not the objects glued to it.
6. Lay the foil over the poster board. Work from the middle outward carefully pressing the foil to the poster board with your fingers.
7. Using a soft, stubby point such as a pencil eraser, rub the foil, bringing out the shapes of the objects beneath.
8. Fold the overlapping foil to the back of the poster board and glue.
9. Using a blunt point, add details to your design to clarify its visual meaning.

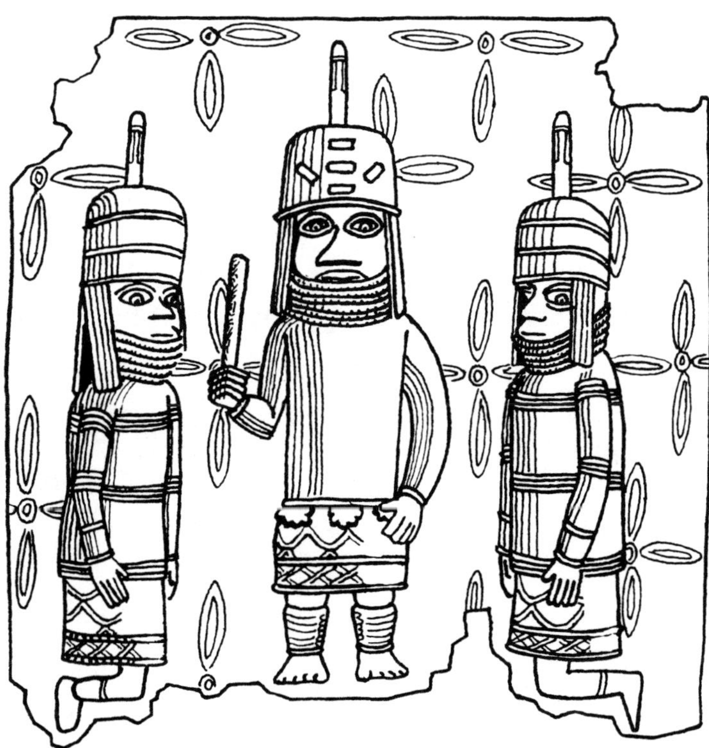

Bronze plaque, sixteenth or seventeenth century, Benin City

Name ______________________________ Date ______________

Project 10: West Africa: Flour Batik

Materials	
For this activity you will need: • light-colored cloth (natural fiber, not synthetic)	• paintbrush • flour • cold-water fabric dye

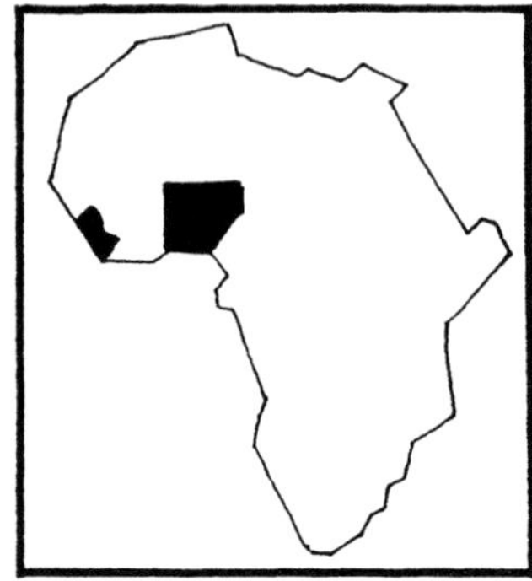

Many Nigerian and Liberian costumes are batik, meaning the design was made with a dye-resisting material. The illustration below shows a batik made in Yorubaland in Nigeria. The light parts of the cloth were covered with dye-resistant cassava starch. When the cloth was treated with dye, only the uncovered parts, black in the illustration, were colored. When washed away, the cassava starch parts remained the cloth color, the white parts of this example. In place of cassava starch, you can work with flour and water.

1. Plan a simple design with the resist portion remaining the color of the cloth itself. Pencil your design on the piece of cloth.
2. Make a thick paste resist of flour mixed with water.
3. Paint your design on the cloth with the flour resist. Use brush handles or sucker sticks to push the paste into the cloth fibers.
4. Also apply the paste to the design on the back of the cloth.
5. Bathe the cloth in a cool-water dye. Avoid agitating it.
6. Lay the cloth flat on newspaper or plastic sheet to dry.
7. When it is dry, wash the cloth to rinse away the resist paste.
8. Display your batik as a hanging or wear it as an African scarf.

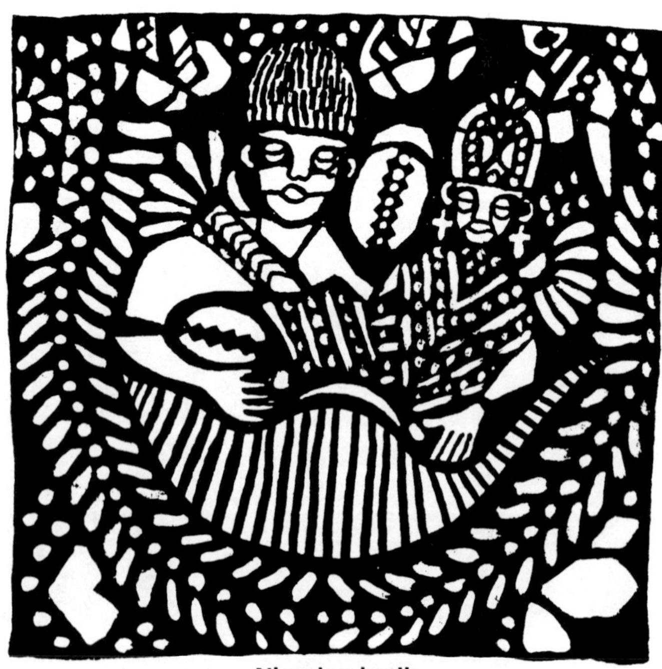

Nigerian batik

Name ______________________________ Date ______________

Project 11: Africa: Drums

Materials	
For this activity you will need:	
• heavy wire	• inner tube rubber or heavy balloon rubber
• wood strips or poster board	• hand drill or hobby knife
• pegs	

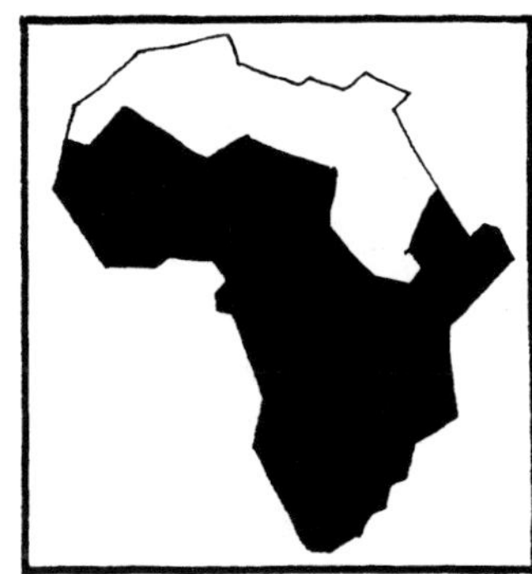

African music is based on rhythm, not harmony. Nothing expresses that fact more than the drums of Africa. Yet, they are used for more than just music. The beating of "speaking drums" once sent messages over great distances. In Senegal, drums announce the beginning of sporting events. Most importantly, drums produce the exciting rhythms of festivals and religious ceremonies. Some are set on stands. Others are hung around the neck to be played on both ends.

Depending on tribal tradition, special artisans make drums carved from wood logs or wooden rods tied around circular rims. Skin is stretched over the top and tied to protruding pegs that stretch the drum skin when turned. Make model drums using these illustrations as a guide.

1. Unless the drum is made from a solid hollow log, it needs a circular support at either end. Twist two pieces of heavy wire into circles for such support.
2. Wire thin strips of wood to the circular supports.

   or

   Roll a piece of poster board into a tube and wire it to the supports.
3. Varnish the wood strips or paint the poster board tube.
4. Decorate the drum with acrylic paint.
5. Drill or cut six holes around the cylinder near the rims. Poke rods through one hole to stick out the opposite hole. Both ends should protrude from the drum.
6. Cut rubber pieces somewhat larger than the drum end.
7. Cut holes into the rubber to stretch over the pegs and close the drum ends.

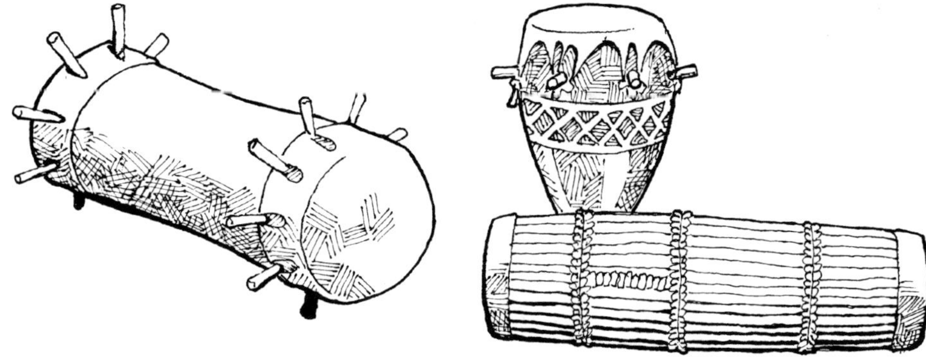

Examples of African drums

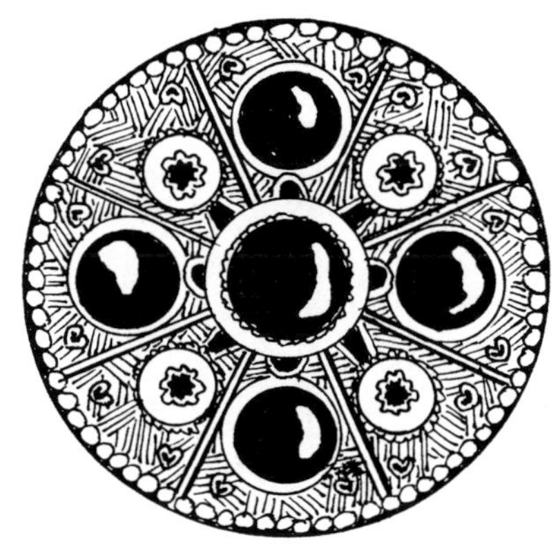

Part III:

North Africa

III. The Arts and Crafts of North Africa

The immense barrier of the Sahara Desert divides North Africa from the equatorial jungles and savannas of the south. With the vast desert at their back, North Africans live in the temperate environment of the Mediterranean. Many of the cultures of this region are Islamic. Because their religion forbids any representation of the human figure in art, Muslim artisans create objects largely abstract in style or else picture animals, birds, and plant life. Abstract designs on tiles, carved in wood, or twisted as filigree jewelry are known as *arabesques*, the very word telling us these are the creations of Arab artists. Although this section introduces North African crafts, the Islamic connection means arabesques and filigree work can also be found in Middle Eastern art.

There is a delicacy, an intricacy to an arabesque. An arabesque provides a useful study in abstract design. When possible, students should study examples beyond those shown here.

Name ______________________ Date ______________

Project 12: North Africa: Arabesques

Materials	
For this activity you will need:	
• drawing paper	• ink
• pencil	• watercolor paint

Muslim craftsmen are forbidden by their religion to represent human forms. Therefore, they design their crafts with intricate patterns of twisting branches and curving leaves. In time, these forms became abstract curves, scrolls, and spirals called *arabesques,* such as those shown here. They are usually symmetrically composed in vertical panels with the space almost completely filled. New shapes are drawn in relation to those already in place to maintain control of the design.

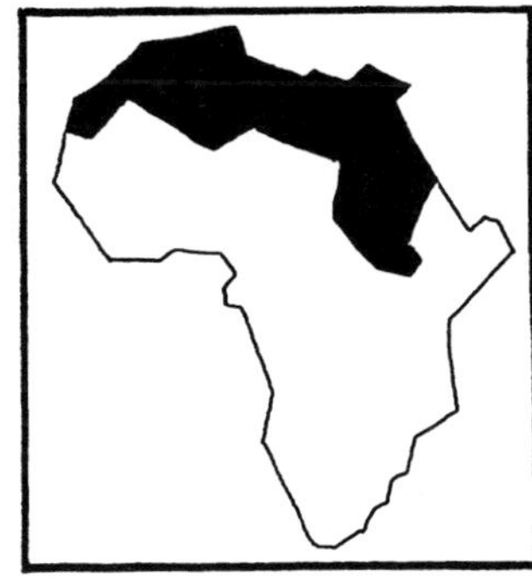

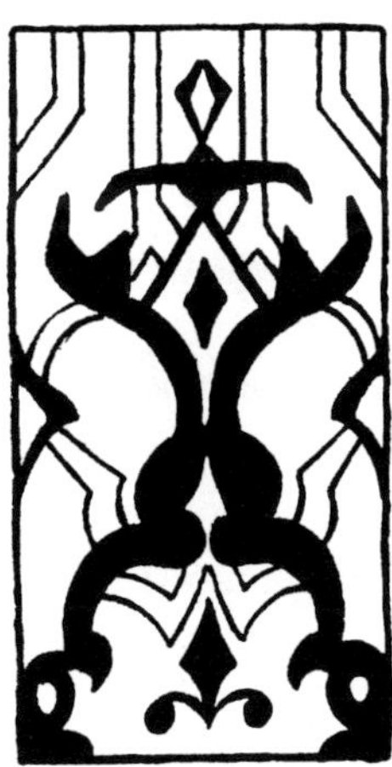

North African arabesques

1. Draw a vertical rectangle and divide it in half with a light line.

2. On the line draw a shape, a leaf, flower, or abstract form. Make the shape the same on the left and right of the line *(Step 2).*

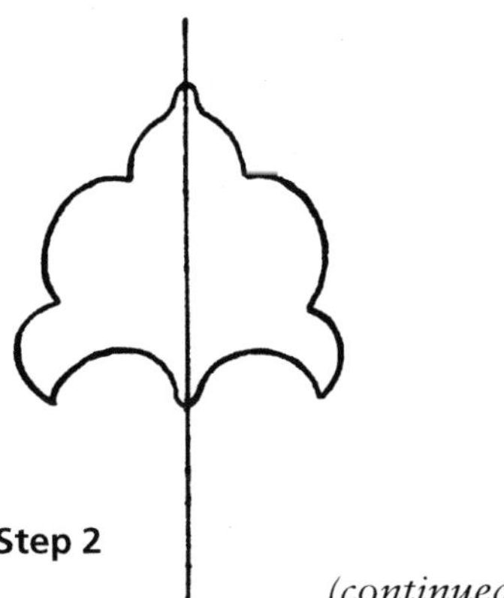

Step 2

(continued)

Name ______________________________ Date ______________

Project 12: North Africa: Arabesques *(continued)*

3. Surround this shape with branching lines or shapes, drawing the identical branching design on both sides of the guideline *(Step 3)*.

4. Let more shapes grow on the branches, twining in and around like vines. New shapes should respond to those already drawn *(Step 4)*.

5. Ink in your finished arabesque. Color in open shapes and the background. Use your design for other projects.

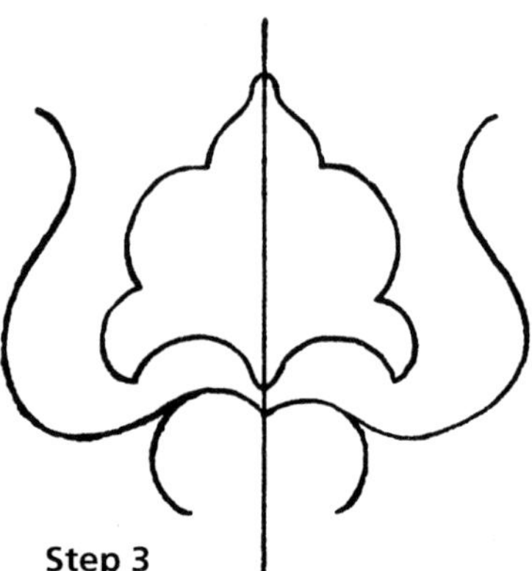

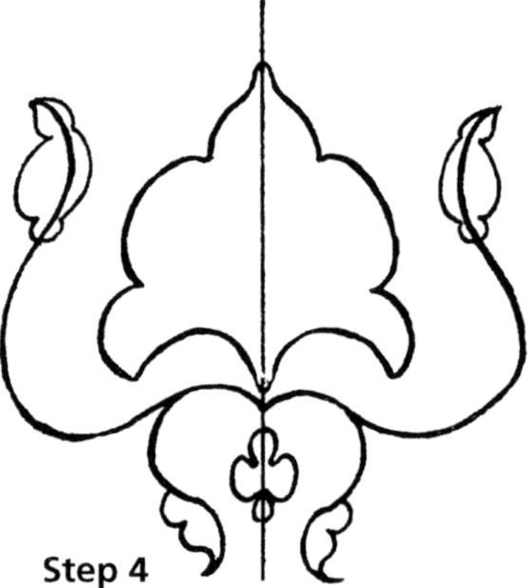

Name ______________________________ Date ______________

Project 13: North Africa: Filigree Jewelry

Materials
For this activity you will need: • wire (silver jewelry wire or ordinary wire) • pliers

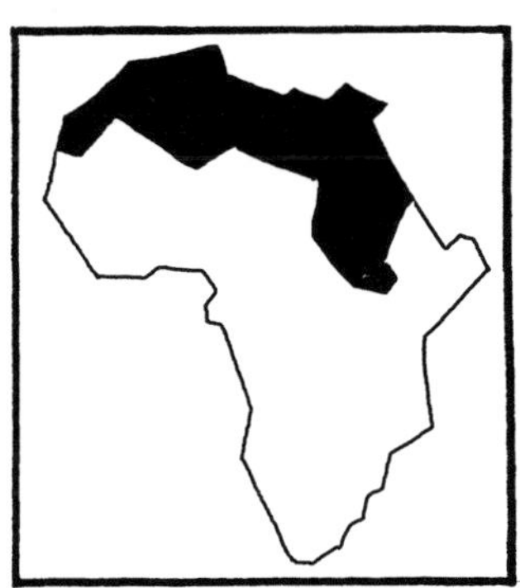

Many peoples of North Africa and the Near East come from nomadic cultures. Because they travel from place to place, nomads prefer small metal utensils and decorative pieces to bulky furniture. Having long ago abandoned their nomadic roots, Arab artisans remain skilled in producing metal pitchers, basins, candelabras, trays and the like, objects to be bought in the bazaars of North Africa. You can try one metal craft practiced by Arab metalsmiths, the making of filigree jewelry.

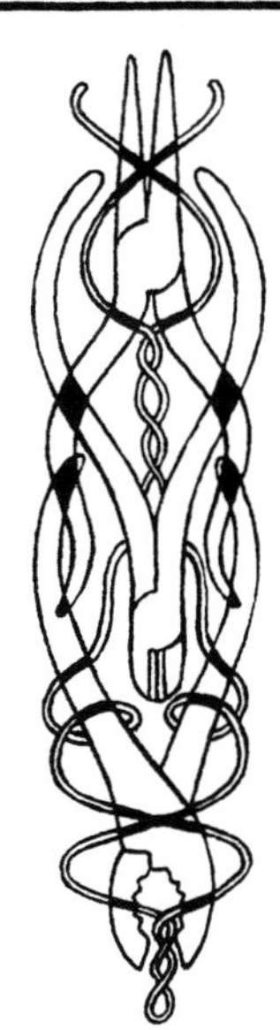

1. Design a filigree pin, brooch, or pendant to hang from a cord. Tight twists, which hold curves to one another, are also part of the design. Do not make it overly complicated.

2. Cut a length of wire with clippers. Use ordinary pliers to make wide bends, needle-nose pliers for smaller twists.

3. Join pieces by twisting together and squeezing with pliers.

4. If the filigree is to hang as a pendant, include a small loop at the top of the design. If it is to be a pin, leave one end long and, sharpened with a metal file, hanging at the back. Here are a few ideas.

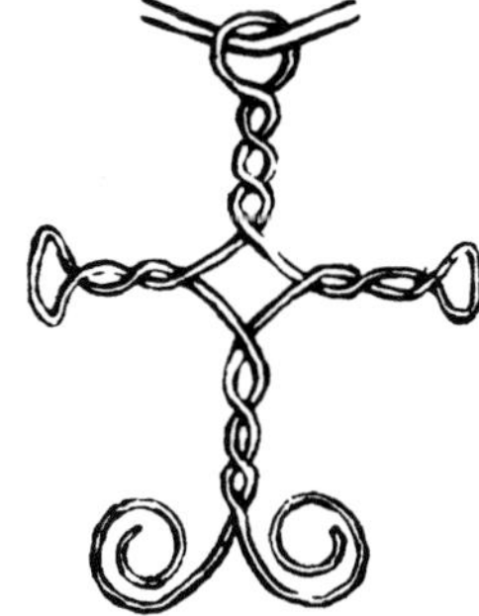
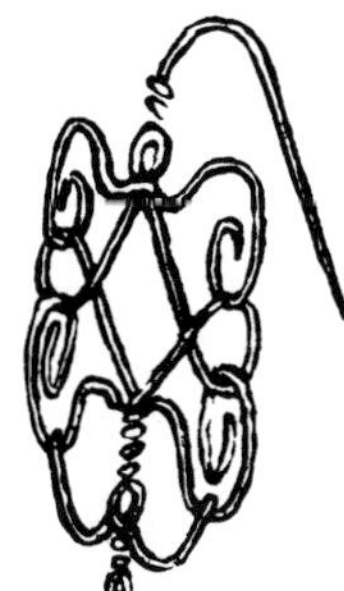
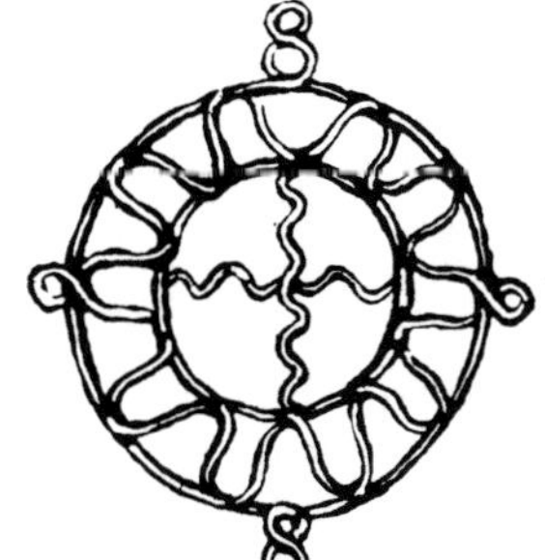
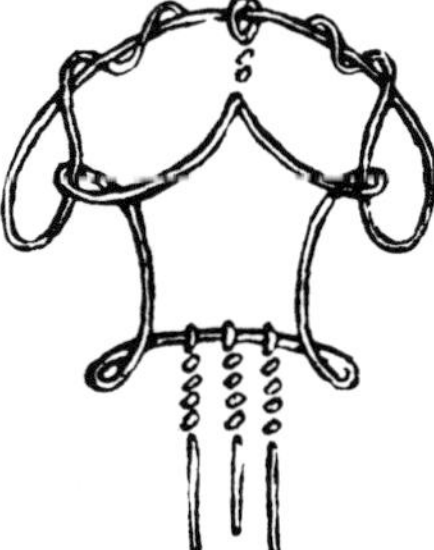

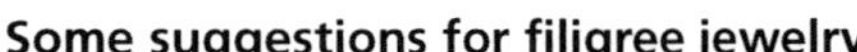

Some suggestions for filigree jewelry

Name ______________________________ Date ______________

Project 14: Algeria: Tabzimt Pendant

Materials	
For this activity you will need: • walled can lid • wire	• enamel paint • paste "jewels" • glue

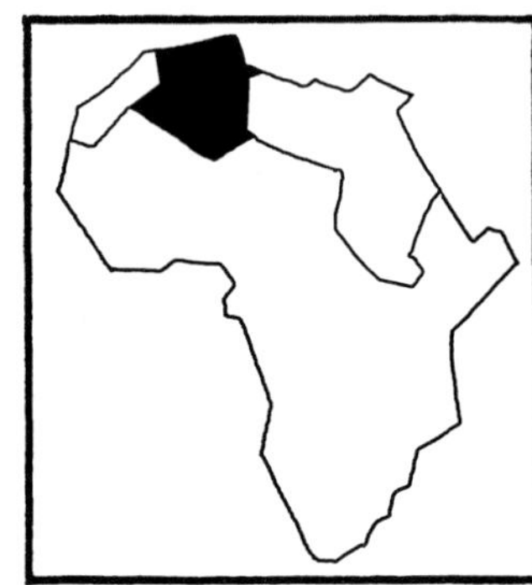

Although Algeria's religion is Islam and its language Arabic, most of its population is non-Arab Berbers. One Berber group is the Kabyle people of northern Algeria. Kabyle artisans specialize in cloisonné work, in which fine wires form tiny walls to hold colored enamel. The eight straight lines in the illustration below represent such walls. Artisans also add jewels to their colorful work, held in wire circles. Called *tabzimt*, the pendants are worn around the neck if granted as part of a woman's dowry. If the jewelry is given by her husband when a child is born, the woman hangs it as a head piece.

1. Your tabzimt base is a walled can lid, the kind found on a coffee or paint can.
2. Work out a design of "jewels" and colored enamel paint to fit into the lid. Draw it to scale on paper.
3. Twist pieces of wire into the shape of the lines between the color areas. The wire will also wall in the jewelry.
4. Spread liquid glue into the can lid. Drop the wire walls into the glue. Set the jewels in place in the glue *(Step 4)*.
5. Once the wire walls and jewels have set and the glue dried, carefully drip enamel paint color between the wire walls.

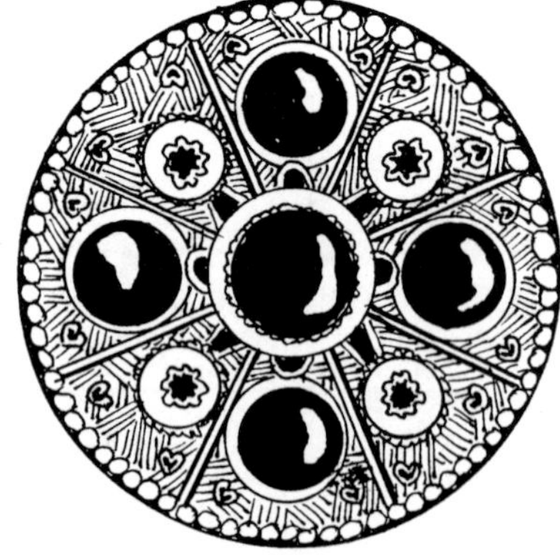

Cloisonné tabzimt pendant

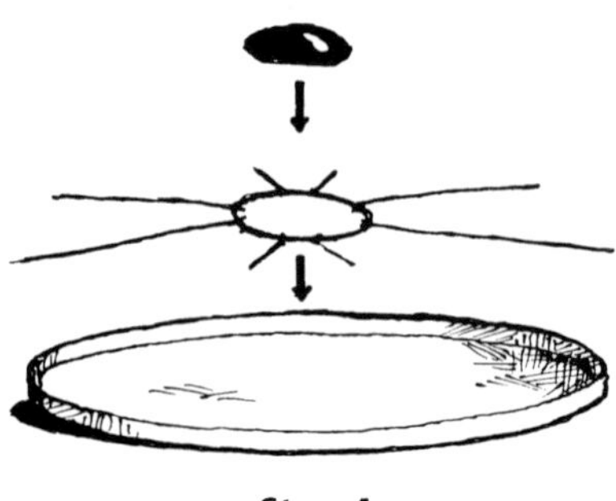

Step 4

Name ______________________ Date ______________

Project 15: Algeria: Berber Headdress

Materials	
For this activity you will need:	• hand drill
• heavy metal foil	• hobby knife
• brightly colored cord	• fine wire

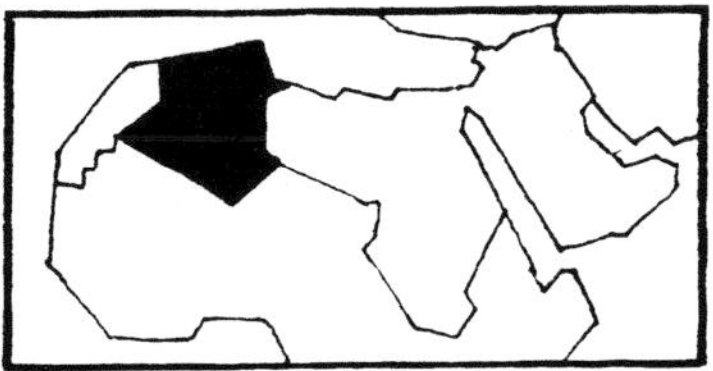

One type of jeweled headdress is worn by the women of several Berber tribes, the original inhabitants of Algeria. For nomadic people without banks, jewelry was a way to store a family's wealth, especially when on the move. Bejeweled nomads need no traveler's checks. Sometimes the economic function was quite direct with the jewelry actually consisting of strung coins. Although real coins are not a part of Berber jewelry today, clusters of metal disks worn over a black head kerchief recall a time when they were.

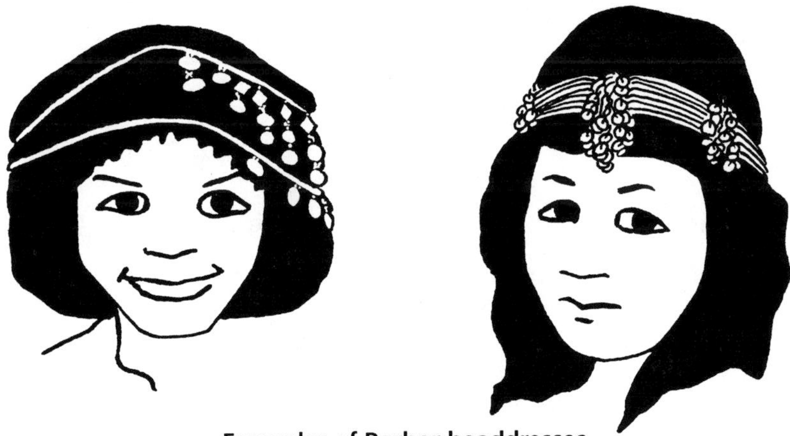

Examples of Berber headdresses

1. Cut a number of small disks the size of a nickel from heavy metal foil, punching a hole in the top of each. (If you prefer, you can collect foreign coins, tokens, metal buttons, etc. Drill a small hole in the top of each.)
2. Make short strands of coins or foil disks by connecting them with fine wire.
3. String the strands on a brightly colored cord. Wear it as a necklace or on top of a head scarf *(Step 3)*.

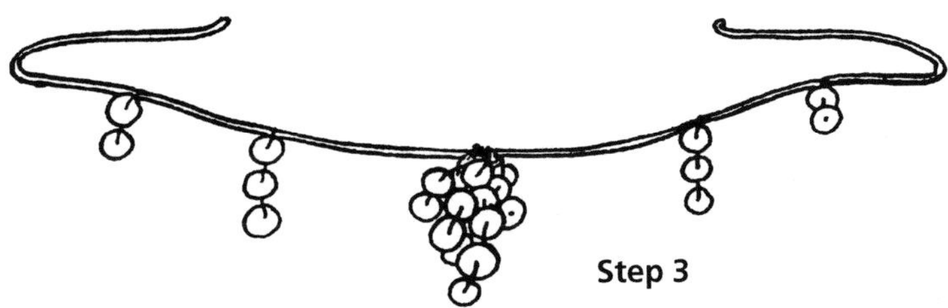

Step 3

Name ______________________________ Date ______________

Project 16: Morocco: Floral Carpet Table Mat

Materials	
For this activity you will need: • scraps of single color cloth or felt	• tempera paints • poster board • white glue

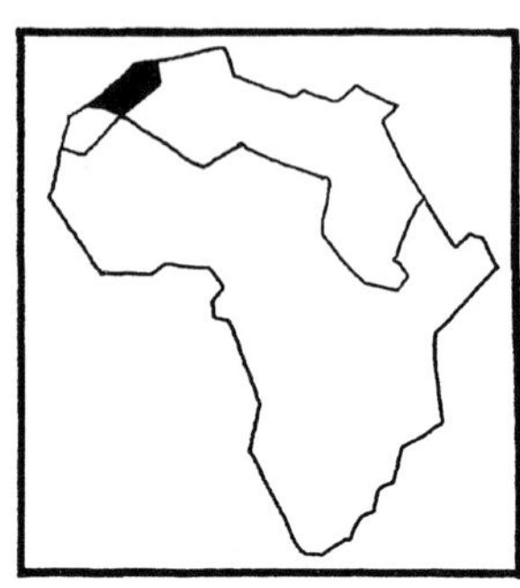

A Moroccan legend tells how ages ago a stork dropped a carpet into the garden of a home. Ever since, the women of Morocco have woven carpets filled with flower designs looking like geometric gardens. Those of Rabat picture birds, animals, trees, and flowers in a composition of seven harmonizing colors. The carpets woven in Marrakesh are designed on a background of several shades of red. Other weavers represent the flowers of their regions, colorful springtime fields, or the valleys of the Atlas Mountains.

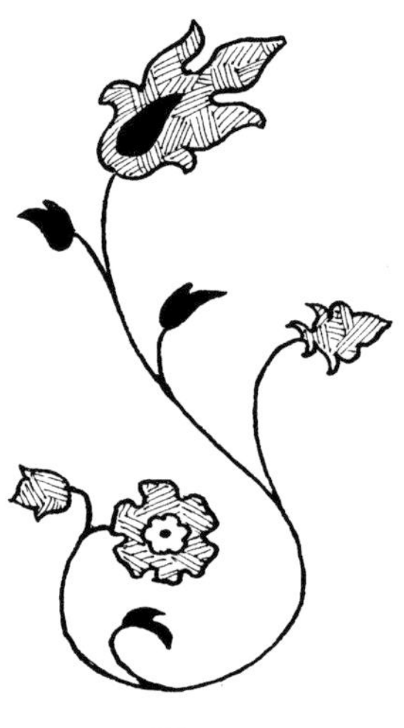

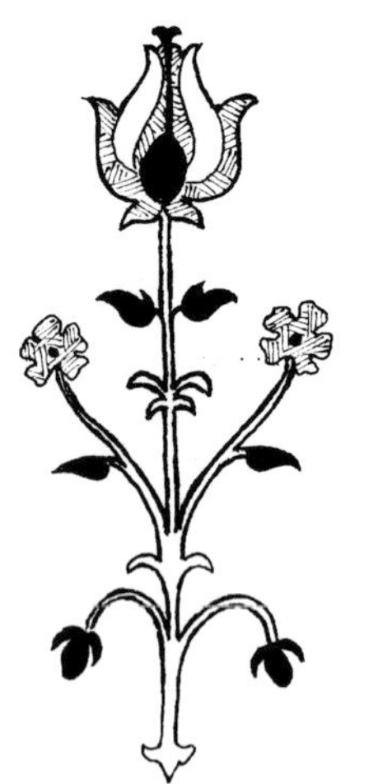

Moroccan flower motifs

1. Draw a carpet design with a floral pattern on a piece of poster board. Note the colors according to the colors of cloth scraps you have collected.
2. Paint thin lines and shapes such as flower stems.
3. Cut pieces of cloth for the flower and leaf shapes.
4. As you cut, glue the cloth pieces onto the design, sticking them flat to the poster board.
5. Use the finished piece as a table decoration.

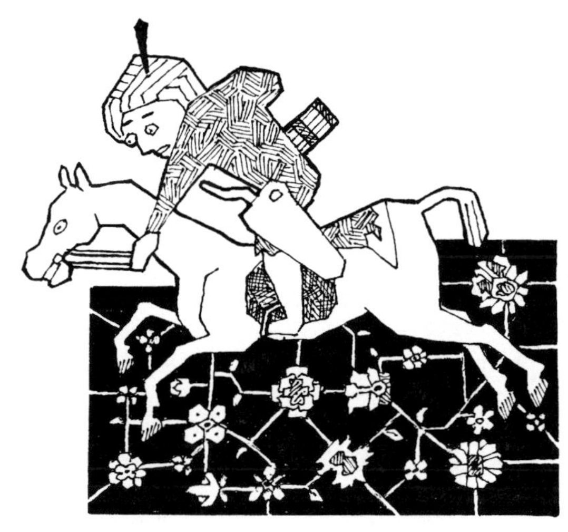

Part IV:

Middle East

IV. The Arts and Crafts of the Middle East

With the exception of Israel and scattered Christian communities in Lebanon and elsewhere, the peoples of the Middle East are Muslim. Of those Muslim nations, all are Arab with the exception of Turkey, Iran, Pakistan, and Afghanistan.

Middle East crafts are at the same time exotic and familiar. Oriental carpets have long graced homes in other parts of the world. This craft provided the flooring for the tents of nomadic Arabs. Their intricate, abstract designs are a result of the Islamic prohibition against using human figures in art. Religion and tradition lie behind the crafts provided in this chapter.

Name ______________________________ Date ______________

Project 17: Middle East: Textile Painting

Materials	
For this activity you will need: • cloth to decorate	• fabric color or acrylic paint

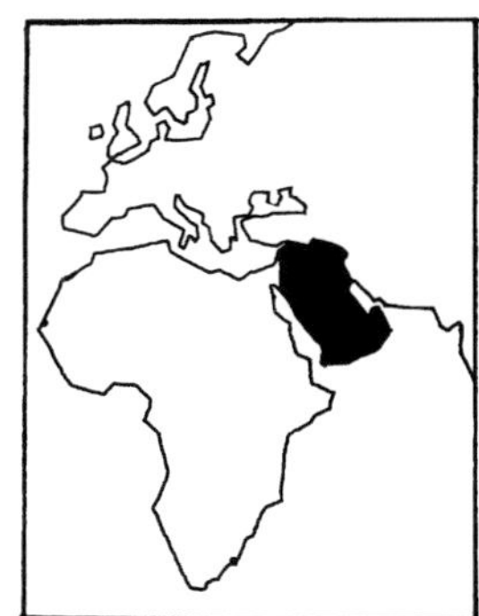

Painting arabesque designs on cloth is an ancient craft in the Middle East. Today machines print most cloth designs. However, craftsmen still practice the art for expensive cloth goods. Decorate napkins, place mats, or a tablecloth with one of the illustrated arabesques shown below or one of your own invention.

1. Plan on a sheet of paper an arabesque design of fine-lined floral or abstract patterns.
2. Select a white napkin for your decoration or hem a piece of white cloth to serve as a napkin or place mat.
3. Rub the back of your design plan with a soft pencil.
4. Pin the design plan to the cloth, pencil-rubbed side down.
5. Draw over the plan's lines, transferring them to the cloth.
6. Remove the plan and paint your design using the pencil lines transferred to the cloth as guides. Acrylic is easier to manage than fabric paint and will remain if washed carefully by hand.

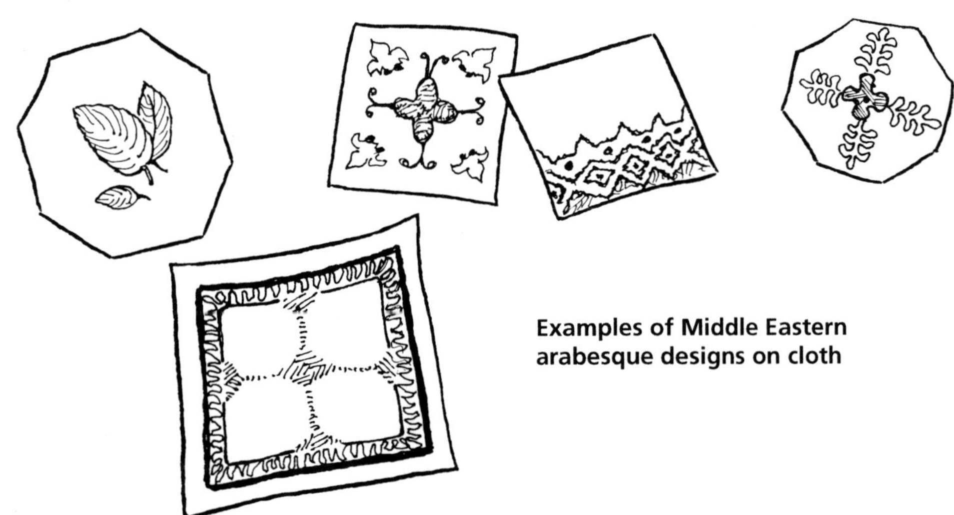

Examples of Middle Eastern arabesque designs on cloth

Name ______________________________ Date ________________

Project 18: Oman: Incense Burner

Materials
For this activity you will need: • clay • poster colors or acrylic paint

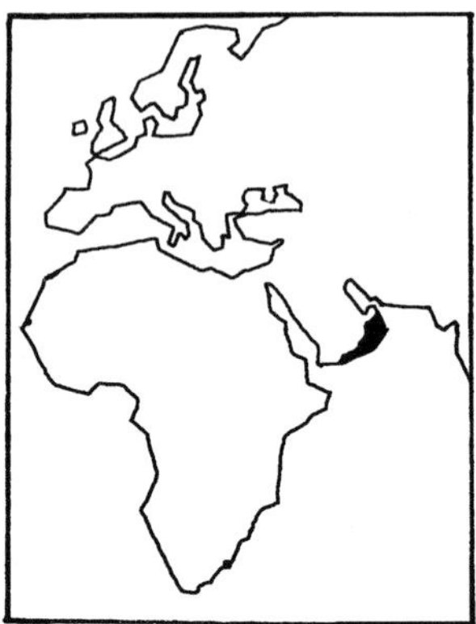

Following the midday meal, your host drops some hot coals from the fire into a clay incense burner. On top of the hot coals he sprinkles incense, then passes the burner around to his guests. You are in Oman, where the world's finest frankincense grows. From here, the hardened tree sap that burns as fragrant smoke was once traded throughout the ancient world.

1. Shape a shallow square bowl about four inches wide from the clay.
2. Shape a second square bowl about three inches wide.
3. Shape more clay into four flat strips one-quarter-inch-thick by one-inch-wide by six-inches-long ($\frac{1}{4}$" × 1" × 6").
4. Assemble the pieces as shown in the illustration *(Step 4)*, dampening the strips where they attach to the bowls.
5. Add other clay shapes to the burner as you wish.
6. When the clay has dried, decorate the burner with paint as illustrated *(Step 6)* or create your own arabesques.
7. Burn purchased incense in your clay Omani incense burner.

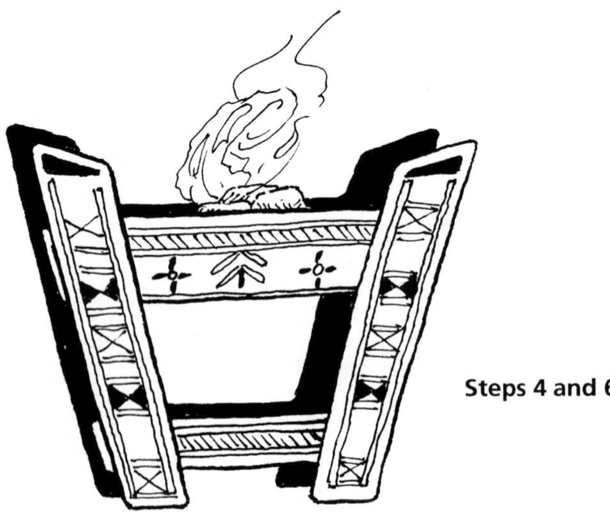

Steps 4 and 6

Name ______________________________ Date ____________________

Project 19: Oman: Amulet

Materials	
For this activity you will need:	
• heavy metal foil	• acrylic paint
• heavy cord	• scissors

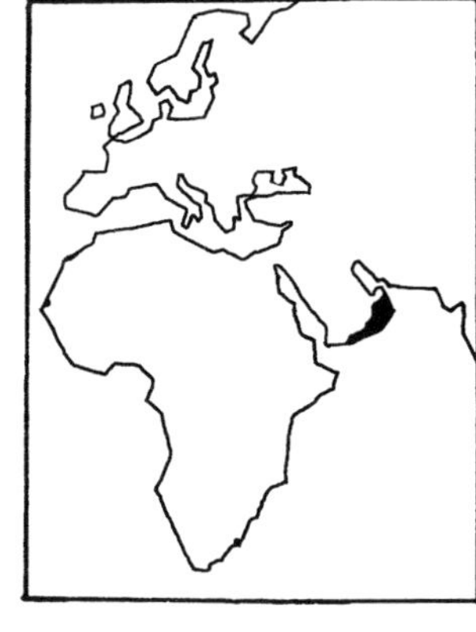

Many devout Muslims wear an amulet, a small metal case containing paper on which is written a passage from the Koran. This Muslim holy book contains the prayers, sermons, and teachings of Muhammad, the prophet of Islam. Wearing an amulet demonstrates one's religious faith and is said to bring good luck.

An amulet is normally made of silver, but you can make one from heavy metal foil.

1. Cut out the illustrated pattern *(Step 1)*. Then, with a felt pen, trace it on a piece of heavy metal foil.
2. Cut the amulet piece from the foil.
3. Paint the amulet with an arabesque using acrylic paint.
4. Insert a written saying inside the amulet as you bend the foil and glue the tabs to the back *(Step 4)*.
5. Thread a cord through the loops to wear or display the amulet *(Step 5)*.

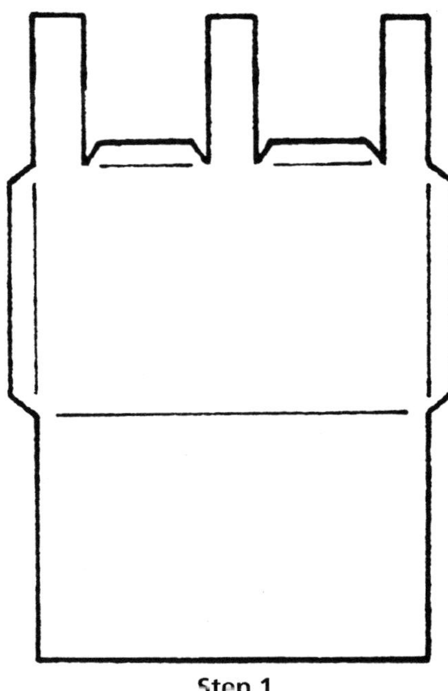

Step 1

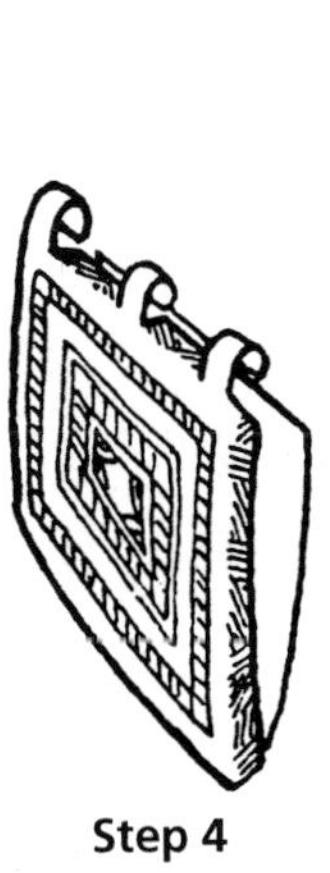

Step 4

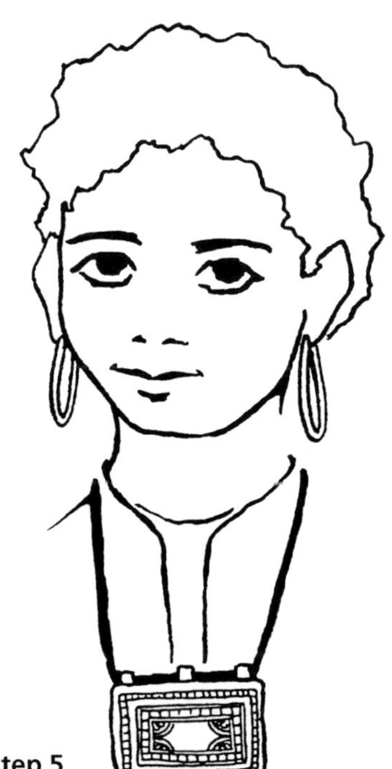

Step 5

Name ____________________ Date ____________________

Project 20: Yemen: Jambiyya Dagger

Materials

For this activity you will need:

- $\frac{1}{2}$-inch-thick plywood
- colored pieces of cloth
- jigsaw
- paste jewels
- foil
- wire

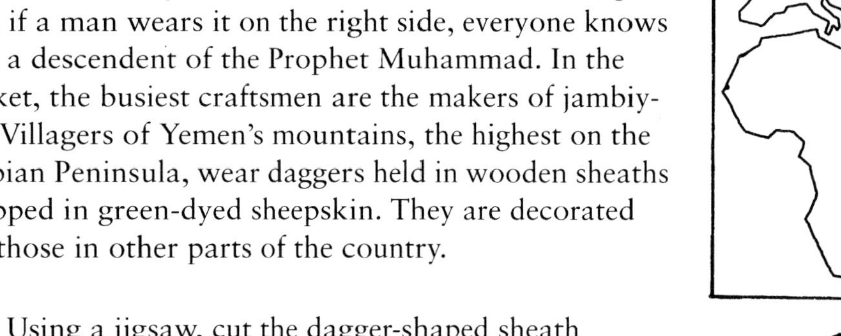

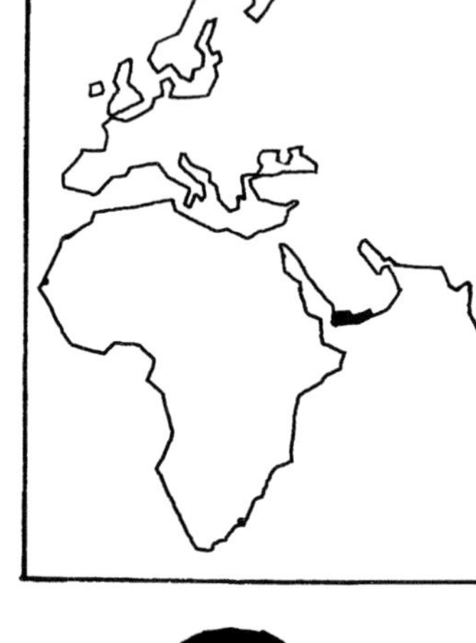

The daggers, called *jambiyya,* tucked into the belts of Yemen men are less about aggression and more about status. The sheaths are richly decorated with jewels or filigree, indicating the wealth of the owner. More important, if a man wears it on the right side, everyone knows he is a descendent of the Prophet Muhammad. In the market, the busiest craftsmen are the makers of jambiyyas. Villagers of Yemen's mountains, the highest on the Arabian Peninsula, wear daggers held in wooden sheaths wrapped in green-dyed sheepskin. They are decorated like those in other parts of the country.

1. Using a jigsaw, cut the dagger-shaped sheath and hilt from a piece of ten-inch-long plywood following the illustrated example *(Step 1).*

2. Paint the hilt black.

3. Glue strips of colored cloth in bands around the sheath.

4. Decorate by wrapping around and/or gluing to the jambiyya costume jewelry, metal foil, and wire.

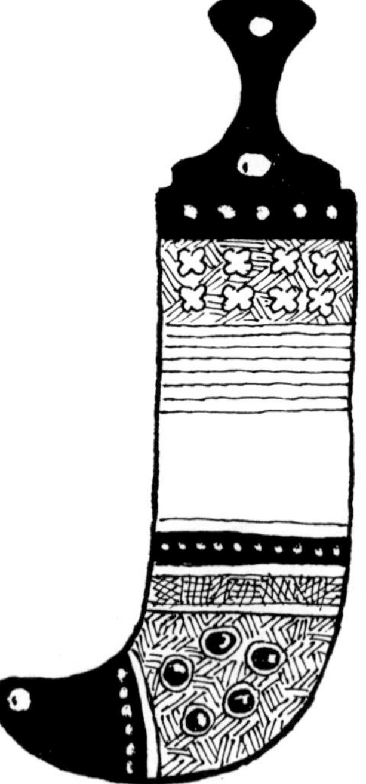

Step 1

Name ______________________ Date ______________

Project 21: Iran: Oriental Carpet Collage

Materials	
For this activity you will need:	• all-purpose white glue
• carpet scraps	• thin poster board
• piece of heavy burlap	• hobby knife

Oriental carpets are made in many parts of the Near East, including Iran. As long ago as biblical times, carpets were made by the nomads of the region for furnishing their tents. They were rolled up for transport whenever the nomads moved on. When Islam became the dominant religion of the Near East, carpets were adapted to the new faith. Covered with arabesques, large carpets decorate mosques. Small rugs are used for prayer rugs. One end of a prayer rug dominates the other, as in the illustration below. A devout Muslim points that end in the direction of the holy city of Mecca, then kneels on the carpet to pray.

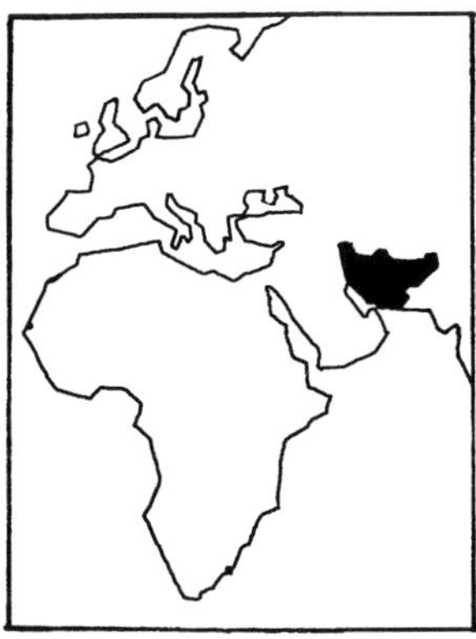

1. Collect scraps of carpet. Ask dealers who sell wall-to-wall carpeting for pieces left from cutting fitted carpets.

2. Design a carpet plan based on the scraps. If any of the scraps have a pattern, make use of it in your design.

3. Make a finished drawing of the design on poster board the same size as your planned carpet collage.

4. Cut the shapes from the poster board. These are the patterns.

5. Lay each pattern on a carpet scrap and draw around it with a felt-tipped pen and cut the shape from the carpet scrap.

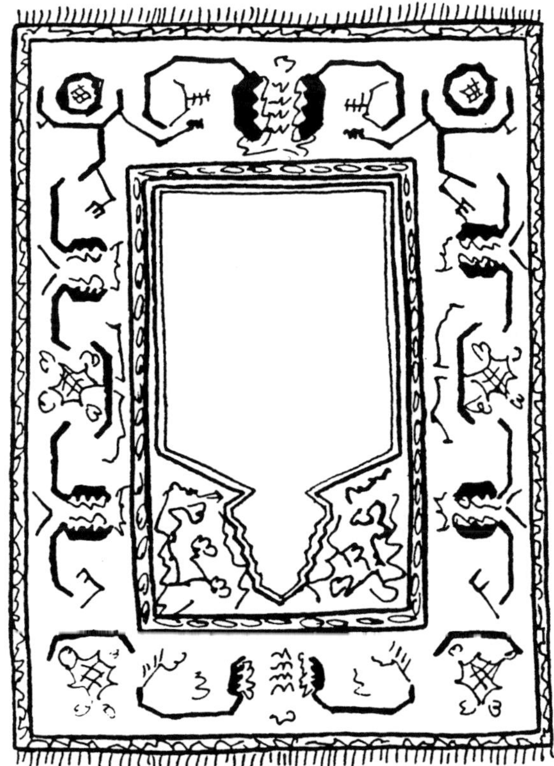

Example of Muslim prayer rug

(continued)

Name ______________________________ Date ______________

Project 21: Iran: Oriental Carpet Collage *(continued)*

6. Cut a piece of burlap slightly larger than the carpet design. This is the carpet backing. Lay it on newspaper to catch glue.

7. Glue the carpet pieces to the burlap working from the center outward *(Step 7)*. Weight down the pieces with something heavy.

8. When the glue has dried, trim the edges of the burlap backing. Use your carpet collage as a floor mat.

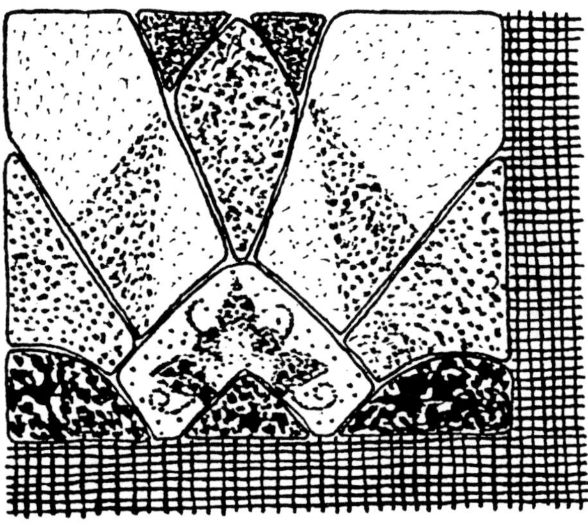

Step 7

Name ____________________________ Date ________________

Project 22: Iran: Kilim Carpet Hanging

Materials	
For this activity you will need:	
• cloth scraps	• white glue
• cotton canvas 12" × 18" or bigger	• rod
	• cord

Iran is especially noted for its kilim carpets, rugs meant to hang on a wall, not to lie on the floor. Woven like tapestries, they are thinner and lighter than floor rugs. Kilims are noted for intricate, abstract designs. Some have pictured hunters in a field of geometric flowers like the illustration below, one of the few occasions when human figures appear in the crafts of a Muslim country.

1. Cut a rectangle of canvas, 12 × 18 inches or bigger.
2. Fold two inches over at the top and sew to make a channel through which a rod can be inserted for hanging.
3. Lay the material on newspaper and then tack to a drawing board.
4. Cut a number of cloth scraps into small shapes.
5. Arrange the cloth pieces on the material, working from the center outward to create a symmetrical design. Arrange for a varicolored border to run around the edge.
6. Move the pieces about until satisfied with the arrangement.
7. Glue the cloth scraps to the backing cloth piece by piece.
8. When it is dry, remove the collage from the drawing board.
9. Insert a wooden rod (two inches longer than the width of the collage) in the cloth channel at the top *(Step 9)*. Tie a cord at the ends and hang for display.

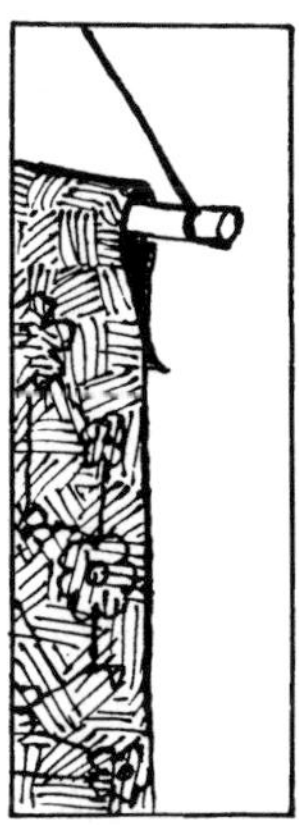

Step 9

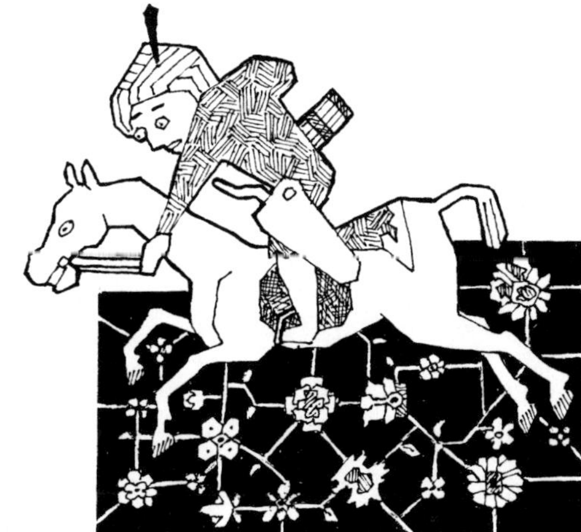

Example of kilim design

Name ______________________________ Date ______________

Project 23: Turkey: Shoeshine Box

Materials	
For this activity you will need: • wooden box • $^1/_8$"-thick plywood • gold-colored foil	• hammer and nails • hinges • jigsaw

The *boyaci,* Turkish shoeshine boys or men, sit in busy parts of towns waiting to polish the shoes of passers-by. The client stands in front of the boyaci (who sits on a low stool) and puts one foot, then the other, on the shoeshine box to have his shoes brushed and polished. Made of brass-covered wood, the box contains the jars of wax and polish and the brushes that the boyaci needs to do his job.

1. Find or build a small wooden box.
2. From the plywood, cut the shapes for the front and back of the box as they appear in the exploded view *(Step 2)*. Cut also the rectangular pieces for the sides.
3. Nail these to the front and back of the box.
4. Nail sides to enclose the box.
5. Nail shelves inside the side compartments for holding bottles.
6. Hinge a wooden top to the main box in the center.
7. Cover with gold-colored foil.
8. Decorate more as you wish, gluing glass jewelry or beads, or drawing designs on the box, guided by the Turkish shoeshine box below *(Step 8)*.
9. Use as a utility box for nails or screws, art supplies, or toilet articles.

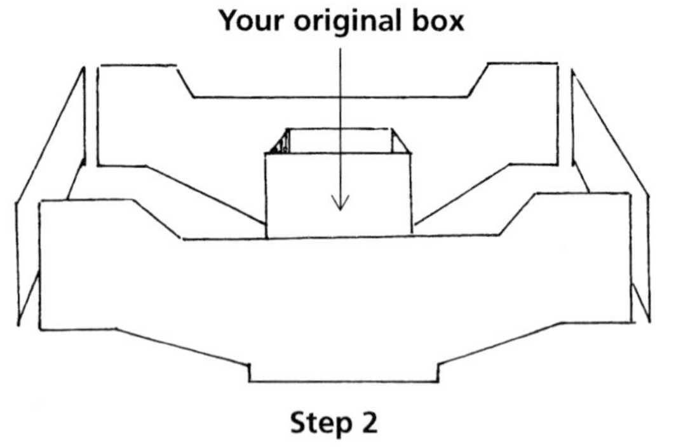

Step 2

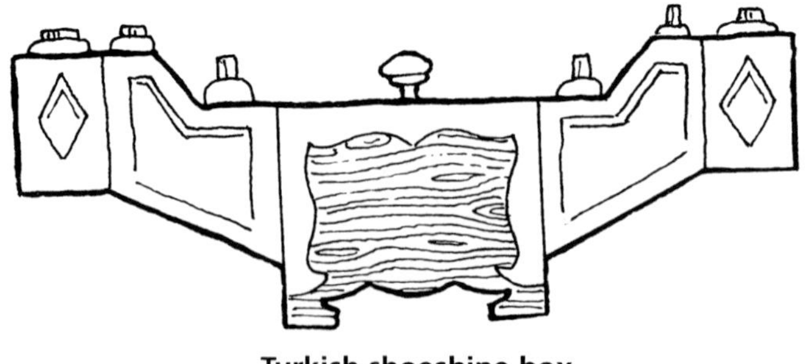
Turkish shoeshine box
Step 8

Name ______________________ Date ______________________

Project 24: Turkey: Shadow Puppets

Materials	
For this activity you will need: • poster board • string • match sticks • 10" stick	• hobby knife • tracing paper • watercolor paint • glue • notebook reinforcements

Folk legend tells how a builder on a mosque held up construction by telling his colleagues stories. Fed up, the sultan angrily ordered him beheaded, but with many stories to tell, the builder's execution was delayed indefinitely. Today Turkish puppeteers perform those stories with shadow puppets made of cardboard and colored semi-transparent paper. The theater is a paper-covered frame with lights arranged to cast shadows and color on the screen while the puppeteer stands behind the lights.

1. From poster board, cut two puppet parts, the head and torso with arms for one, the legs for the other. Together they make a puppet about twelve inches high. Make the sultan illustrated at right or design your own.
2. Cut inner holes with a hobby knife, one where torso joins the legs, two at the shoulder.
3. Glue strong tracing paper to the puppet.
4. Color the paper puppet with transparent watercolor.
5. Reinforce the holes where the torso is to be joined to the legs and the two holes at the shoulder with circular note-book paper reinforcements.
6. Make joints with match sticks and short string as shown *(Step 6)*.
7. Tie a string from the shoulder holes to the end of a stick *(Step 7)*. Move the stick and the puppet jumps and flops about.

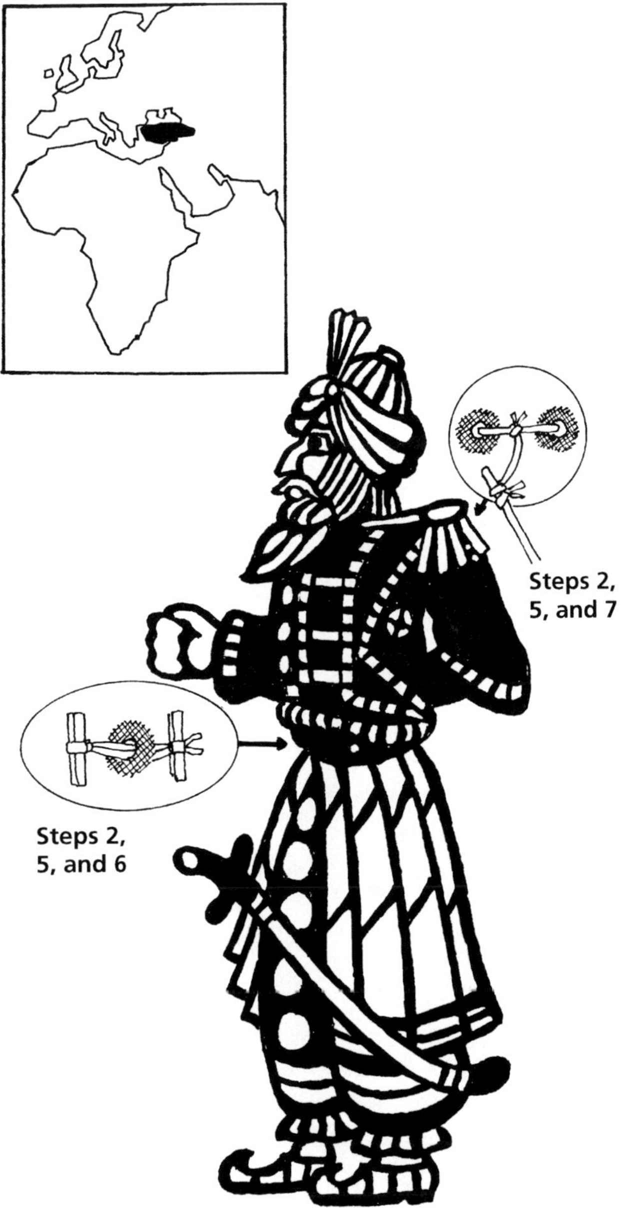

Shadow puppet of a sultan

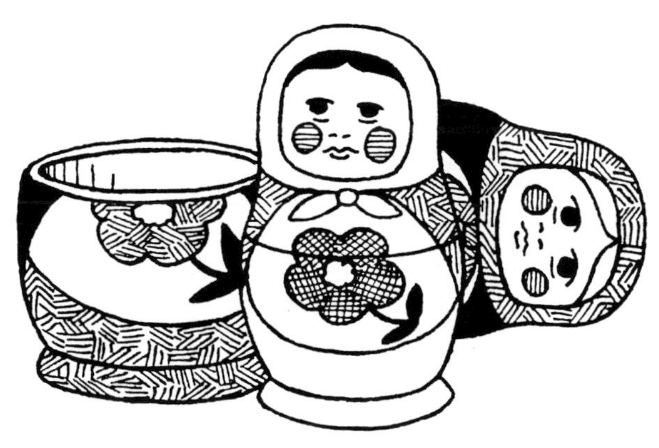

Part V:

Europe

V. The Arts and Crafts of Europe

Traditional crafts can tell much about a region. For example, handpainted inn and trade signs hang in many European towns that have held onto their centuries-old appearance. They show the pride those communities take in their ancient traditions and their desire to preserve those traditions. Political borders are not necessarily cultural. Finely decorated Easter eggs are common throughout Eastern Europe. Crafts can even tell a political story. Since Communism fell in Russia, for example, some nested dolls have been made to represent President Yeltsin, inside of which rests Gorbachev, then Brezhnev, and so on, creating a Russian political history.

Italy's Renaissance, Spain's New World contributions, and France's taste have made the crafts of these countries among the most influential in the western world. One need speak only of glassware and lace from Venice, appliqué and Limoges china from France, and Toledo swords and leather goods from Spain to understand how craft work can be raised to art. It is no coincidence that many words for craft techniques are French. Cloisonné, découpé, appliqué, repoussé, collage, and silhouette are all examples of how French tradition has led the crafts world.

Name ______________________ Date ______________

Project 25: Northern Europe: Inn and Trade Signs

Materials	
For this activity you will need: • plywood • wood strips	• enamel or latex paint • varnish • jigsaw

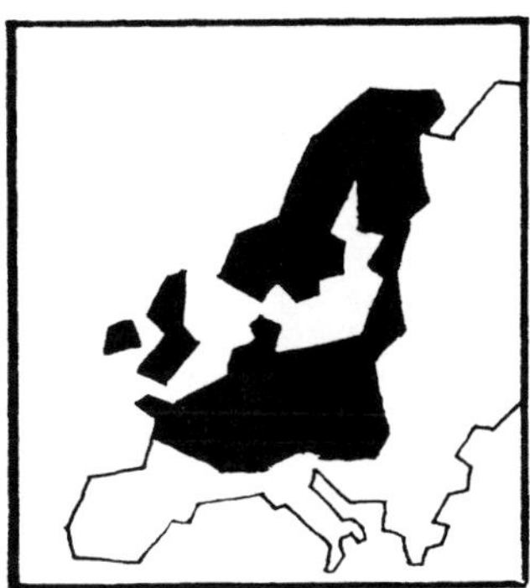

Spot two interlocked yellow arches or a revolving striped pole in front of a business and you know whether you will get a hamburger or a haircut inside. For centuries, signs outside have told people what goes on inside. Even though modern signs might be factory plastic or flashing neon, European sign painters still create traditional signs, especially in towns that keep their centuries-old appearance to appeal to tourists. Illustrated below are some examples. Could there be a place for such signs in your town? Perhaps a local business would be interested in a sign like this. For classroom decoration, make inn signs using French *(auberge)*, German *(Gasthaus)*, or whatever language you are studying on the sign.

1. Select a local business for a sign, whether they would be interested in having one made or not.
2. Design the sign using an illustrated example or your own idea.
3. Cut the design with a jigsaw if it is of unusual shape. If it is rectangular, glue and nail strips as a frame on the front and back.
4. Paint your sign design on the front and back.
5. Cover with several coats of clear varnish to protect the sign from weather.

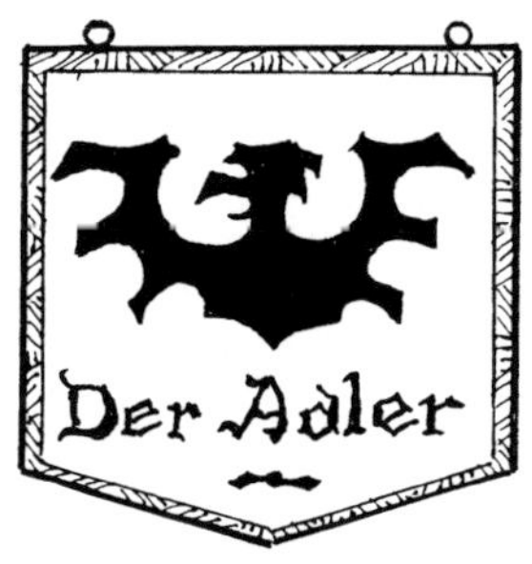

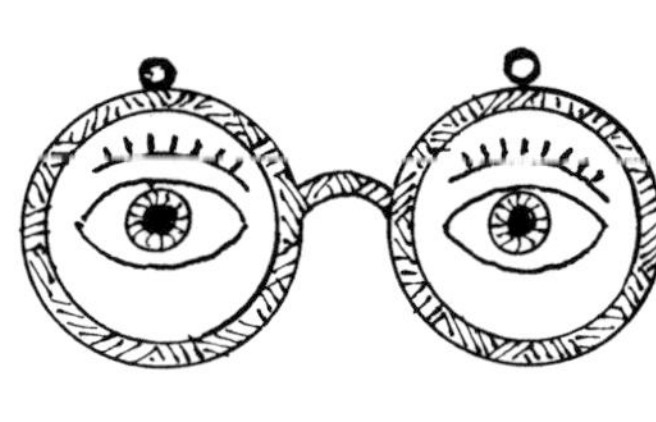

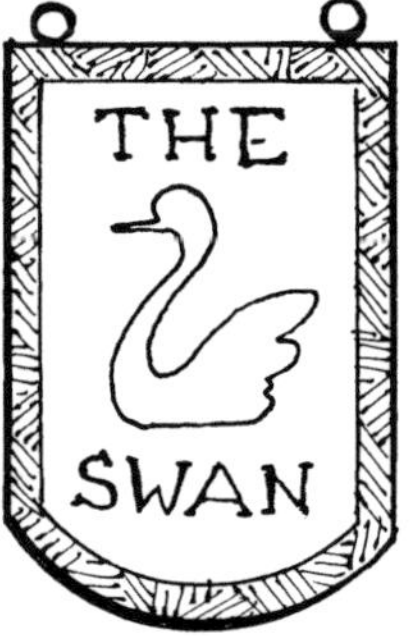

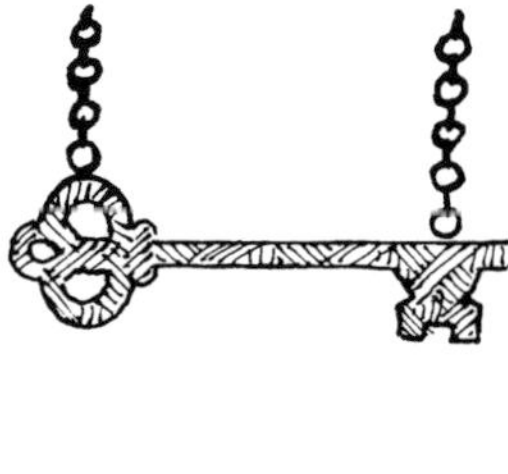

Examples of traditional, European hand-painted signs

Name ______________________ Date ______________

Project 26: Central Europe: Behind-Glass Painting

Materials	
For this activity you will need: • acrylic paint	• piece of clear glass or plastic • drawing paper

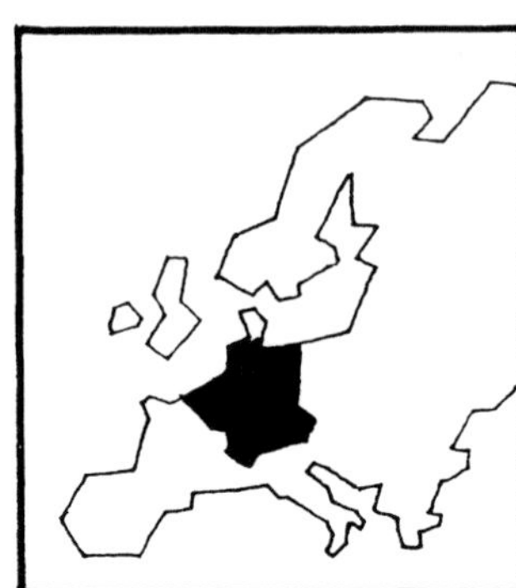

With this craft the artist paints on glass. When it is framed, the plain glass side, not the painted side, is turned toward the viewer. This craft is practiced in Roman Catholic Bavaria and Austria. Religious themes, such as images of saints, are the traditional subject. Hung in the home, these objects recall colored church windows.

At the beginning of the twentieth century, artists in Munich, Bavaria's capital, used modern art styles to paint on glass.

A behind-glass painting must be painted in the reverse of the usual painting order. For example, foreground foliage and details must be painted first, then the background over that. Portraits and figures are especially complicated since details, such as mouth and eyes, must be painted first, before flesh and dress colors are painted over the details.

1. Plan a picture on a piece of paper the size of the glass or plastic. Acrylic paint will stick better to plastic than glass. Tape the plan face down on the glass or plastic.
2. Turn the glass over and use the plan to guide your painting. First, paint details such as facial features or costume decoration *(Step 2)*. You might need to paint a second time for the paint to completely cover the glass or plastic.

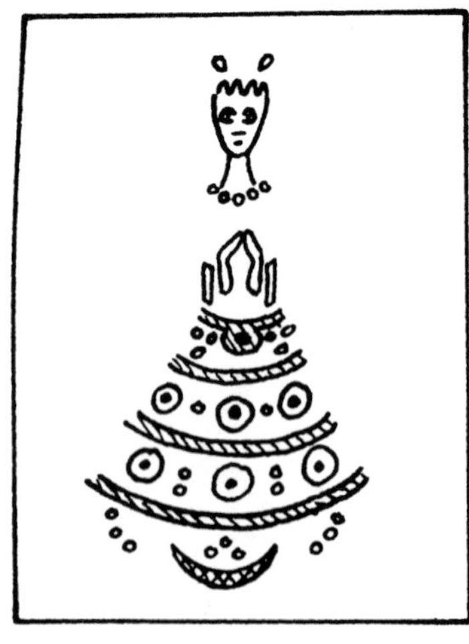

Step 2

(continued)

Name ______________________ Date ______________

Project 26: Central Europe: Behind-Glass Painting *(continued)*

3. When details have dried, paint in the background color *(Step 3)*.

4. When all the paint has dried, turn over the glass. The details and foreground objects will lie in front of the background.

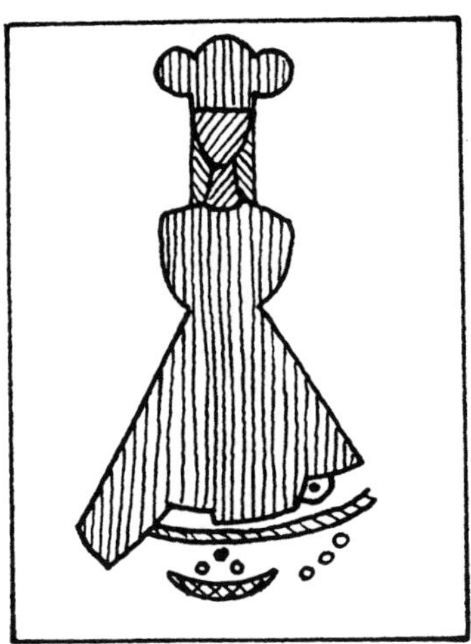

Step 3

Some artists in Holland, which borders Germany, have used behind-glass painting for special three-dimensional landscapes. They painted foreground objects on one sheet of glass, middle-ground objects on a second, and background on a third piece of glass as illustrated below. Bound together, the foreground is nearer the viewer and the background farther away: a three-dimensional painting.

5. If you try this special kind of art, tape together the painted glass or plastic with plastic tape once all three pieces have been painted.

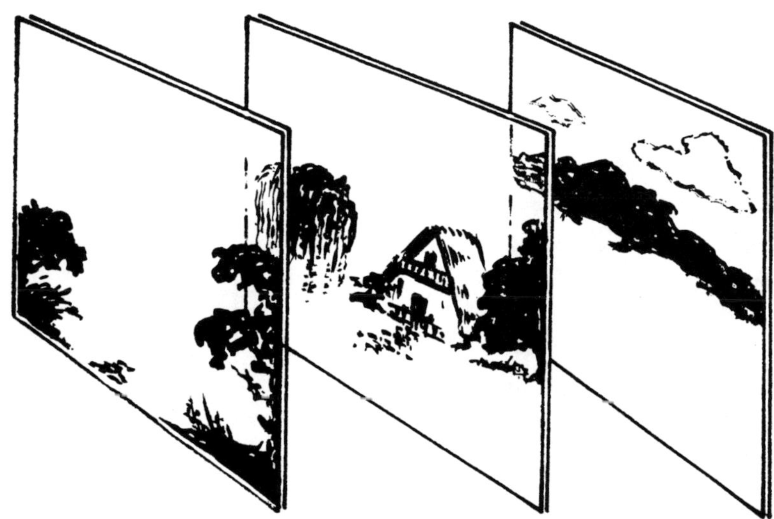

Example of three-dimensional behind-glass painting

Name ______________________________ Date ______________

Project 27: Poland: Wycinanki Paper Cutting

Materials	
For this activity you will need:	
• black construction paper	• white poster board
• glue	• hobby knife

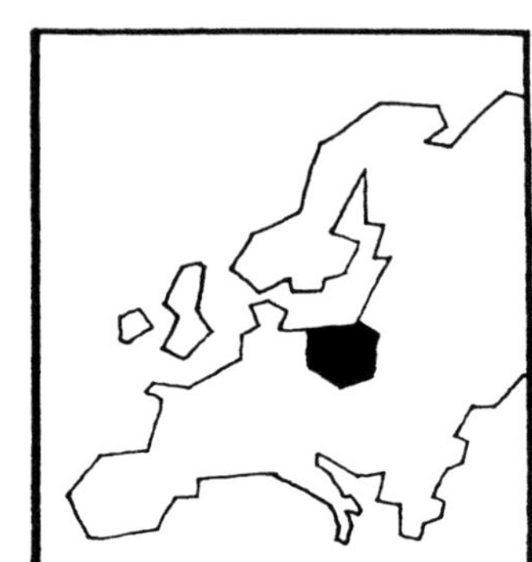

Wycinanki is a paper-cutting craft made popular in Poland in the late nineteenth century. The designs, usually symmetrical, are of stylized birds or flowers as illustrated below. Originally, wycinanki designs were cut from only black paper. Today, however, colors are often added to enliven the decoration. Once cut, the paper designs are used to decorate furniture, trays, kitchen utensils, and the like.

1. Plan one half of a symmetrical design on thin paper.
2. Fold a piece of black construction paper in half. With a few drops of glue fix your paper plan to the folded black paper, resting the middle of the design along the fold.
3. Using the plan as a guide, carefully cut out your design. For fine cuts use manicure scissors or a pointed hobby knife.
4. Open your cut design, tear away the plan, and scrape off any glue that remains.
5. Carefully glue your finished wycinanki design to a white paper background such as poster board or notebook cover.
6. Cut out details from colored paper to enhance your design—red and yellow patches for bird wings or flowers, for example—and glue them to your wycinanki paper cutting.

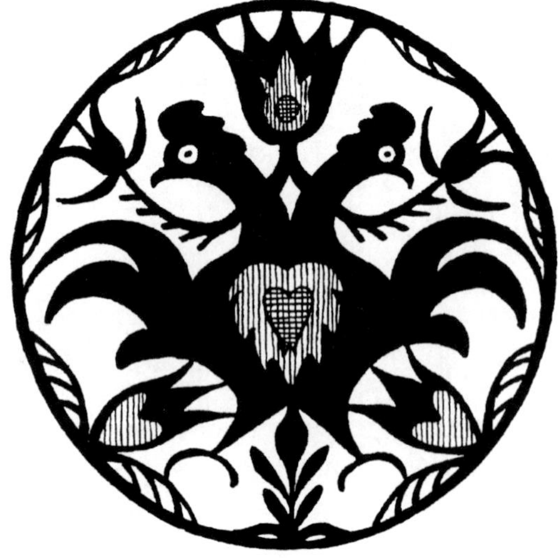

Examples of Wycinanki paper cutting

Name ______________________________ Date ______________

Project 28: Czech Republic: Cornhusk Dolls

Materials	
For this activity you will need: • dried cornhusks cut in convenient strips • glue	• wire • string • poster paint

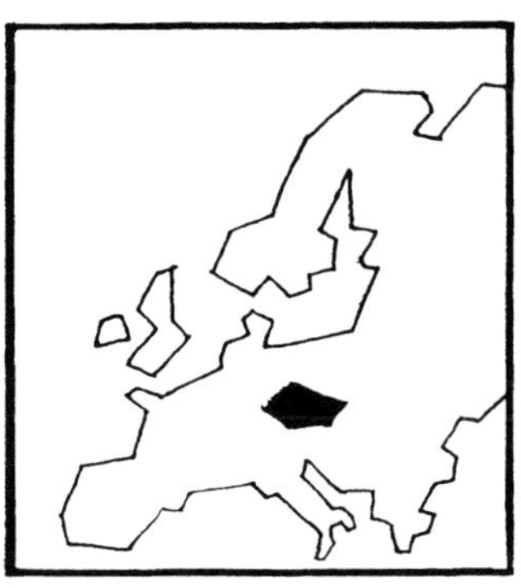

Folk artists are very resourceful, crafting objects from all available materials. Cornhusk dolls have been made in many places. This cornhusk doll (below left) is for village children in the Czech Republic.

1. Roll some pieces of husk into a ball for the head. Wrap the ball neatly with a cornhusk strip and twist the end into a point *(Step 1)*.
2. Wrap a piece of wire with a cornhusk to serve as sleeved arms *(Step 2)*.
3. Double several cornhusk strips over the center of the arms to serve as fill for the body.
4. Cover the body with one broad cornhusk strip for the skirt. Glue to the arms where it passes over the wrapped wire. Tie it together with a string around the waist *(Step 4)*.
5. Poke a hole in the top of the covering husk. Dab glue along the long point of the head and stick it into this hole.
6. Paint a simple face on the doll. Wrap the head with a strip of cornhusk to serve as a head scarf.

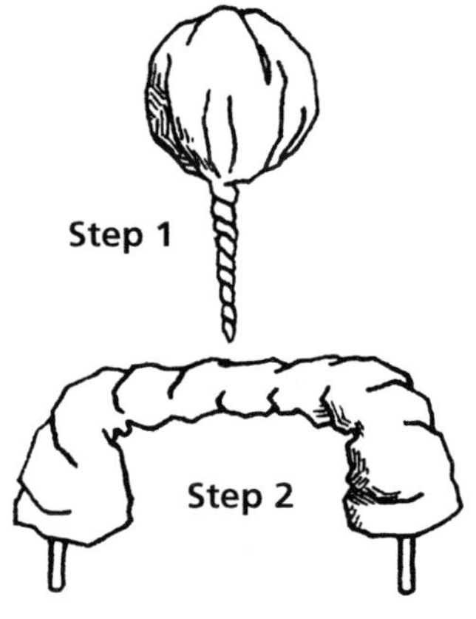

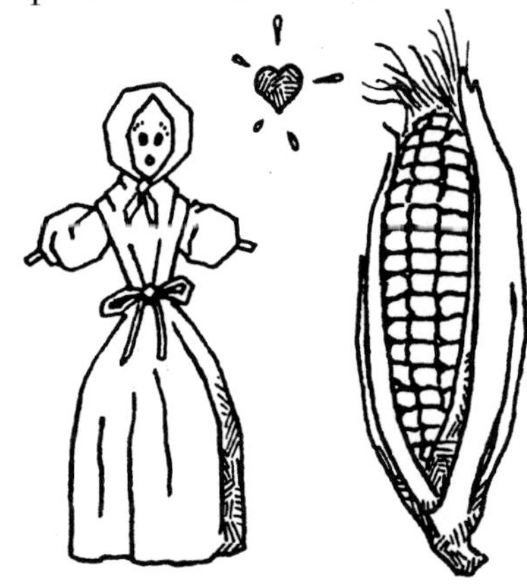

Czech cornhusk doll

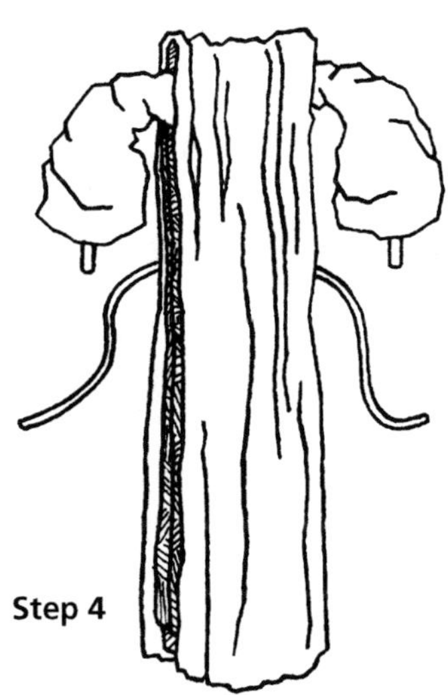

Name ____________________ Date ____________________

Project 29: Eastern Europe: Easter Eggs

Materials	
For this activity you will need:	
• a raw egg	• paraffin or candle wax
• match stick	• cold water egg dye

Elaborately decorated Easter eggs are a craft tradition throughout Eastern Europe. The single egg illustrated here (below left) is from the Czech Republic. The collected eggs (below right) are Russian designs. These eggs are colored with a batik technique in which the decorator covers part of the shell with a dye-resistant wax. You can do the same, or simply use a brush to paint an egg in the decorative manner of Eastern Europe.

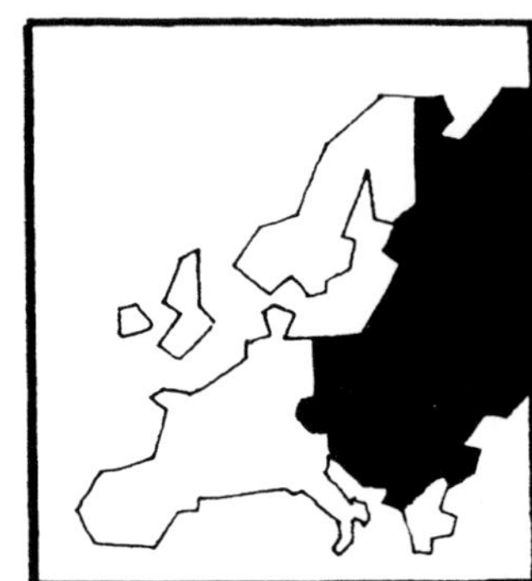

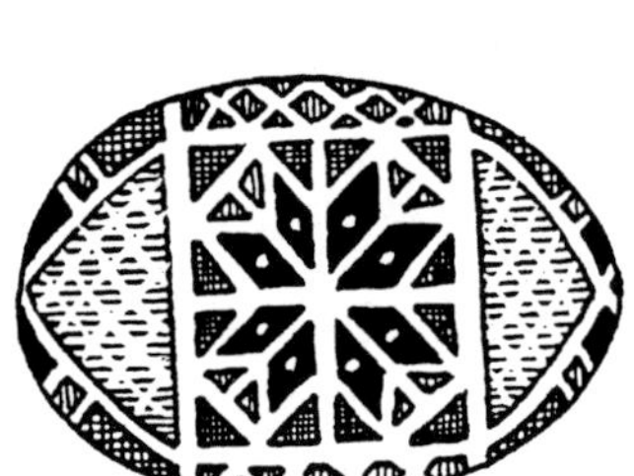

Czech Easter egg

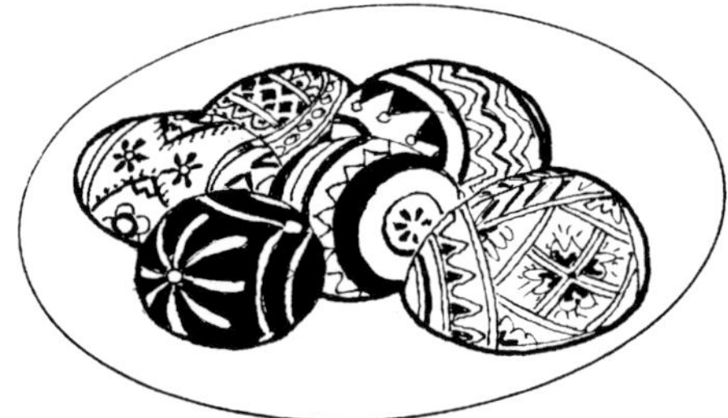

Russian Easter eggs

1. Because egg designs are so intricate and beautiful, these eggs are kept for many months and years. To prevent rotting, the yolk and white are blown out. Poke a hole in each end of the egg with a needle and then use the needle to break the yolk inside. Blow hard through one hole to force the white and yolk out the other.

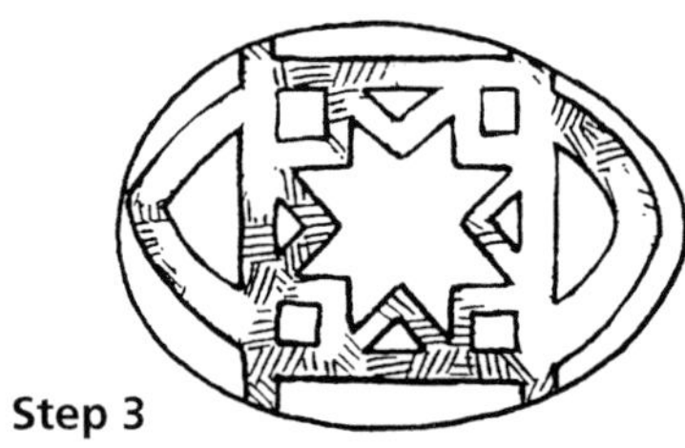

Step 3

2. Plan a simple design for a first try. Let the natural egg color be part of the design with two other colors.
3. Use a match stick to apply melted wax to those parts that are to remain free of dye *(Step 3)*.
4. Dip the egg into lighter colored, cold-water dye.

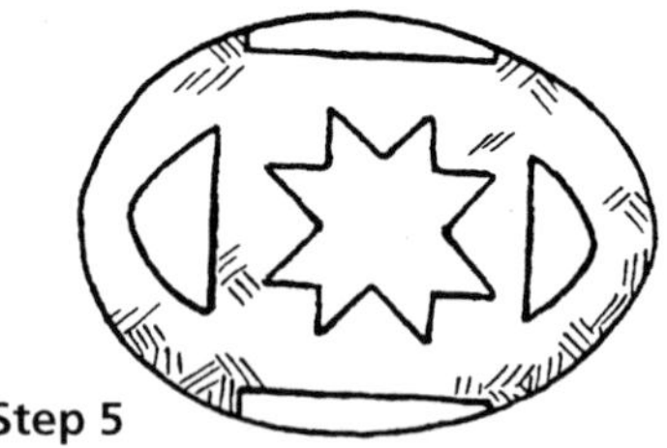

Step 5

5. Once it is dry, wax the egg where the lighter color is to remain *(Step 5)*.
6. Dye the egg with the darker second color.
7. When the second color has dried, hold the egg near heat to melt the wax. The egg will have two colors plus the shell color *(Step 7)*.

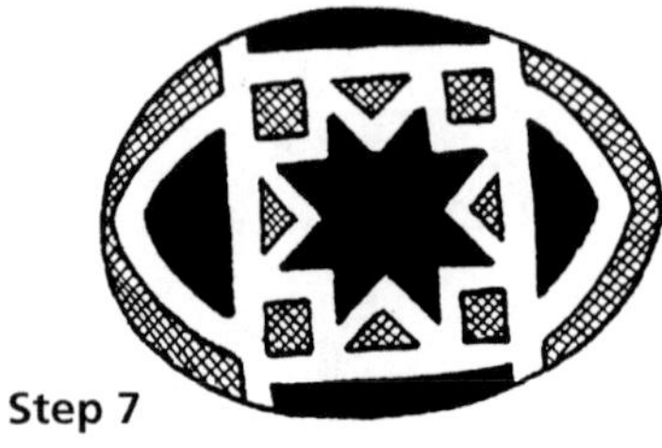

Step 7

Name ____________________ Date ____________________

Project 30: Russia: Nested Dolls

Materials	
For this activity you will need:	• white latex paint
• gift boxes of various sizes	• poster paint or crayons

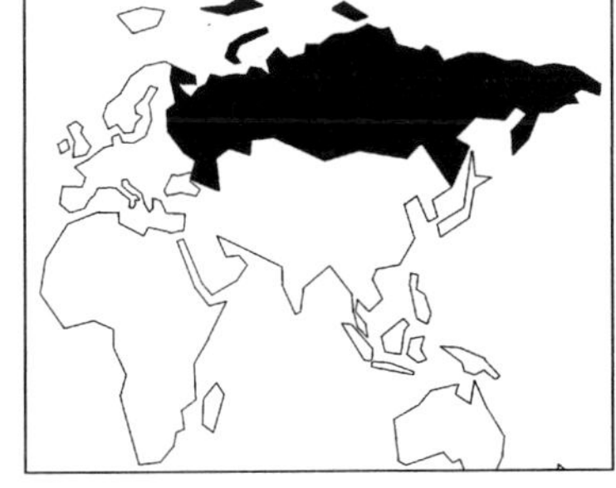

Sold in gift shops around the world, nesting dolls are an example of Russian wood carving, a natural craft for this forest-rich country. The doll below is dressed in a traditional costume with a head scarf called a *babushka*, the Russian word for grandmother. When the head is removed, a second doll is found inside. Remove its head and another doll appears.

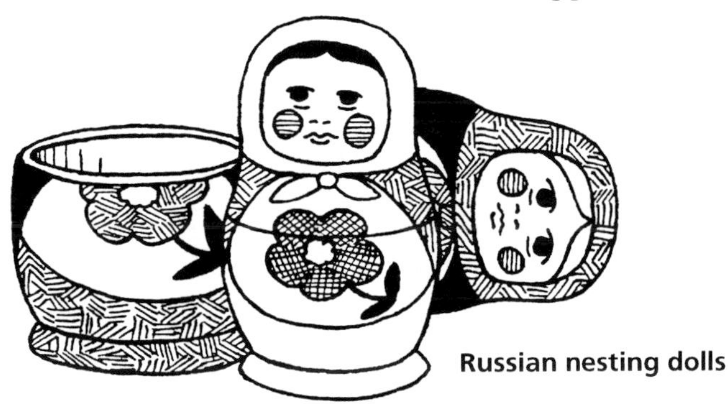

Russian nesting dolls

1. Choose three or four gift boxes that will fit into each other in a nesting series: the smallest inside the next smallest, and so on. All should fit inside the largest box.
2. Paint the boxes with white latex paint.
3. On one side of each box draw peasant women in traditional Russian costumes. Then paint them in color.
4. Nest the boxes and give them as a gift.
5. You can draw other figures as well, such as historical Russian figures, American personalities, or entertainment figures. The nested dolls have a time sequence. First the outer box is removed, then the next, and so on. If you decide on historical figures, draw the most recent on the outer box, the person preceding on the next box, and so on back in time.

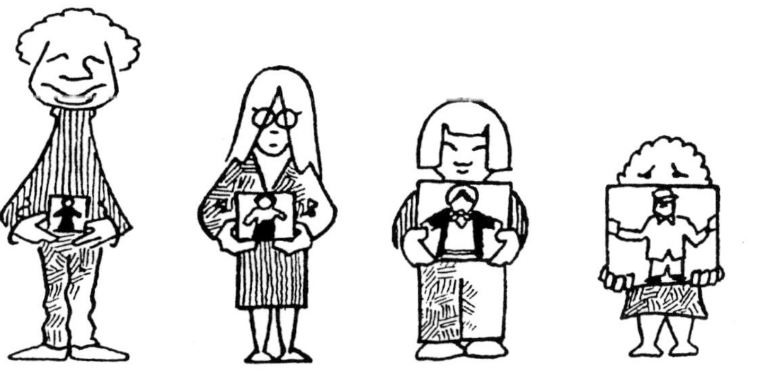

Nested boxes painted with dolls

Name ______________________________ Date ______________

Project 31: Spain: Leather Purse

Materials
For this activity you will need: • soft leather large enough to cut an 8" circle • 24"-long leather thong

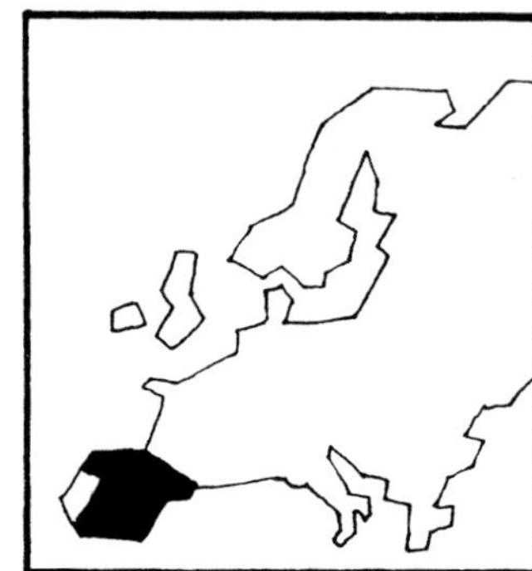

For centuries, Spain was part of the Muslim world. Cordoba, its capital, was Europe's most civilized city in the Middle Ages. From Cordoba, Europeans learned Arabic numerals and the use of the decimal point. They also learned how to tan animal hides to make leather. One type of fine leather, cordovan, was named for Cordoba.

In centuries since, Spanish leather has continued to be famous. Besides making shoes and jackets, Spanish artisans have used leather in furniture making and even utensils, such as wine-skins. This project shows you how to make a simple but practical object from leather, requiring no sewing.

1. Cut a circular piece of leather eight inches in diameter.
2. On a circle one-half inch in from the outer circumference, punch or cut small holes every inch. There will be twenty-one holes on this inner circumference.
3. Thread the leather thong through the holes all the way around the purse. Let the ends hang outside one exit hole *(Step 3)*. Knot the thong ends. Pull them to close the purse.

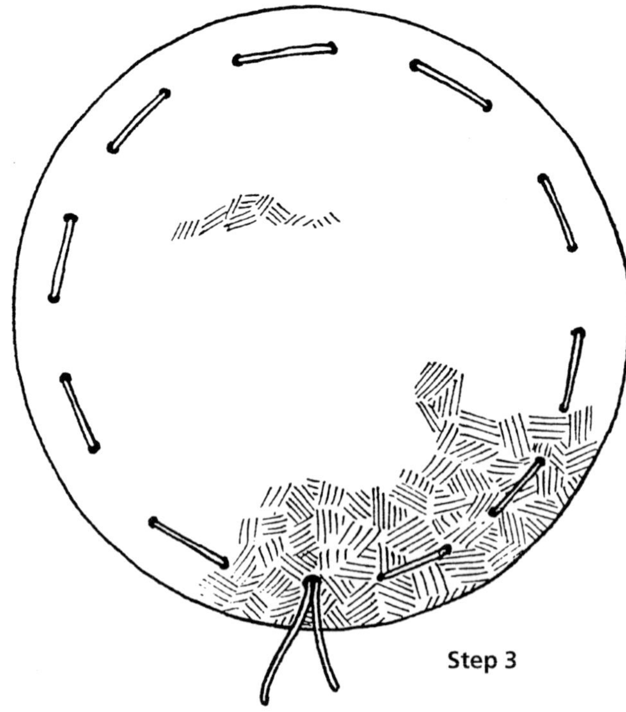

Step 3

Name ____________________ Date ____________

Project 32: France: Appliqué

Materials	
For this activity you will need: • pieces of cloth that do not fray easily (taffeta, linen, velvet, felt)	• colored thread • sewing needle • backing cloth

Although *appliqué* is a French word meaning "to apply," it has a history extending far beyond its borders to Asia and even ancient Egypt. The knights of the Crusades, many of them French, used appliqué decorations for their tents, cloaks, and horse coverings. Your theme can be based on a Crusader's coat of arms, a medieval religious motif, a French scene, or a design based on the modern art of Braque, Leger, or another famous French artist.

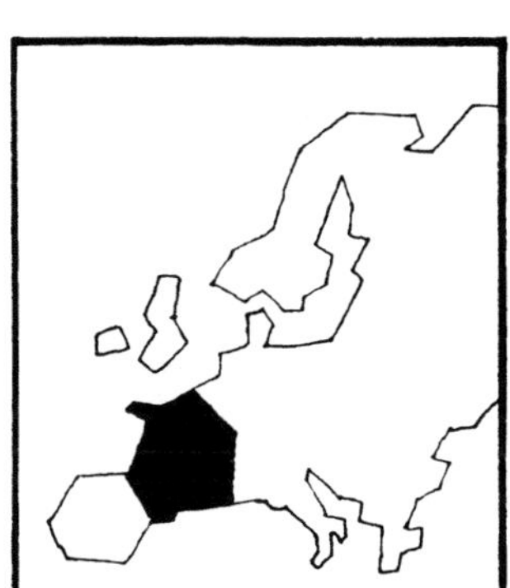

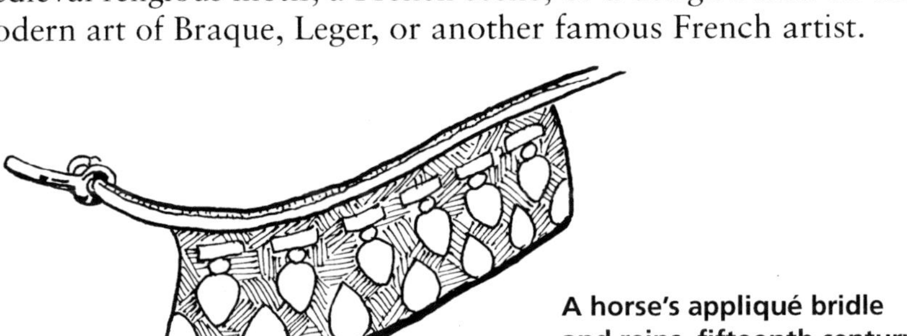

A horse's appliqué bridle and reins, fifteenth century

1. Plan a panel picture on a sheet of heavy paper. Color it according to the colors of the cloth scraps. If cloth pieces have decorative patterns, use them as part of the picture plan. A flower pattern can become a garden in the picture.
2. Cut out the shapes from the picture plan.
3. Pin each paper pattern to the cloth of the matching color. Adjust each pattern so the threads of the cloth pieces all run at the same angle.
4. Cut the cloth pieces according to the pinned paper pattern.
5. Arrange and pin the cloth pieces to the backing cloth *(Step 5)*.
6. Using whatever stitch you know, sew each cloth shape along its edges to the backing cloth. For neatest results, turn under the edges of the patches before sewing.
7. The completed appliqué picture can be used in a variety of ways. Sew a backing piece to it, stuff, and sew closed for a cushion *(Step 7)*. Or sew loops at each upper corner for hanging on a wall.

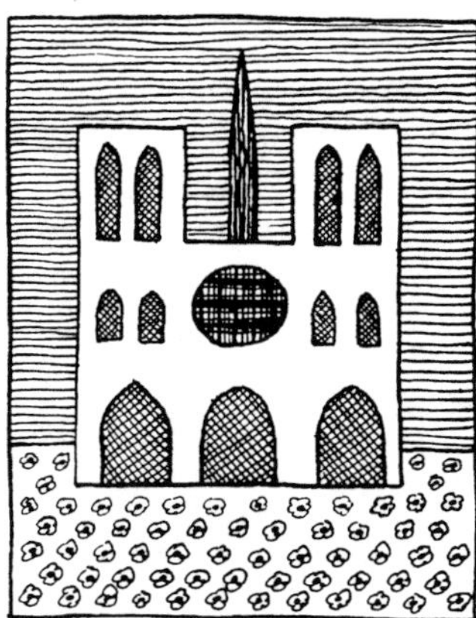

Step 5

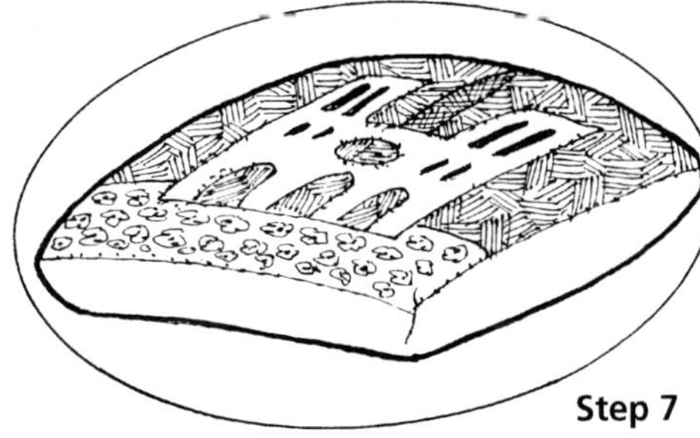

Step 7

Name ______________________ Date ______________

Project 33: France: Découpé

Materials	
For this activity you will need:	
• three or four pieces of colored felt, each approximately 6" square	• colored thread
	• sewing needle

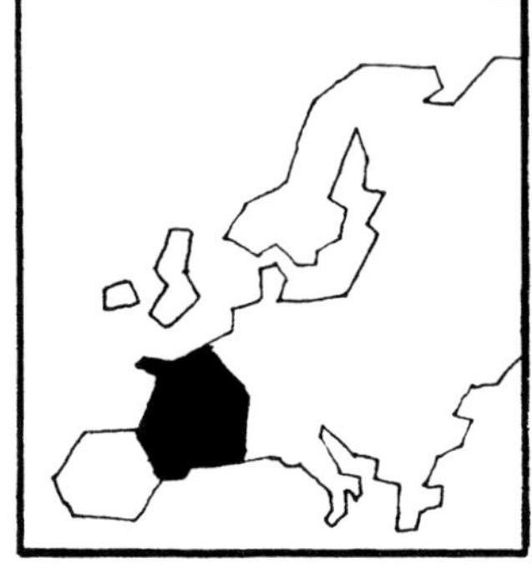

Découpé, another French term, is best understood as reverse appliqué. Rather than adding pieces of cloth to a design, as in appliqué, you cut away pieces of cloth. Traditional découpé has been used for decorating the vestments of priests. These directions show you how to make a small découpé panel.

1. Plan a design such as a French fleur-de-lis or an abstract design of geometric shapes. The colors include the background of the panel plus the design.
2. Arrange the felt (or other cloth) pieces one on top of the other, the background color on top, the smaller design shapes on the bottom. Sew the pieces together around the outside edges *(Step 2)*.
3. Draw your design on the top piece of cloth.

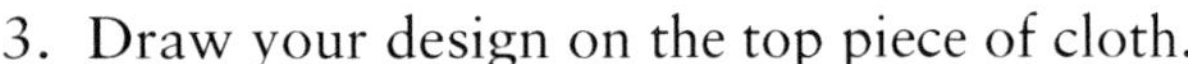

4. Cut away all the shapes of your plan from this upper piece *(Step 4)*.
5. Cut away smaller shapes of the plan from the second cloth below. If there is a fourth piece, reveal it by cutting away the smallest shapes from the third cloth *(Step 5)*.
6. Leave the last piece of cloth intact *(Step 6)*. The design has been created by cutting away shapes from the pile of cloths.
7. With colored thread, stitch down the edges of the cut shapes.
8. Make a small loop from one of the cut away pieces, sew to one corner of the découpé square to make a potholder, and hang on a kitchen hook.

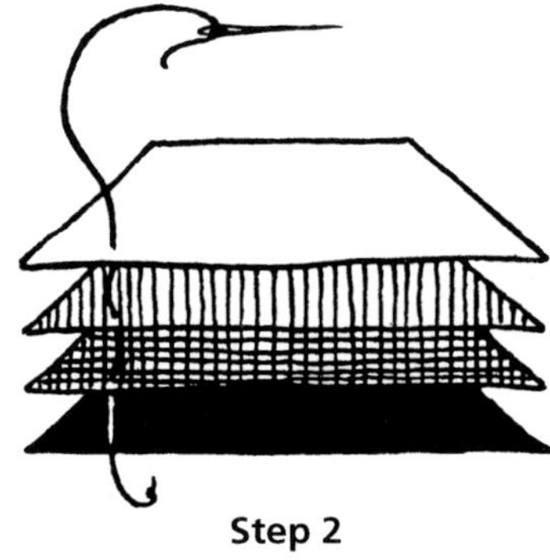

Step 2

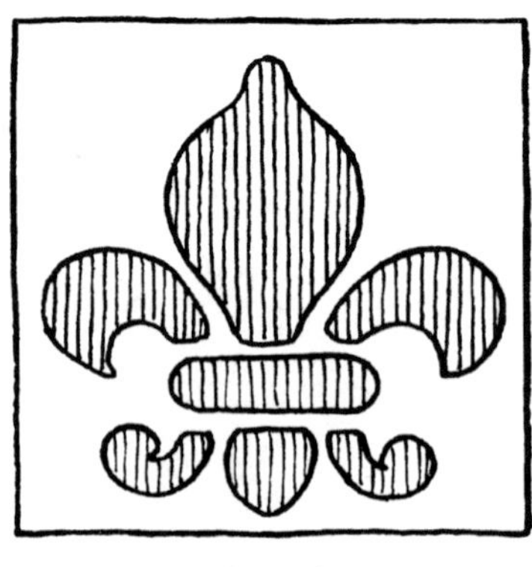

Step 4

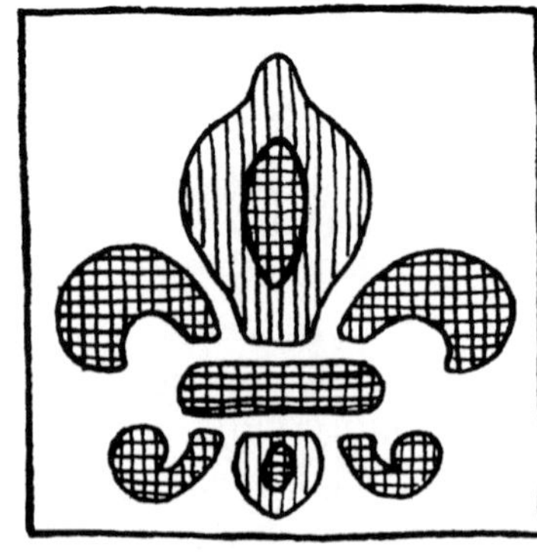

Step 5

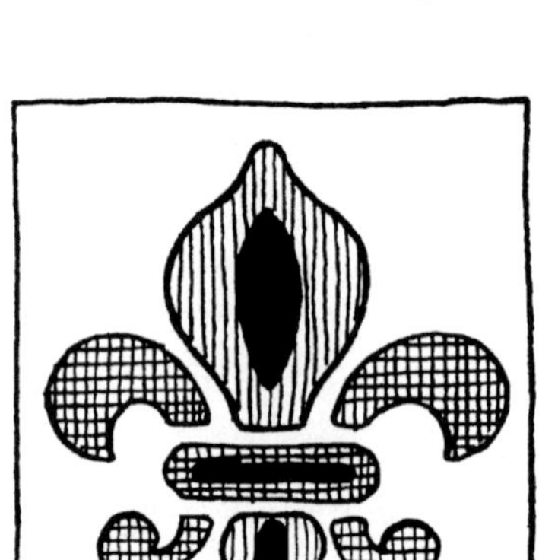

Step 6

Name ____________________ Date ____________________

Project 34: France: Jumping Jack Puppet

Materials	
For this activity you will need:	
• poster board	• string
• poster paint	• paper fasteners

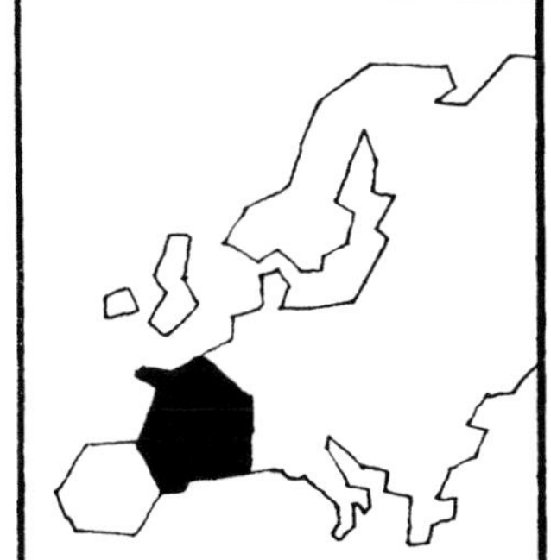

Jumping Jack puppets have long been favorite toys in France. They were once so popular that a police order of 1746 banned them from public. They often depict the classic pantomime characters of Columbine, originally from an Italian story, especially popular in France. Make classic Columbine puppets or turn them into modern characters. Improvise and perform with your Jumping Jack puppets.

1. Design your puppet. You can use traditional characters such as Columbine and her company using the illustrations on page 58 as a guide.
2. Draw the puppet parts (head, body, upper arms, lower arms, upper legs, lower legs) as illustrated on white poster board.
3. Decorate the puppet parts with poster paint.
4. Cut out the pieces for the puppet.
5. Assemble each puppet as shown with paper fasteners.
6. Tie a string to each hand and the head as illustrated. Tie the other ends to a stick.
7. Tie strings on the back as shown, connecting the upper arms and legs.
8. To make the puppet perform, hold the stick with one hand, then pull the string hanging below.

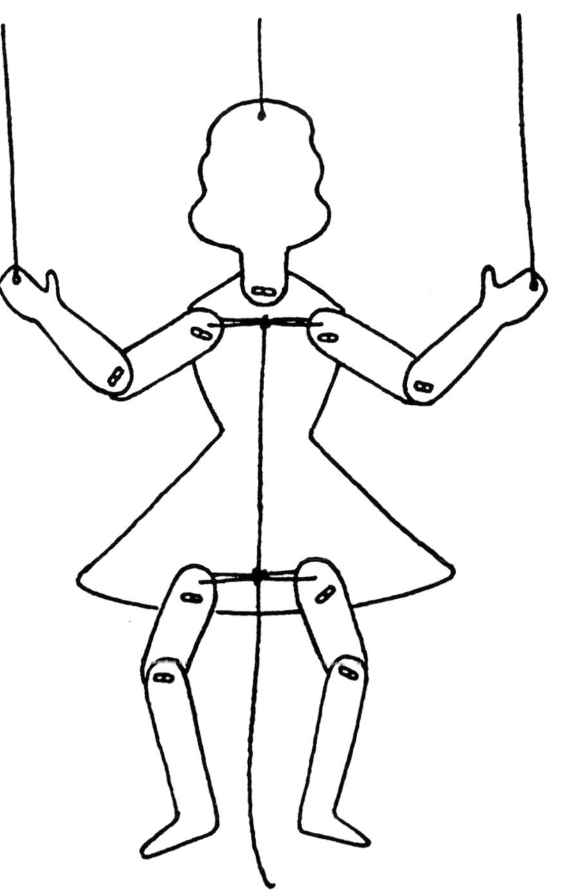

Steps 2, 5, 6, and 7

(continued)

Name ____ Date ________________________

Project 34: France: Jumping Jack Puppet *(continued)*

The Story of Columbine

Columbine's father Pantaloon forced her to mind his vegetable shop, ordering his servant Clown to watch over the spirited girl. Because Clown could not keep up with the girl, Pantaloon asked his neighbor Pierrot to mind Columbine. Pierrot, wearing a white costume with large black buttons, secretly loved her. But Pierrot was too serious for Columbine and she spent all of her time with a jolly fellow named Harlequin.

Sadly, Pierrot left their town and Columbine quickly forgot him. However, she was growing tired of Harlequin and ever sadder with her life. One day a traveling group of players appeared. To lift her spirits, Harlequin took her to see their performance. When the curtains parted, she saw herself played by an actress along with actors as Harlequin and Pierrot in their familiar costumes. The story they told was of how Pierrot lost Columbine to the frivolous Harlequin.

Columbine

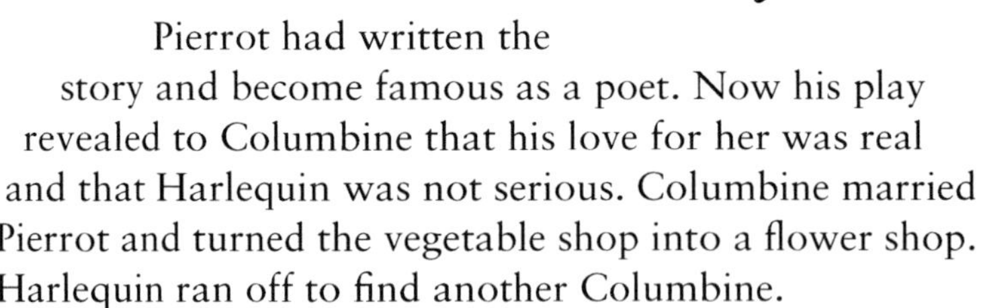

Pierrot had written the story and become famous as a poet. Now his play revealed to Columbine that his love for her was real and that Harlequin was not serious. Columbine married Pierrot and turned the vegetable shop into a flower shop. Harlequin ran off to find another Columbine.

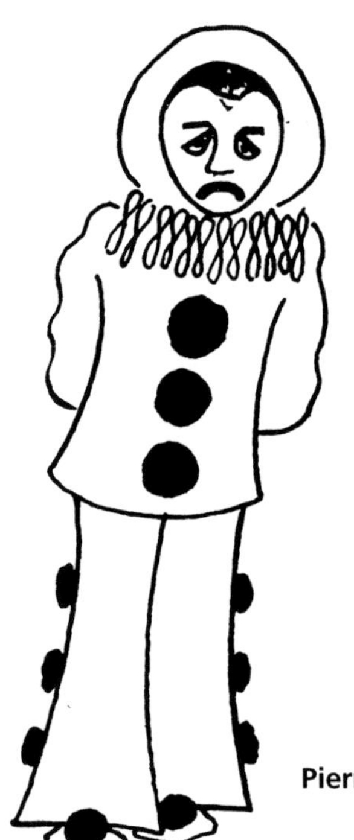

Pierrot

Name ______________________ Date ______________

Project 35: Italy: Lace Panel

Materials	
For this activity you will need: • heavy-gauge thread • four wood strips for a frame • short brads	• corner plates • stain • varnish or paint • hammer

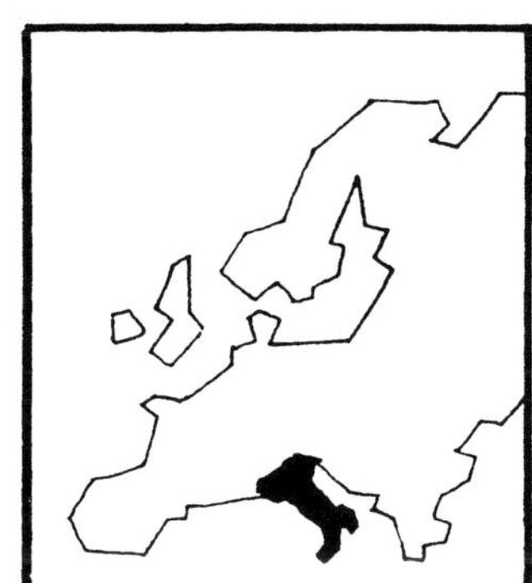

Venice has long been famous for lacemaking, with the Venetian island of Burano still noted for handmade lace. Unlike embroidery, which is decoration sewn on cloth, lace is decoration made by looping, tying, braiding, twisting, and interlacing thread without a supporting cloth. Create a decorative thread panel by combining any of these methods.

1. Make a supporting wooden frame approximately nine by twelve inches with the wood strips. Screw metal corner plates on the back, leaving room to nail brads along the inside edge of the frame *(Step 1)*.

2. Nail brads every one-eighth of an inch along each inside edge of the frame. Each brad protrudes one-quarter of an inch.

3. Stain, varnish, or paint the frame.

4. Tie lengths of thread from one brad to another across the frame without pulling the threads tight *(Step 4)*.

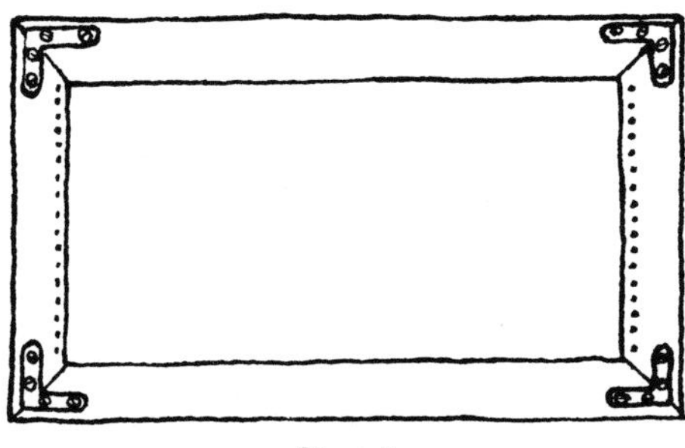

Step 1

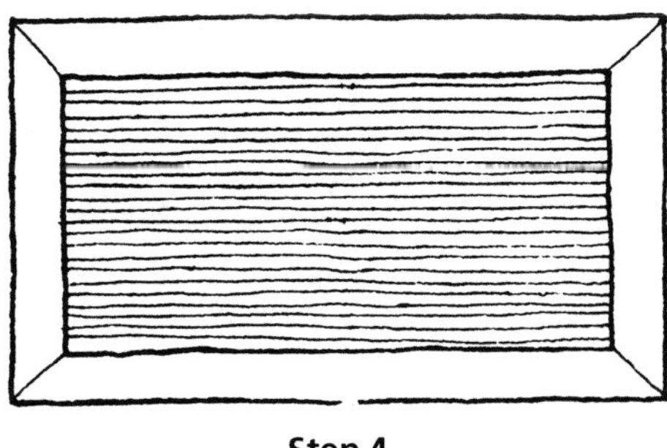

Step 4

(continued)

Name ______________________________ Date ______________

Project 35: Italy: Lace Panel *(continued)*

5. Plan a simple design. Notice it is to be developed by tying vertical threads to the horizontal thread network *(Step 5)*.

6. Tie in the design by looping, interlacing, or any other method. Add other pieces to the horizontal threads if necessary.

7. Cut away threads within shapes as in the sun *(Step 7)*. With practice, you will be able to create elaborate panels.

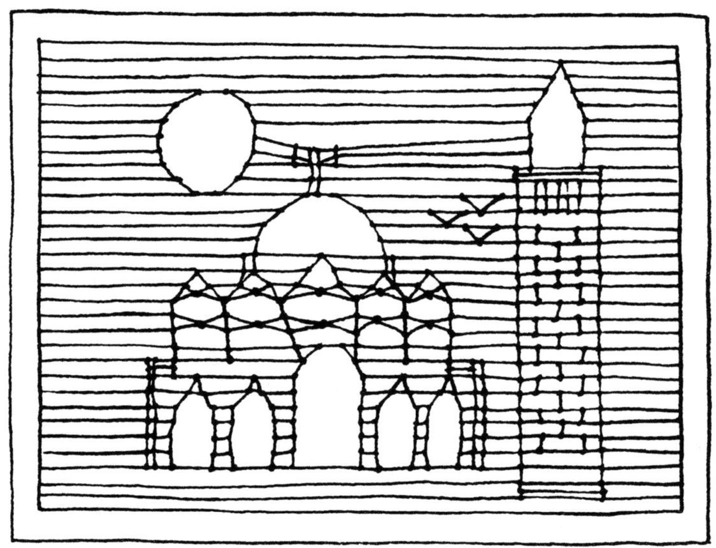

Steps 5 and 7

Name ______________________________ Date ______________________

Project 36: Italy: Bookbinding

Materials	
For this activity you will need:	
• two pieces of heavy cardboard, each $8\frac{1}{2}" \times 11\frac{1}{4}"$	• covering fabric
• wire-bound notebook, $8\frac{1}{2}" \times 11"$	• white glue
	• newspaper

In the centuries prior to the Renaissance, learning was largely confined to monasteries and cathedral schools. All books dwelt on religious themes. This was natural, since most writers and readers were either priests or monks. The Renaissance atmosphere changed that. Writers began concerning themselves with many subjects besides religion. At the same time, more and more people began reading books. When Johann Gutenberg invented the printing press in fifteenth-century Germany, a book revolution was on throughout Europe.

Book printing means book making, and book making means bookbinding. Bookbinding is the process of sewing together the pages of a book and mounting them in a cover. For centuries bookbinding was a special craft. In fifteenth-century Italy, bookbinders created some of the finest book covers ever made. Sometimes they were decorated with an overall pattern like the cover from Renaissance Florence illustrated at right. Sometimes they were made of leather with an embossed motif as in the second example below. By the middle of the fifteenth century, bookbinders in northern Italy were even using tooled gold on book covers. This, more than anything else, gave Italian craftspersons the lead in European bookbinding during the Renaissance.

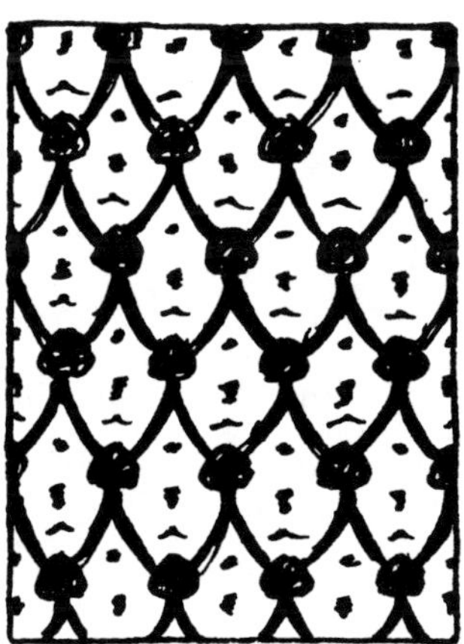

Decoration from Renaissance Florence book cover

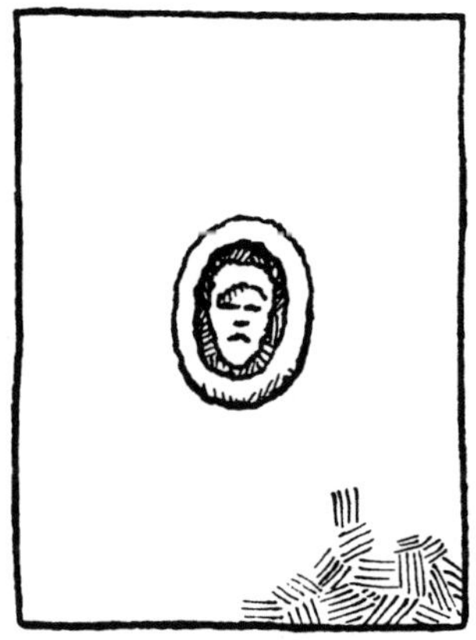

Example of embossed leather book cover

Today virtually all books are bound by machine. A few special editions of high-priced books are bound by hand. Specialty shops in large cities repair old books by hand rebinding. Some people practice hand bookbinding as a hobby. The following directions simplify the standard technique, allowing you to experience the craft of bookbinding by making a hard cover for a book. (You can adjust the measurements given to bind other books as well.)

(continued)

Project 36: Italy: Bookbinding *(continued)*

1. Because you will be doing a lot of pasting, work on a surface protected with many sheets of old newspaper.
2. Select a fabric for the cover. It should be cotton or other heavy fabric. You might decide on an overall pattern such as a plaid or something similar to the illustrated Florentine cover. Or you might use a solid color, especially if you plan an embossed design. If you do not make an embossed cover, skip to step 5.
3. If you wish to make an embossed cover, plan a design. Make it simple—a central motif such as a rosette, a flower, or your initial. Draw the motif in the middle of one of the pieces of cardboard. This will be the front cover.
4. Mix a small amount of papier-mâché pulp by tearing some newspaper into small pieces and soaking it for a while. Take a large pinch of the wet pulp, squeeze out the water, and mix with white glue. Then shape the sticky pulp on the cardboard, using your drawn design as a guide to model the pulp. Add more pulp, mixed with glue, when necessary. Do not let the motif stand too high from the cover. Let the pulp dry.
5. To connect the two cover cardboards, lay them side by side along the longer edges with a $1\frac{1}{2}$-inch gap between them. Cut a strip of the covering fabric (or white cotton) 2 inches wide and $11\frac{1}{4}$ inches long. Run diluted white glue up and down each edge of this cloth band. Glue to the inside edges of the cardboard, leaving a half-inch gap *(Step 5)*. Let dry.

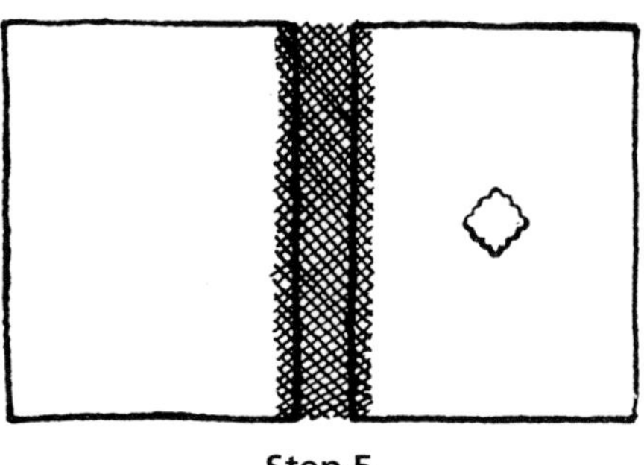

Step 5

6. Cut a piece of your selected covering fabric $12\frac{1}{4}$ inches wide and $19\frac{1}{2}$ inches long.
7. Spread diluted white glue over the front sides of the cardboard pieces, the fabric connecting strip, and the papier-mâché motif (if there is one). Carefully and neatly lay the covering fabric over the glued cover cardboard, leaving one-half inch of fabric extending beyond the cover edges all the way around.

(continued)

Name ______________________________ Date ______________

Project 36: Italy: Bookbinding *(continued)*

8. Smooth the fabric over the cardboard with your fingers, working from the inside edges outward. Use a blunt instrument, such as a small paint brush handle, to push the fabric into the recesses of the papier-mâché motif. Lay flat weights (books, small boards) protected by plastic over the fabric-covered cardboard. Do not weight the embossed design. Let the fabric dry tightly to the cardboard.

9. When the glue is thoroughly dry, remove the weights. The two cardboard covers are now connected and covered. Turn them over. Run diluted white glue along the edges of the cloth where it extends beyond the cardboard. Turn the cloth over the cardboard edges, being careful to make neat corners, and glue down *(Step 9)*. Weight down the edges to dry.

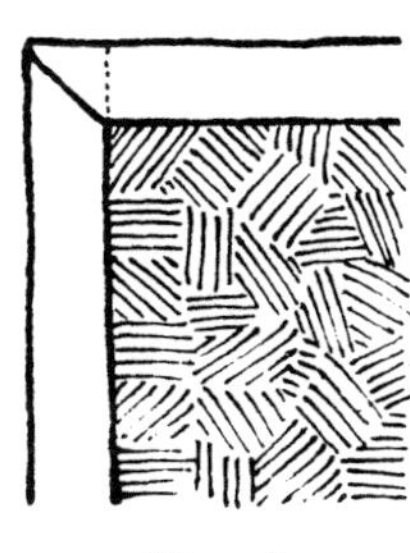

Step 9

10. When the completed cover has dried, you are ready to cover your notebook. Turn the book back side up. Spread diluted white glue over the book's back cover up to the holes where the wire rings enter the book.

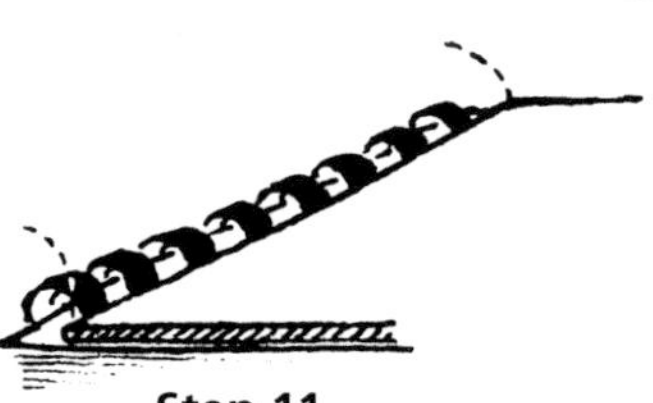

Step 11

11. Lay your back cover (not the half with the embossed design), nonfabric side down, on the glued notebook cover. The inside edges of the cardboard should lie along the line made by the holes of the ring binding *(Step 11)*.

12. Turn the book over so it is front side up. Spread diluted white glue over the book's front cover. Paste the nonfabric side of your front cover onto this glued surface. Again, the inside edge of the cardboard should just meet the line made by the holes of the wire rings. Weight down the newly bound book to dry. (Do not put weights on the embossed motif.)

13. When the glue has thoroughly dried, remove the weights. You have bound this book as a hardcover.

14. If you wish, you can add some color to the cover, but only sparingly. You can add touches of gold paint or use acrylics. You can also use acrylic paint to letter the name of your book along the spine.

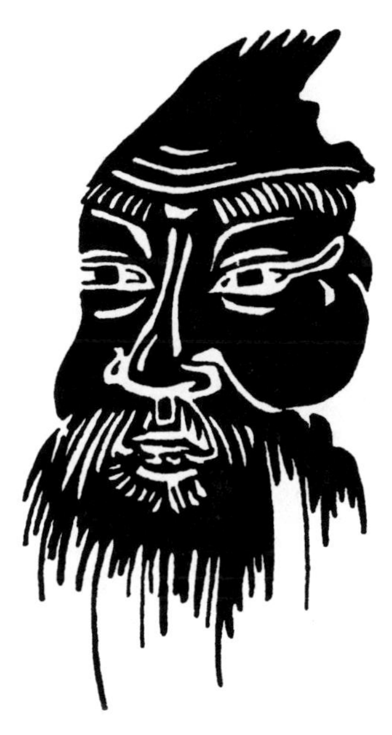

Part VI:
Asia

VI. The Arts and Crafts of Asia

Several of the world's greatest craft countries lie within this region. Handcrafted objects from India, printed cotton, inlaid boxes, engraved brass, and lacquered trays still find their way into American stores. There are two reasons for this rich survival of Asian Indian crafts. One is the caste system, now slowly disappearing, with an Indian tied to the caste in which he or she is born. Each caste has its own traditional occupation, with children of the craft caste continuing the family art, then passing it on to their own sons and daughters.

Another reason is political. When the great leader Mohandas Gandhi began his campaign to awaken Indian nationalism, he stressed Hindu values, rejected foreign products, and encouraged a return to traditional crafts. The *charkha*, the ancient spinning wheel of India, became the symbol of Gandhi's independence drive.

Archaeological excavations have unearthed craft objects made in China's Shang Dynasty over 3,500 years ago. Remarkably, many of the craft techniques and decorative motifs of the Shang have continued in use throughout the many centuries since then. As remarkable is how Chinese artisans and artists lifted many of their craft objects to the highest level of art, while influencing the crafts of cultures throughout Asia, especially that of Japan. Chinese and Japanese craft products are noted for their unusual nature, good taste, and delicate beauty. At the same time, they have a simplicity that makes them ideal for students' experiments.

Name ______________________________ Date ______________

Project 37: India: Mica-Inset Embroidery

Materials	
For this activity you will need: • cloth	• embroidery thread • heavy silver foil

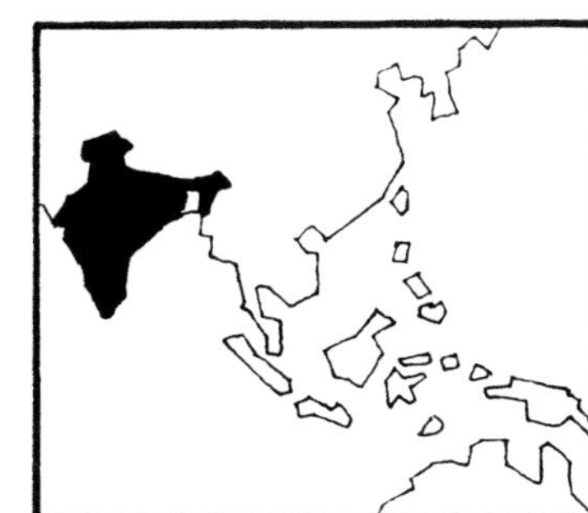

Indian cloth embroidered with brightly colored thread is often enhanced with mirrorlike pieces of mica, a mineral crystal that flakes into thin layers. The four round shapes in the illustrated detail of an Indian embroidery below are such mica insets. Rather than obtain mica flakes, use thin pieces of metallic plastic or disks made of metal foil to make a spectacular embroidery.

1. Select a cloth to embroider. Indians delight in strong colors, bright red or orange, deep purple, or hot pink. They also often use black cloth to contrast and highlight the color of the bright thread they choose.
2. Plan an abstract design of geometric shapes.
3. Lightly sketch your design on the cloth with a soft pencil. Embroider the design using stitches you know. The cross-stitch and parallel stitch of the illustration at the bottom of the page are typical. If you are unfamiliar with embroidery, work as if "drawing with thread."
4. Position a penny-sized disk of metal foil on the cloth. Draw a line around it. Sew two loops of thread inside the line slightly smaller than the space the disk will occupy. Fit the disk beneath the loops. Sew the loops down with colored thread to create a frame holding the disk in place *(Step 4)*.
5. Sew the remaining disks in place and complete the embroidery.
6. Hang the embroidery, make a pillow cover, or sew it to a blouse.

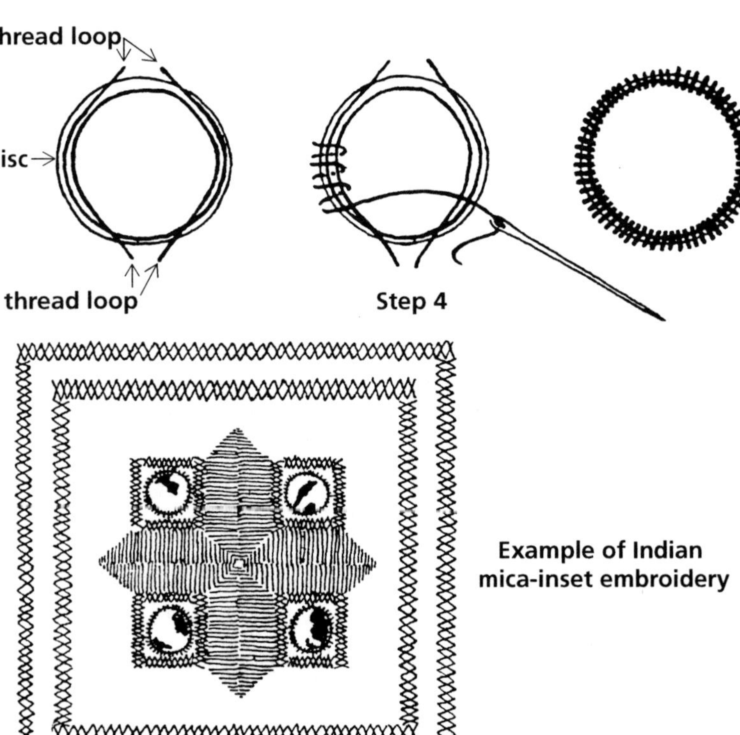

Example of Indian mica-inset embroidery

Name ______________________ Date ______________

Project 38: India: Papier-Mâché Trays

Materials	
For this activity you will need: • papier-mâché material • tray or foil baking pan to use as a mold	• plastic cling wrap • gesso • acrylic or poster paints • water-based varnish

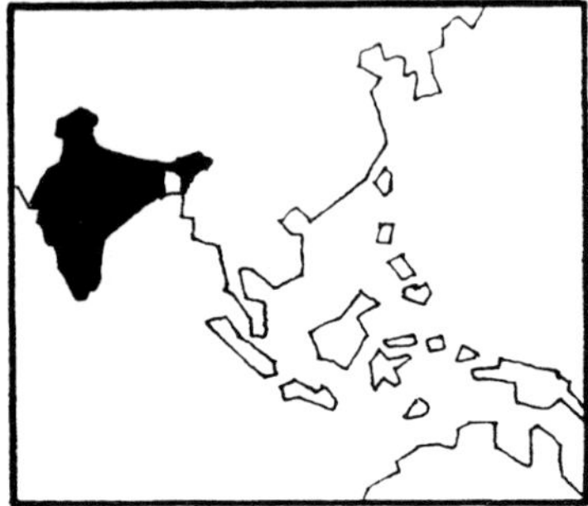

Indian artisans have turned papier-mâché into practical utensils. Illustrated here are several typical Indian papier-mâché trays, as attractive as the Indian cuisine served on them is savory.

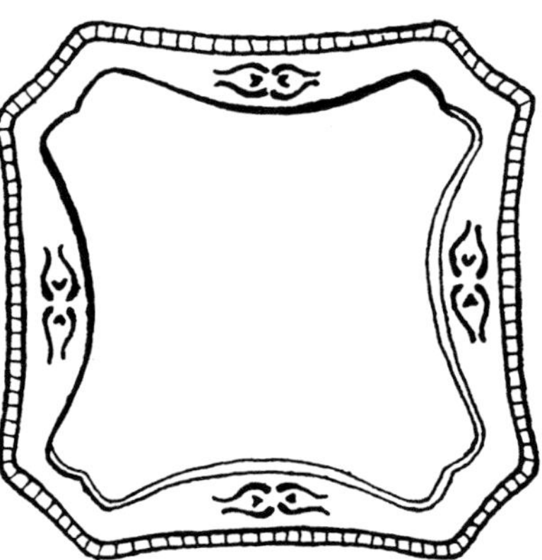

1. Plan the tray shape and decoration design.
2. Place the tray or plate upside down on a work surface. Cover it thoroughly with plastic cling wrap. This will keep the papier-mâché from sticking to the tray.
3. Dip torn strips of newspaper into wallpaper paste or a paste made of flour and water. Lay several layers of wet strips across the plastic-covered tray.
4. When the bottom has dried, remove the tray mold. Lay several layers of wet papier-mâché strips across the top. Add layers to make the tray edge. Shape the tray by laying thinner or thicker layers of paste-soaked strips.
5. Once it is dry, spread one or two coats of gesso over the tray.
6. When the gesso is dry, sand it smooth.
7. Paint the tray an overall bright color.
8. Decorate the tray with contrasting bright colors.
9. Seal the finished tray with water-based varnish.

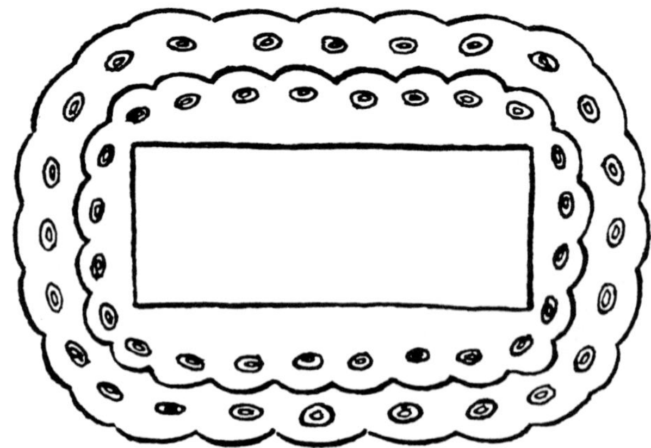

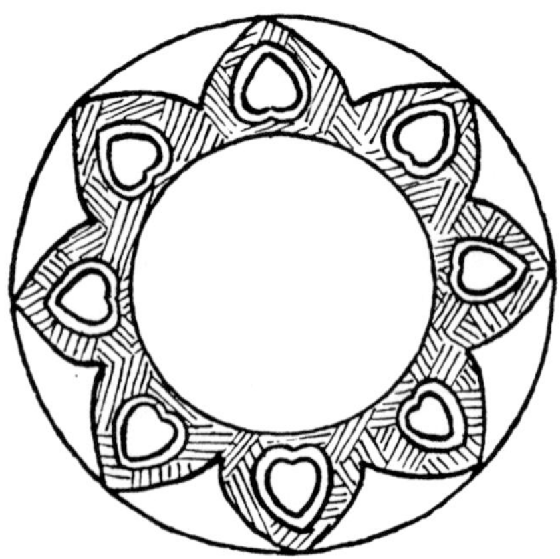

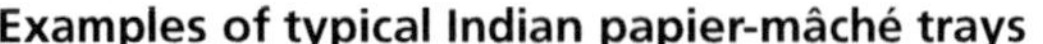

Examples of typical Indian papier-mâché trays

Name ______________________ Date ______________

Project 39: India: Painted Wooden Dolls

Materials	
For this activity you will need: • discarded wood • enamel or acrylic paint • clear varnish	• hobby knife • sandpaper • screws • screwdriver

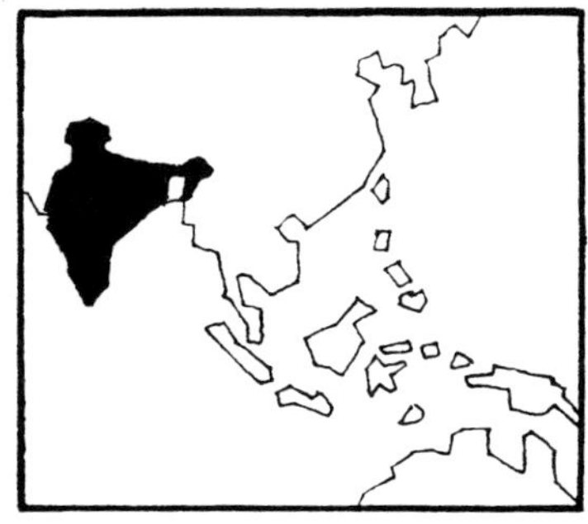

Modern India has developed new folk arts to join traditional ones. One example is a wooden doll, turned on a lathe to an approximate human shape. Its painted decoration brings out the form intended. You do not need to actually turn the wood on a lathe. Instead, use discarded turned wood, such as a rod from a chair arm or back, a bannister railing, or a wooden candlestick. Use books on the life and culture of India or the illustrated examples below to provide clothing ideas for your Indian doll.

1. Find a piece of discarded turned wood. Let its shape suggest a form for the doll, which will be decorated in a traditional style of India. Sketch your idea.
2. Cut away any parts of the wood not needed for your design *(Step 2)*.
3. If the wood piece is too thickly covered with old paint, sand away the gloss.
4. Cut a wooden base and screw to the bottom of the doll *(Step 4)*.
5. Paint the doll, following your sketch.
6. When the decorative paint has dried, cover the doll with a coat of clear varnish.

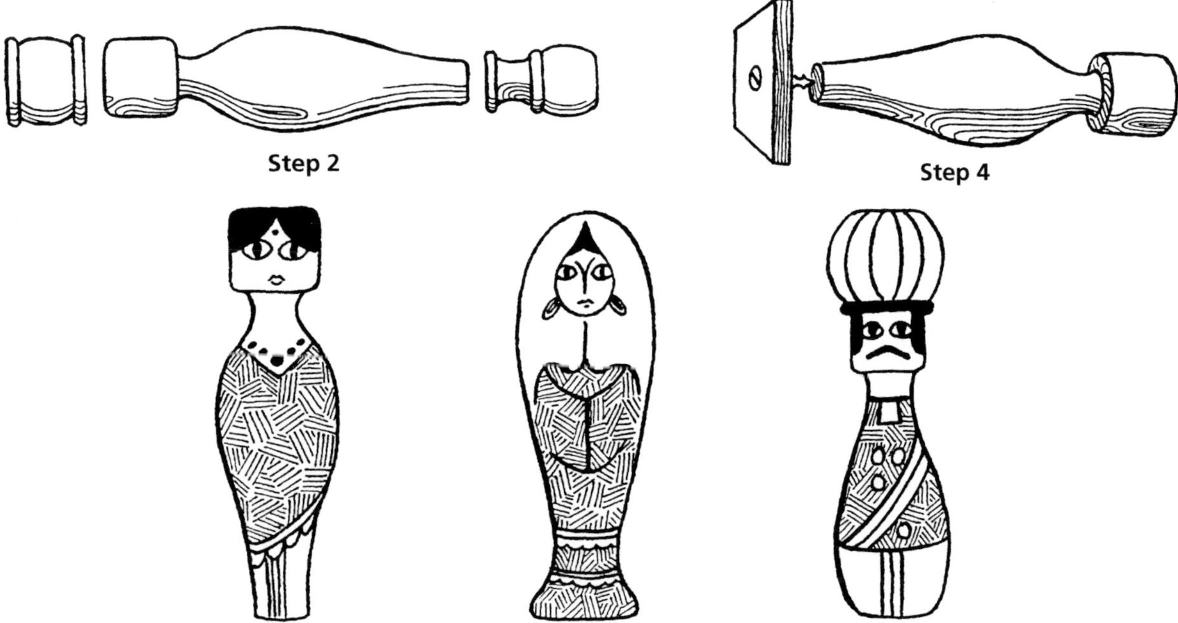

Examples of Indian painted wooden dolls

Name ____________________ Date ____________

Project 40: India: Hand-Printed Patterns

Materials	
For this activity you will need: • heavy paper • foam-rubber pad	• raw potato • colored inks • hobby knife

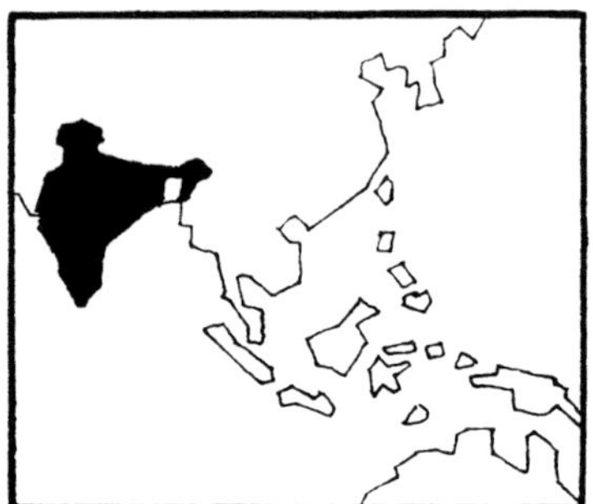

Have you ever seen hand-printed cotton from India? It comes from an age-old tradition. The oldest examples of cotton cloth ever found were in the ruins of Mohenjo-Daro, an ancient city of the Indus Valley. These fragments were woven some five thousand years ago. An Indian hymn in the Hindu Rig-veda, written about 1500 B.C., mentions cotton. In the fifth century B.C., the Greek historian Herodotus wrote that the patient hands of the women of India pulled cotton fiber from the seeds of the plant, carded it, and then spun it into cloth. Few countries can look back on such a long craft tradition as can India with the weaving, printing, and sewing of cotton cloth.

Below is a copy of a fifteenth-century Indian painting. It shows how important printed fabrics have always been in India. The woman's skirt is an overall print. Two more printed fabrics serve as sheet and mattress cover.

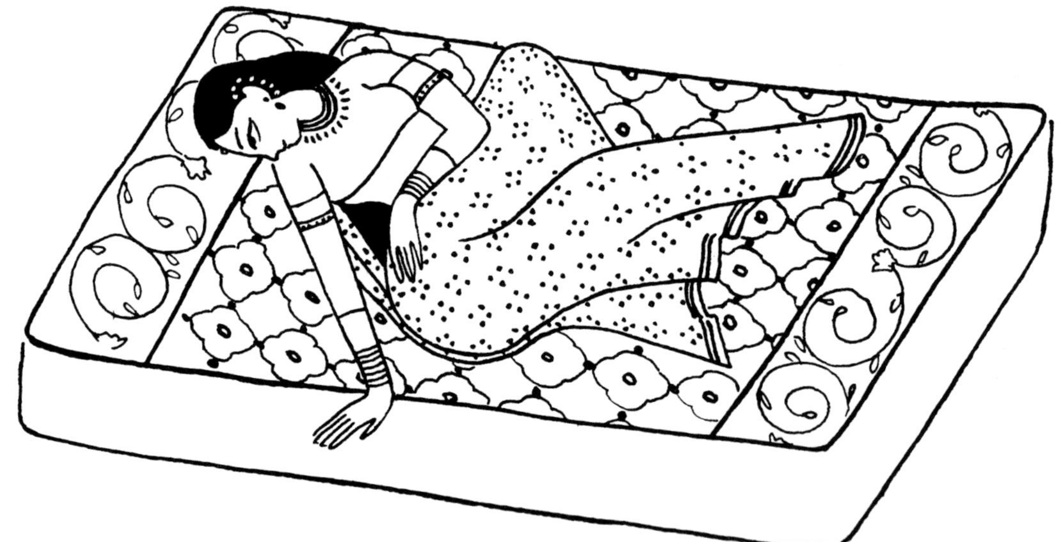

Fifteenth-century Indian painting shows importance of printed fabrics

When modern Indians cut wood blocks to print cotton by hand or to mass print with machine presses, they continue using traditional colors and motifs. The blocks are usually small and printed closely together, producing an overall pattern. Only on close inspection can you discover the birds, animals, flowers, or abstract motifs that are the basis of the complicated print design.

(continued)

Name ______________________________ Date ______________________

Project 40: India: Hand-Printed Patterns *(continued)*

You can practice making hand-printed patterns by cutting motifs into potatoes. You can use the potato stamp to print paper with ordinary colored inks. The potato stamp can also be used for printing cotton, but you need fabric dye for that. The following project shows you how to print paper place mats.

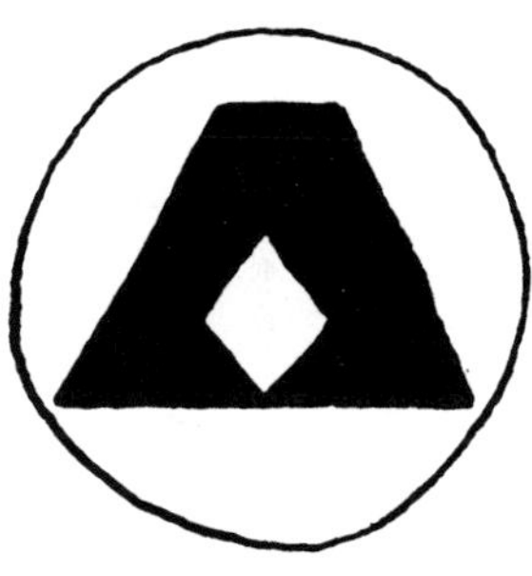

Step 1

1. Design a single motif for your print. Make it relatively simple. Books about India can give you some ideas for a motif *(Step 1)*.
2. Slice a raw potato in half. Draw your motif on the flat face of the potato with a felt-tipped pen.
3. Using a sharp knife, cut away the background portion of the potato, leaving the motif raised about one-quarter inch from the surface.
4. Brush colored ink onto a foam-rubber pad or clean stamp pad. Press the raised potato face on the inked pad. Then press on paper to print the motif. Practice printing a few times before printing a place mat.
5. Cut a blank place mat about ten inches by fifteen inches from a sheet of heavy paper. For guidelines, lightly draw a line across the middle from top to bottom and another line across the middle from left to right. You can later remove these lines with a soft eraser.
6. Using the guidelines, begin printing in the center and work outward *(Step 6a)*. The print motif need not always be in the same position. Alternating the position will create different and more interesting designs, as in the illustrated example *(Step 6b)*.

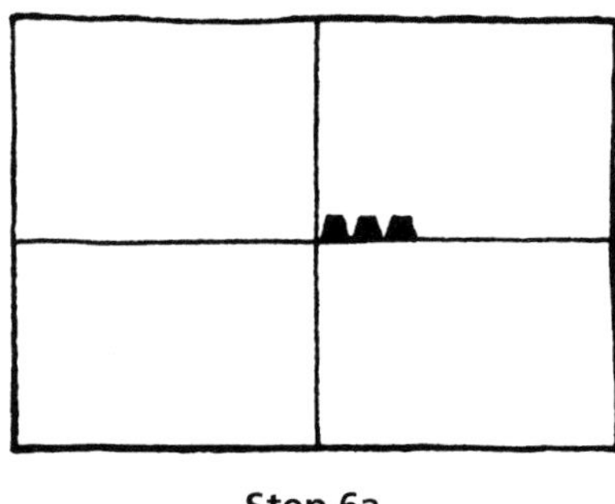

Step 6a

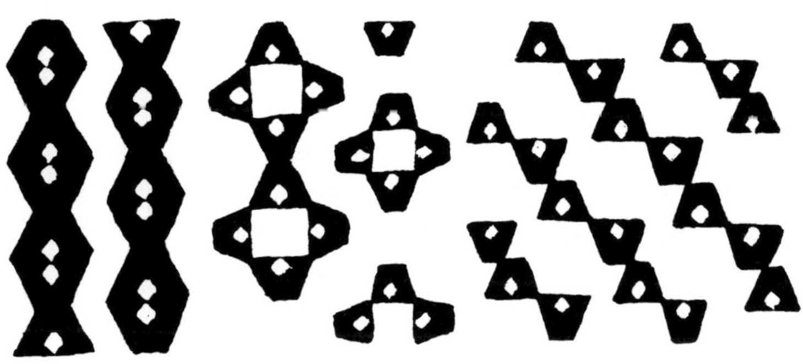

Step 6b

(continued)

Name ______________________ Date ______________

Project 40: India: Hand-Printed Patterns *(continued)*

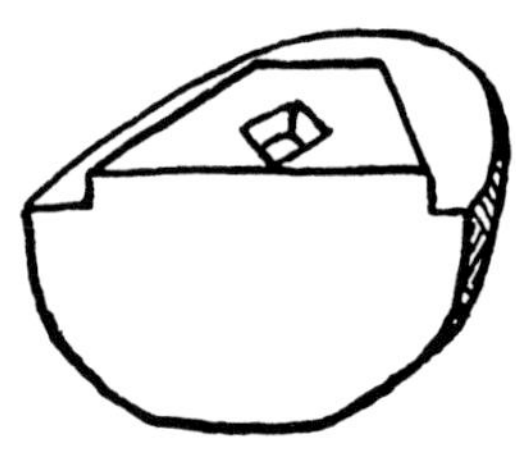

Step 7

7. If you intend that one motif meet another, slice away the non-printing part of the potato *(Step 7)*. Then you can more easily see where the potato edges are to match up.

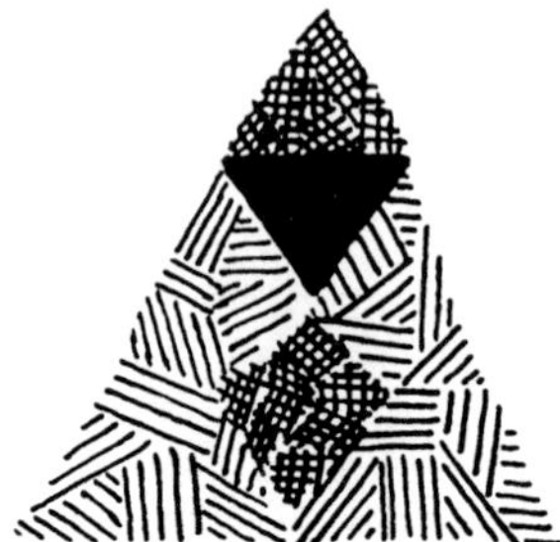

8. You can cut another potato for a second color *(Step 8)*. Choose the color carefully. Where it overlaps the first there will be a mixture of the two colors. Test your choice by first brushing one color on a piece of scrap paper. After that has dried, overbrush the second color. When printing, clean out the foam-rubber pad before using the second color, or use a second pad.

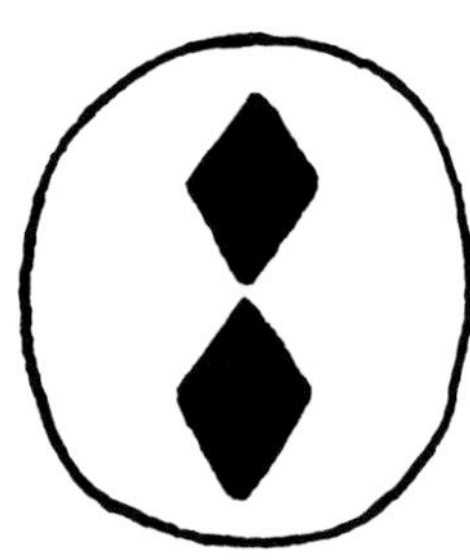

Step 8

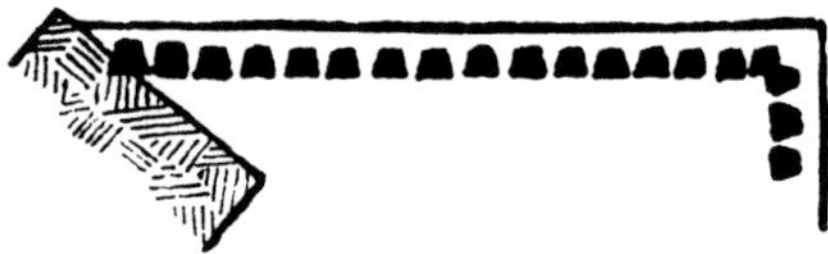

Step 9

9. If you are printing a border, lay a paper at a 45-degree angle across the corner *(Step 9)*. Then you can make a properly angled meeting of adjacent motifs at the corner.

10. You can use a potato stamp for printing cloth. The procedure is the same as with paper. However, you will need to use fabric dye to make it colorfast. Because normal dye will run, it must be thickened in order to print with it. The dye instructions or your dealer will tell you what thickening agent to use. Craft shops sometimes sell fabric printing dyes already thickened.

11. When printing cloth, do not mark the guidelines with pencil. Instead, fold the cloth in half vertically and then again horizontally, dividing it into quarter sections. Iron the folded cloth. Use these folds as guidelines. The printing procedure is the same as for printing on paper.

Name ______________________________ Date ______________

Project 41: China: Stone Rubbing

Materials	
For this activity you will need: • high-quality paper	• stone-rubbing wax or black crayon

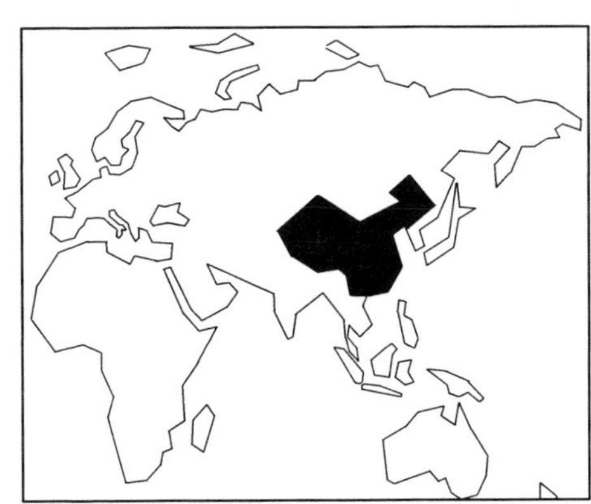

In the second century, emperor Ling Ti had stone tablets of the writings of Confucius placed before the Imperial Academy. To copy the quotations, students had the clever idea of making rubbings of them. So began the stone rubbing craft. The illustration below copies a centuries old stone-rubbed portrait of Confucius.

Have you ever rubbed a pencil over a piece of paper covering a coin to make the image of the coin face? You were using the stone-rubbing principle. Locally, you can make rubbings of stone or metal reliefs on memorial plaques in a church or on the bases of statues, from gravestones or from decorative building details.

1. Select high-quality paper, thick enough not to tear easily but not so thick that it is difficult to work with. Rag paper with a slight texture is best.
2. Soak the paper. Let surface water run off.
3. Lay the paper over the surface to be rubbed.
4. Press the paper into the relief, though not deeply, taking care not to tear the paper on edges. Do not press under any undercuts in the relief or the paper will tear when removed.
5. When the paper has dried, rub the raised surface with stone-rubbing wax (from a hobby shop) or thick black crayon.
6. Remove the paper and you have a rubbed relief image.

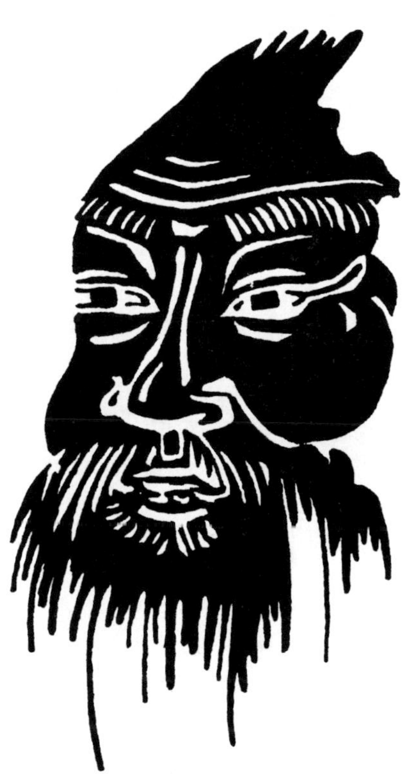

Stone-rubbed portrait of Confucius

Name ______________________________ Date ______________

Project 42: China: Paper Cutting

Materials	
For this activity you will need:	
• white tissue-type paper	• hobby knife
• colored ink	• tape

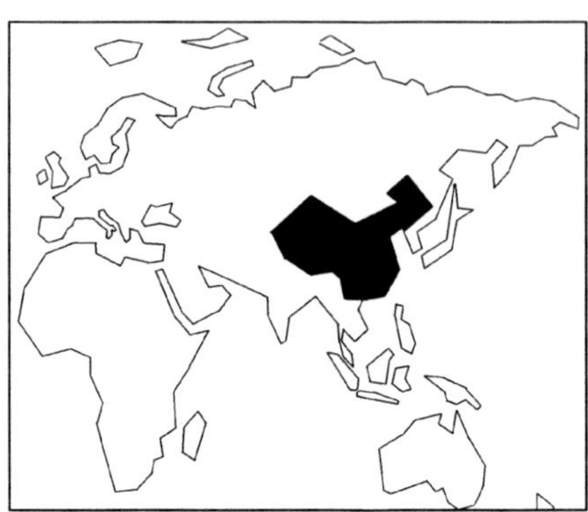

Paper cutting, a traditional Chinese craft, continues to be practiced. The designs are *asymmetrical* (not the same on both sides). Cut from thin paper, they are hand-colored dark blue, maroon, or red. Once made to be handed out at Chinese funerals, today they are given at many functions. The traditional method of paper dying and cutting is described below. You can modify it as you see fit.

1. Experiment to find a paper thin enough that ink will soak through but strong enough not to disintegrate when wet.
2. Stack ten sheets together. Glue all four edges to stick the sheets together in a package, one on top of the other *(Step 2)*.
3. Tape the bundle to a drawing board along all four edges *(Step 3)*.
4. Brush the top sheet with colored ink. Do not leave pools on the paper. When it is dry, brush a second time, darkening the color. The ink soaks through the sheets, coloring the paper beneath in decreasing intensities.
5. When the paper is dry, untape the bundle but leave the edges glued.
6. Draw a design on a piece of typing paper. Tape or staple it to the top of the bundle and another piece of typing paper to the bottom.
7. Following the design on the typing paper, cut the entire bundle at one time, interior details first, with a hobby knife. Use scissors for broader cuts. Cut the outside shape last, releasing the separate sheets from the bundle.

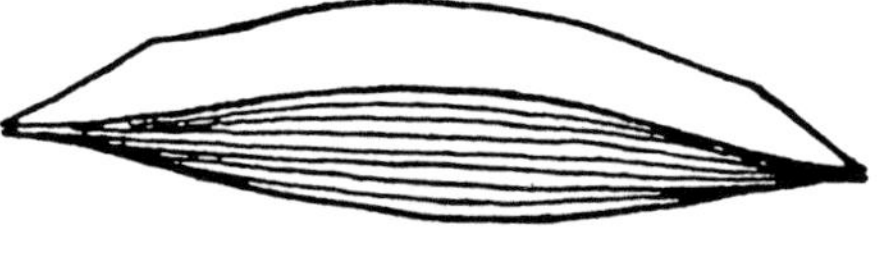

Step 2

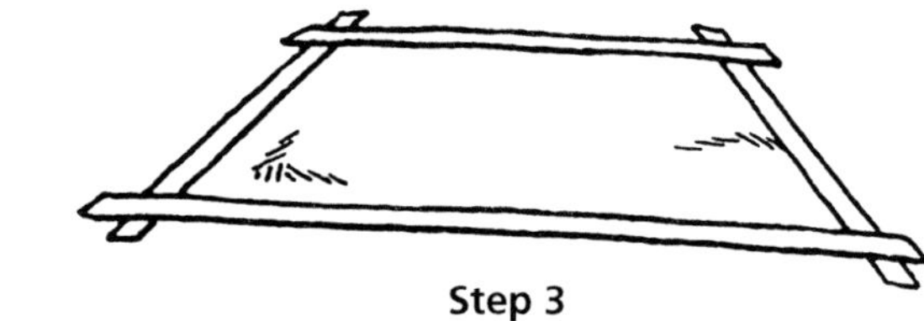

Step 3

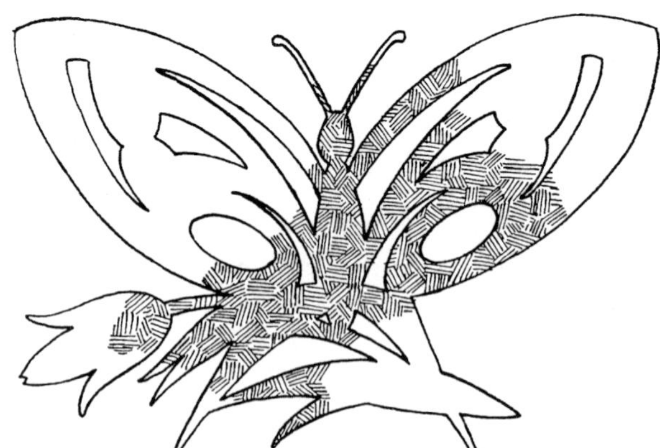

Typical Chinese paper cutting design

Name ______________________ Date ______________

Project 43: China: Calligraphy

Materials	
For this activity you will need:	• India ink
• writing paper	• Chinese brush or one similar

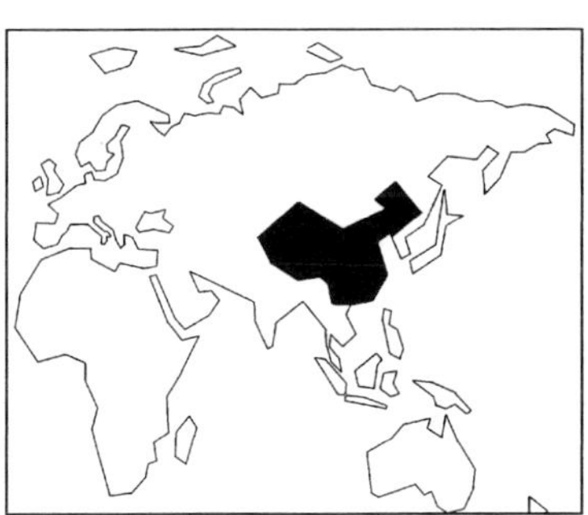

The word *calligraphy* means "fine writing." Chinese calligraphers use a brush to write Chinese word symbols. Held vertically, a Chinese writing brush is grasped firmly by the finger tips with the forearm held parallel to the paper as illustrated below. Writing is made by arm movements, not with fingers. The word *yung,* meaning "eternity," contains all the basic writing strokes, here written vertically as is all Chinese writing. Students of calligraphy practice these strokes until becoming master calligraphers. Then they write poems, expressing themselves not only with words but with their writing style.

1. With a Chinese brush or a long-bristled, fine-pointed watercolor brush, practice writing the character for yung.
2. Compose a poem or select a favorite quotation that you will express in your own calligraphic manner. The quote written here is one of the principles of Taoism, a major religion of China.
3. Through your writing style, express the meaning of your words.

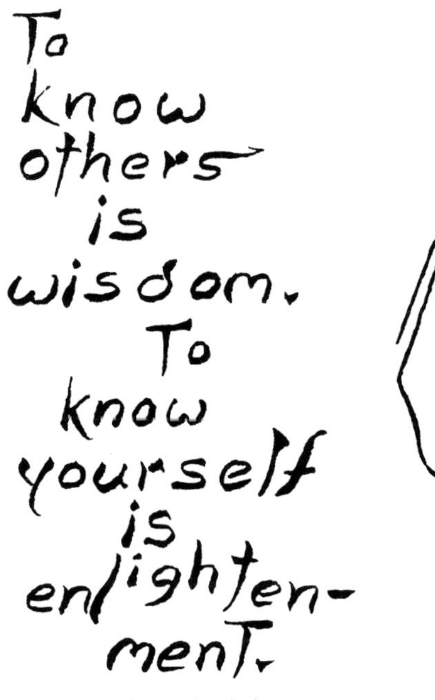

Taoist principle

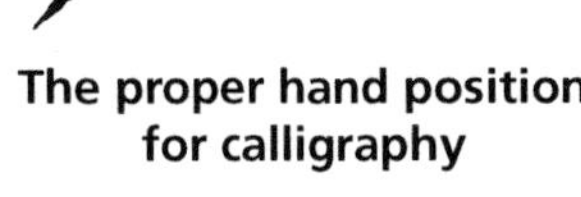

The proper hand position for calligraphy

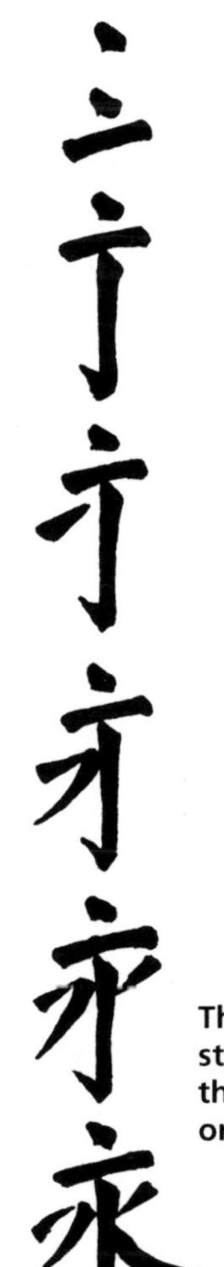

The calligraphic steps in writing the word yung, or eternity

Name ______________________________ Date ______________

Project 44: China: Room Screen

Materials	
For this activity you will need:	
• drafting tracing paper	• four small door hinges
• half-inch-wide wood trim strips	• glue
• black or dark red paint	• screws

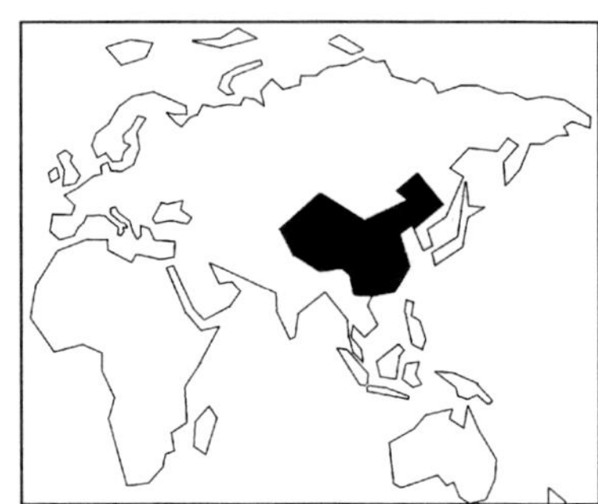

Chinese homemakers often divide rooms with paper screens. A screened-off corner can be used for a television or work area. The screen's painting often shows an imagined landscape with large, bold natural shapes that leave much of the screen empty. These directions tell you how to make a miniature screen. If you want, you can enlarge the frame to make a full-size screen.

1. Cut the wood trim strips as follows. Cut 6 twelve-inch-long pieces, 6 four-inch-long pieces, and 12 two-inch-long pieces.
2. Cut the ends of the two-inch lengths at 45-degree angles. Use these to brace the corners of the screen frames *(Step 2)*.
3. Assemble the three screen frames, leaving five inches below for legs. Screw the braces in at the corners.
4. Connect the three frames with hinges, cutting away some of the wood so that they will fit flush to the wood uprights *(Step 4)*.
5. Paint the legs and outer edges of the frames, including the hinged edges, traditional Chinese black or dark red.

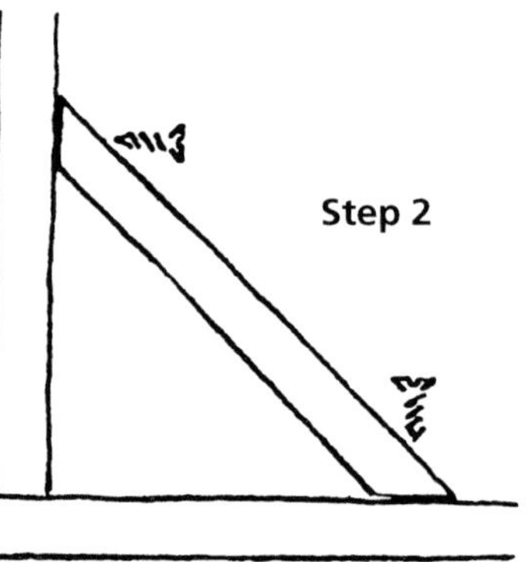

Step 2

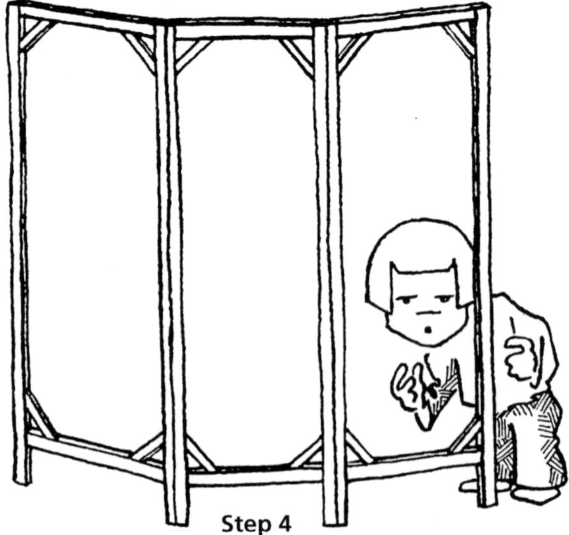

Step 4

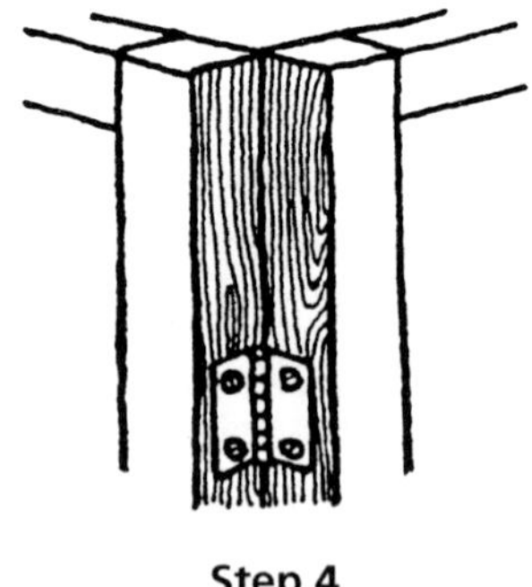

Step 4

(continued)

Name ______________________ Date ______________

Project 44: China: Room Screen *(continued)*

6. Glue a sheet of paper to one side of each frame, running glue along the edges. Take care there are no wrinkles or folds.

7. Glue sheets to the other sides of the frames.

8. Moisten each sheet of paper by wiping with a wet cloth. Do not soak the paper. The paper will shrink and tighten.

9. Paint a watercolor landscape on the screen *(Step 9)*.

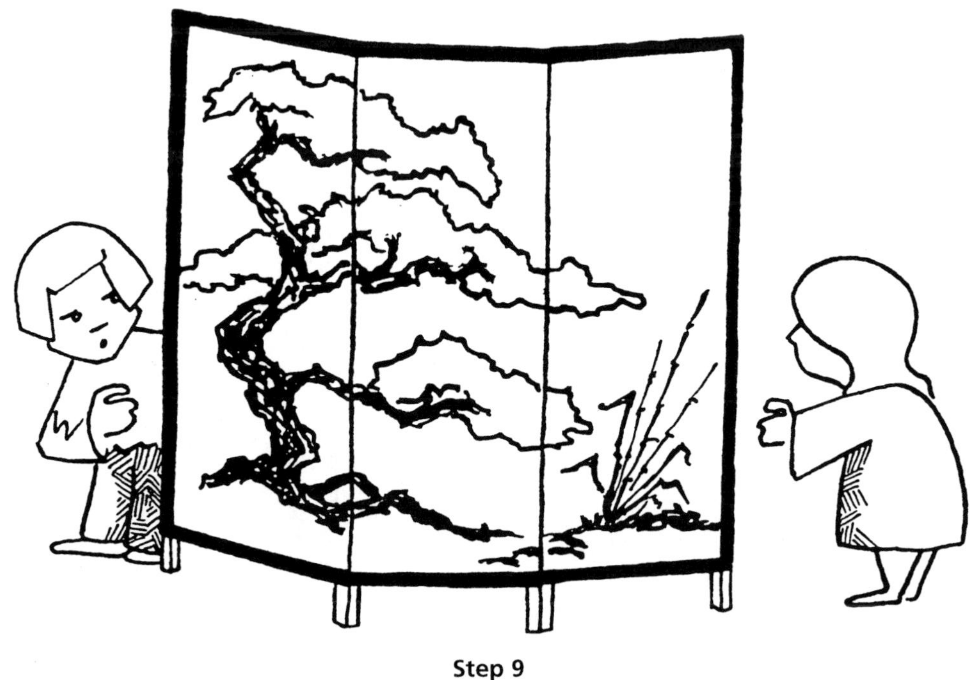

Step 9

Name ______________________________ Date ______________

Project 45: Japan: Origami

Materials
For this activity you will need: • 6"-square piece of origami paper or other smooth, thin paper (such as typing paper)

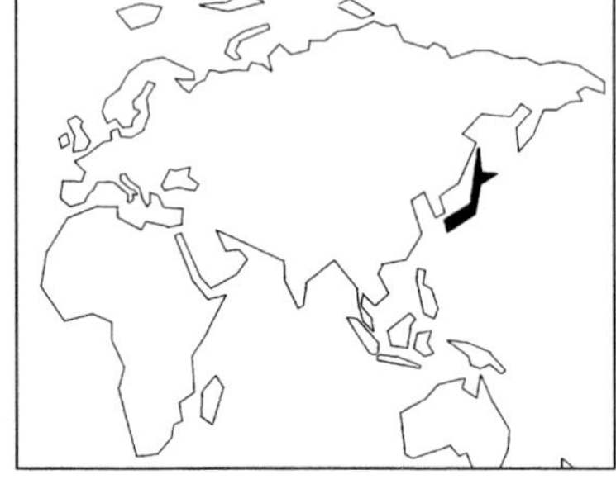

Origami is the Japanese craft of paper folding. There are two kinds of origami, traditional and creative. Traditional origami dates back to 1682 and follows strict rules. Each piece must be done with one 6"-square piece of paper, with no paper added. Once all white, the paper is now often colored on one side so that the finished origami has two colors. In creative origami, which appeared in the mid-twentieth century, the artist invents new shapes, beginning with paper of any size and adding more as the figure develops. There are one hundred figures in traditional origami, of which the samurai helmet shown is one. The samurai, warrior knights who controlled Japan for seven centuries, wore helmets like the one illustrated here.

1. Origami folds are exact and creases sharp. Use your fingernail to crease the folds. Follow the illustrated steps 1–8 to make the samurai helmet.
2. When folding the front fold upward in step 7, the back flap will also fold upward. Make the corners neat, then fold the back flap down once again.
3. Step 8 illustrates the completed origami helmet.

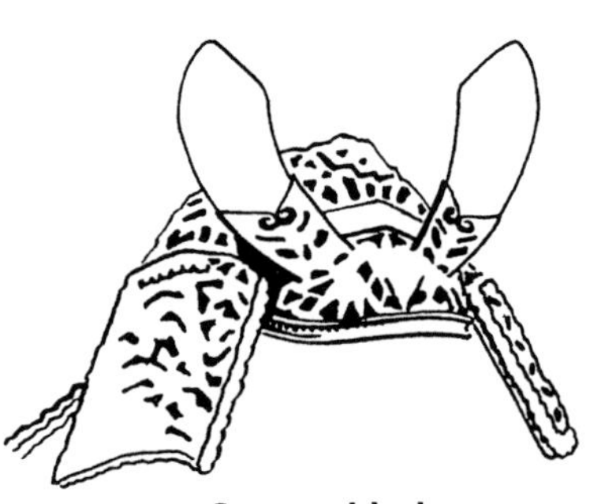

Samurai helmet

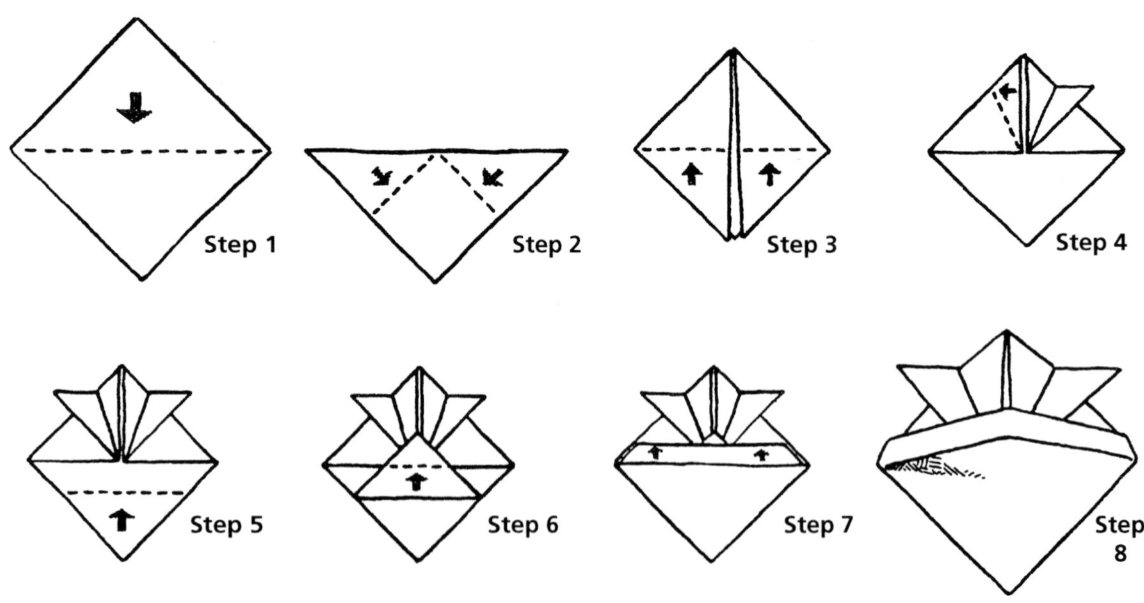

Name ______________________________ Date ______________

Project 46: Japan: Kites

Materials	
For this activity you will need: • $\frac{1}{2}$" light wood strips • tracing paper or newsprint paper • watercolors	• glue • roll of string • rod • hobby knife

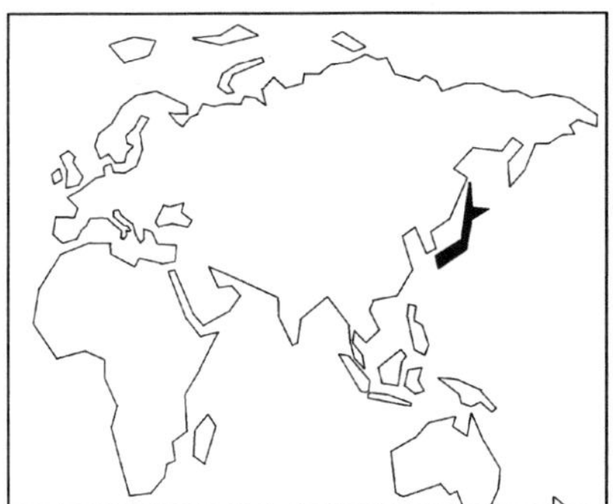

Making kites is a popular Japanese folk art. Made of cloth as well as paper, they are shaped and decorated to resemble birds or insects or have humorous or abstract motifs. The kites are sometimes so large that teams of half a dozen people are needed to handle them. Create a kite design or use one of the Japanese designs illustrated here. Its shape depends on the design of its supports.

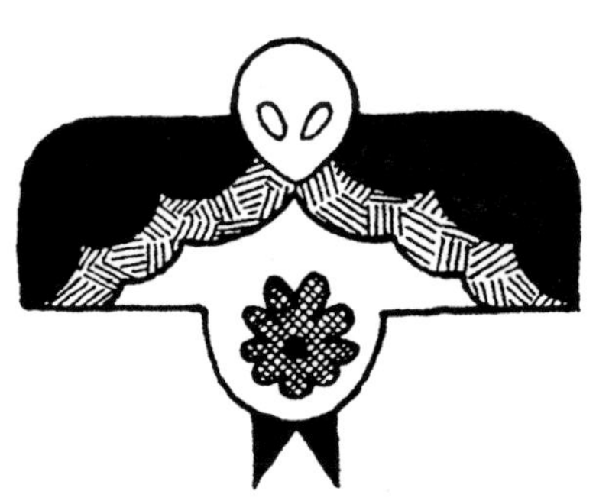
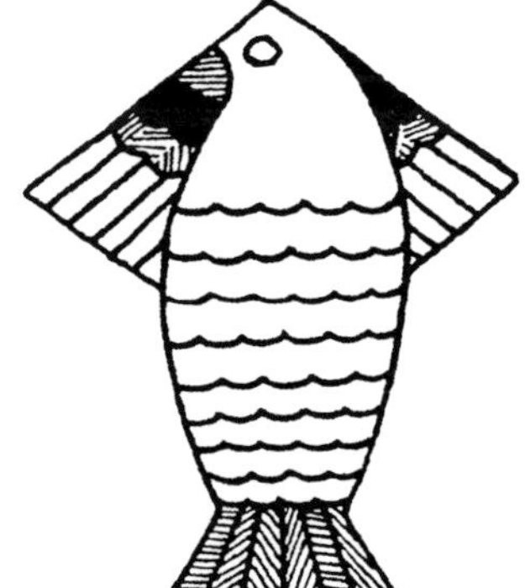
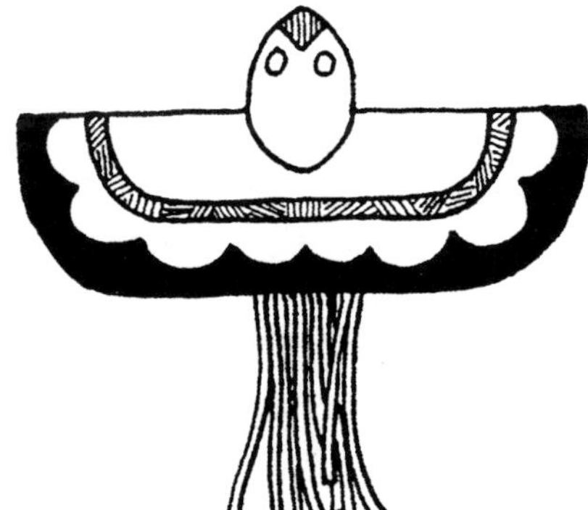

Various Japanese kite designs

1. From the half-inch-thick wood strips, make the supports (shown in heavy black lines in the diagrams below) (*Step 1*). A two-foot kite is a reasonable size.

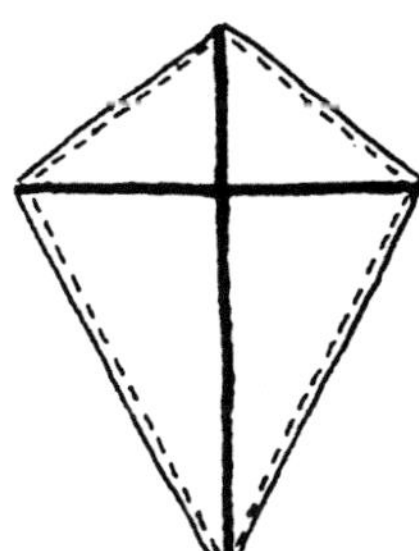
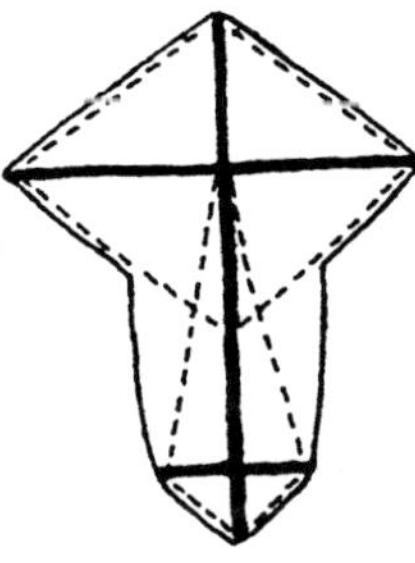
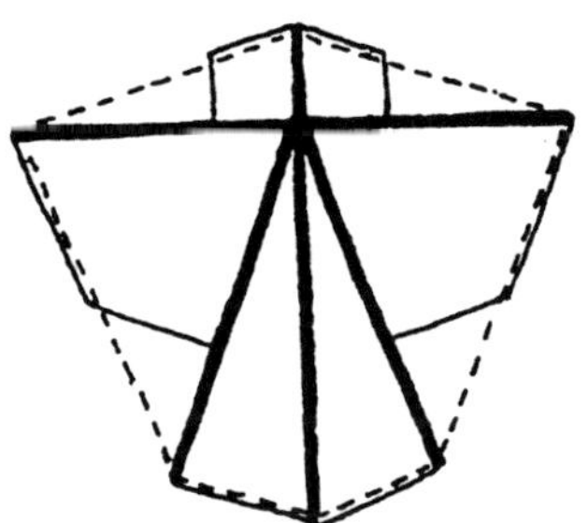
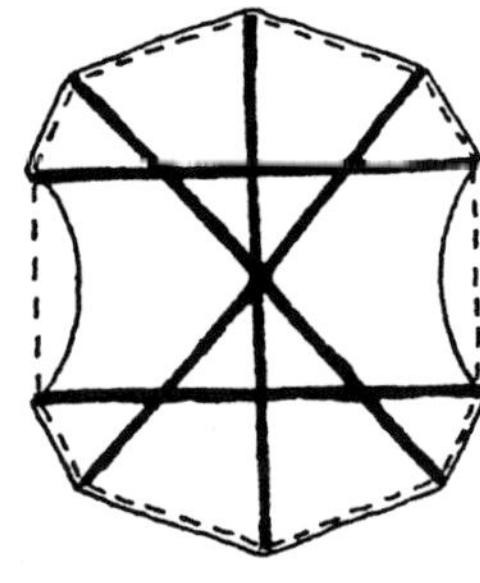

Step 1

(continued)

Name ______________________________ Date ______________

Project 46: Japan: Kites *(continued)*

2. Tie the support pieces in place. Hold them in the middle and make adjustments until they balance exactly. Glue them at the joints.

3. Cut a notch across the ends of each of the wood supports.

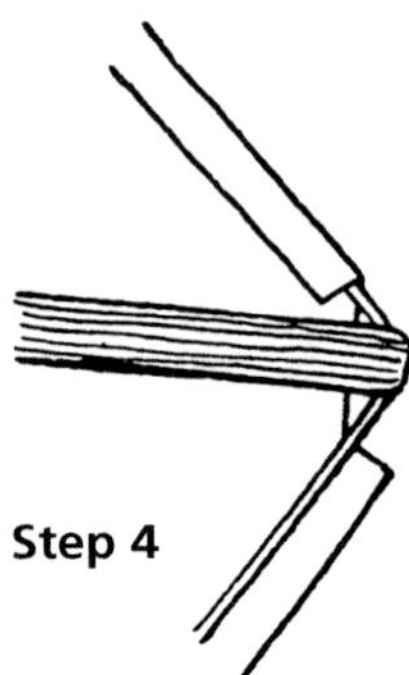

4. Run string through the notches of the stick ends (dotted lines in the diagrams in Step 1). Draw the string taut but not so tight that the frame bends *(Step 4)*.

5. Design the kite paper to fit the shape of the frame. Glue pieces together if needed. Draw and then color the design.

6. Cut the kite paper (thin lines in the diagrams in Step 1) slightly larger than the support frame.

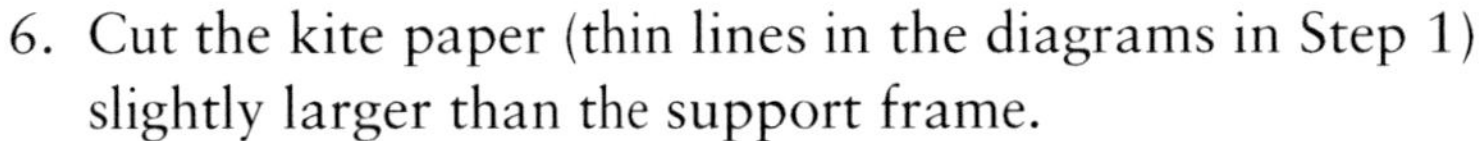

7. Cover one side of the support frame with glue. Carefully lay the kite paper, decorated side up, over the string between the supports and glue it down. Press the paper to the frame until it sticks.

8. When the glue is dry, turn the kite over. Fold the edges of the paper over the string between the support ends and glue down.

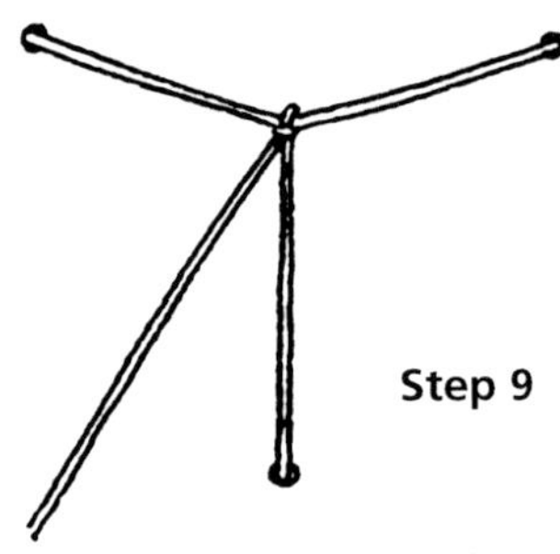

9. Make a string bridle by punching holes in the paper and tying string to three arms of the support. Tie the two ends of one string equidistant from the middle of one horizontal stick. Tie one end of a second string to the middle of the first string and the other end lower down to the middle vertical stick. Adjust these strings so that they will pull about one foot away from the face of the kite. You will tie the kite string where the two bridle strings join *(Step 9)*.

10. Make the tail with short lengths of paper tied to a string attached to the bottom of the kite. This steadies it when flying. If the kite cartwheels, it needs more tail.

(continued)

Name ______________________ Date ______________

Project 46: Japan: Kites *(continued)*

11. A simple reel is a rod around which the string is wrapped in a figure-eight pattern to keep it from tangling. Illustrated at right is a more complicated Japanese type reel *(Step 11)*.

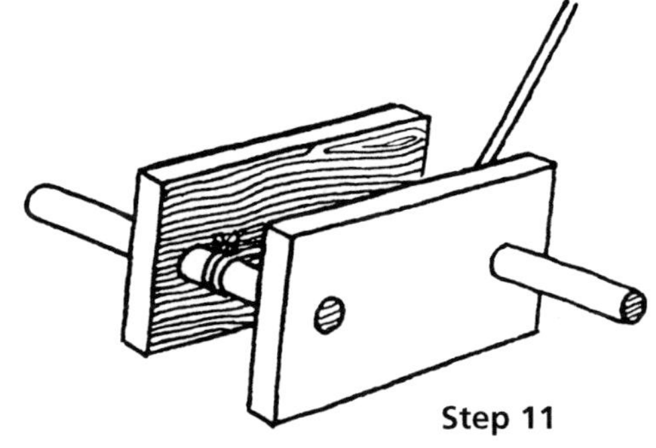

12. Flying a kite means more than just running with it. Choose a windy day. A friend holding the kite standing a few yards away tosses it up into the wind. Let the wind take it up. You help by keeping the string taut. When it drops and the string sags, pull the string with steady jerks to slowly raise the kite. As you jerk it upward, let the wind pull the string from the reel.

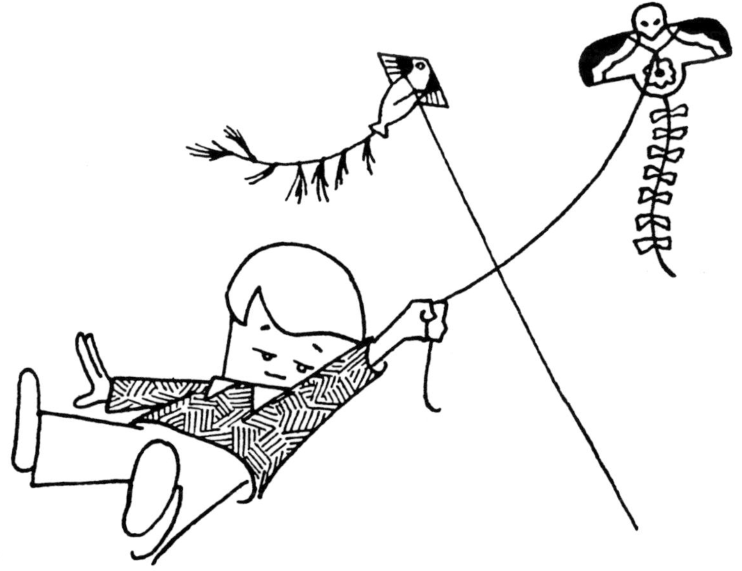

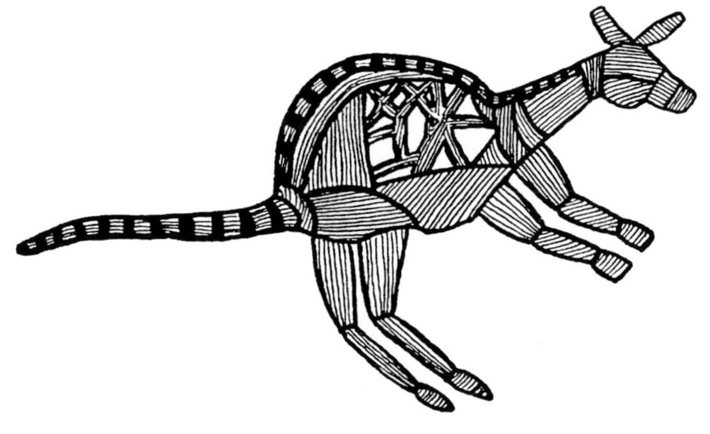

PART VII:

Southeast Asia and Oceania

VII. The Arts and Crafts of Southeast Asia and Oceania

The crafts of this region, coming from countries as modern as tonight's stock market report, seemingly belong to the exotic past. Yet, as elsewhere, a revival of traditional crafts has been pursued in order to maintain a cultural identity in the face of an increasingly uniform world culture. Wayang puppets continue to delight audiences. Indonesian batik is a popular amateur craft in the United States and a dress material worn on the fashion runways of New York, London, and Paris. Maori wood carving is making a comeback after decades of neglect.

Two Wayang puppet projects appear here. The more complicated wooden puppet can be worked on by several students, each making one part of the doll. Maori wood carving can be attempted on any size wood or designs can be painted on wood, as sometimes occurs with Maori building decoration.

The native Maori of New Zealand boast the traditions of Oceania. Native Australians do not. However, two crafts of the island continent are included here.

Name ____________________ Date ____________________

Project 47: Thailand: Princess Ring

Materials	
For this activity you will need: • wire	• clay • gold-colored paint

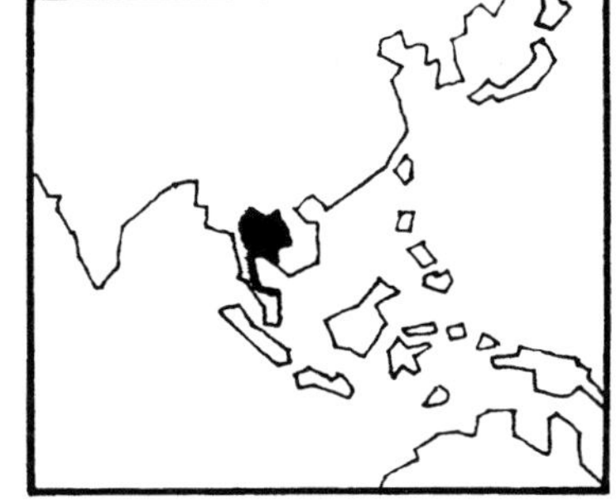

Thailand is the oldest independent nation of Southeast Asia. As throughout most of the region, Buddhism is the religion of the Thai people, with the tall towers of Buddhist temples dotting the skyline of Bangkok, the capital. *Garuda* statues, the bird-men of myth who are the Thai national symbol, wear tall crowns as they protect those temples (below right). Performers of the classic *khon* dance wear elaborate towering crowns (below left). And goldsmiths make the Princess Ring, a cone-shaped ring resembling the towers and crowns of Thailand.

1. Cut a short piece of wire and wrap it *loosely* around your finger. Let one end project one-half inch in the air. Wrap the other end around the base of this projecting piece.
2. Shape a cone of clay around this projecting piece and some clay along the circular finger part of the ring *(Step 2)*.
3. Use a pointed instrument to shape the ring cone into the crown of a Thai Princess Ring.
4. When the clay has dried, paint it gold.

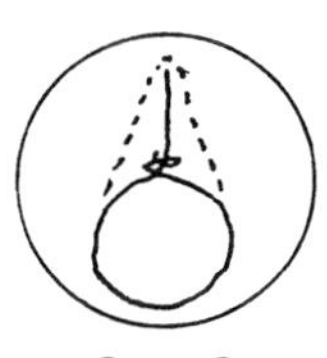

Step 2

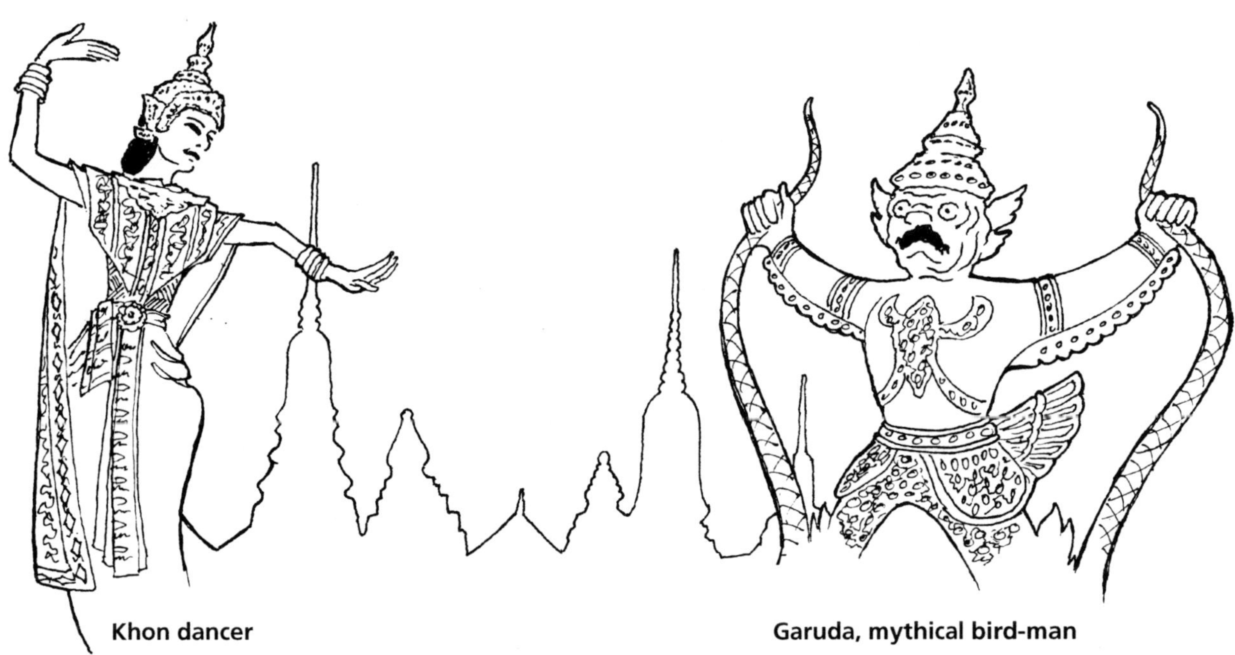

Khon dancer

Garuda, mythical bird-man

Name ______________________________ Date ______________

Project 48: Malaysia: Ikat Dyeing

Materials	
For this activity you will need:	
• white natural fiber yarn (or cord or string)	• ribbon
	• fabric dye

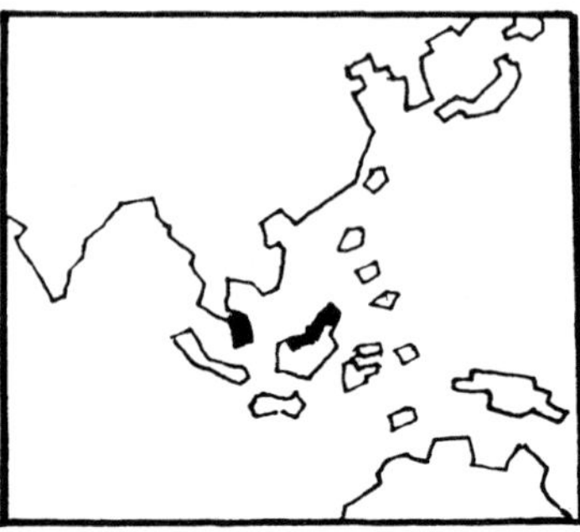

Malaysia lies at the tip of the Malay Peninsula, then leaps over water to include islands of the Malay Archipelago and the northern coast of Borneo. This land mixture is home to a cultural mix, including native Malaysian, Chinese, Indian, and Pakistani cultures. One craft, ikat dyeing, is common to all Malaysian cultures. The ikat method dyes thread or yarn with an accentual fall of color combinations. Ikat dyeing is also practiced in neighboring Indonesia and parts of Africa.

1. Leave yarn in the skein. If using cord or string, wrap the cord or string into a large loop like a skein of yarn.
2. Fix the skein in some planned fashion such as tying knots in the loop or tying ribbons around the skein at regular intervals, or plan to dye one end of the skein, then the other *(Step 2)*.
3. Prepare fabric dye according to manufacturer's instructions.
4. Dye the material. If combining two color dyes, let the first one dry before dyeing with the second.
5. Use the dyed material for knitting or other craft projects. The resulting color effect can be surprising.

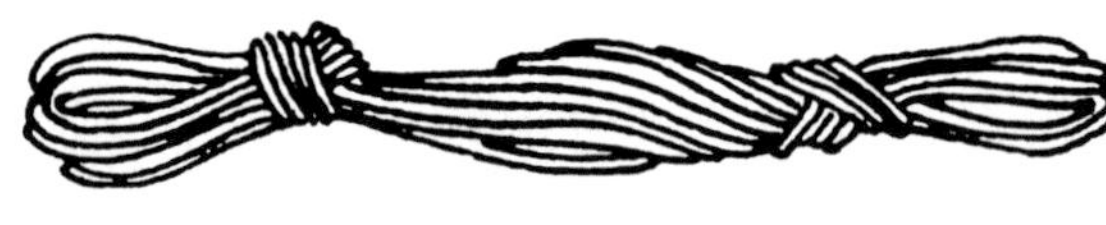

Step 2

Name ________________________________ Date ____________________

Project 49: Indonesia: Batik

Materials	
For this activity you will need:	
• white natural fiber cloth	• fabric dye
• white candle	• iron

Indonesia has one of the world's largest populations. It is an oil-producing nation and critical to global economics. In the world of craft, the Indonesian island of Java is home of the popular batik method of dyeing fabrics. One piece of Javanese batik survives from 1750. The main tool used in batik dyeing is a *tjanting*. This resembles a small metal funnel with a fine opening at the tip. It allows the artisan to drip wax on cloth. After waxing, the cloth is dyed. The wax resists the dye. When the cloth is waxed again and dyed another color, a complex multi-color design can be created. This simple batik project does not require a tjanting.

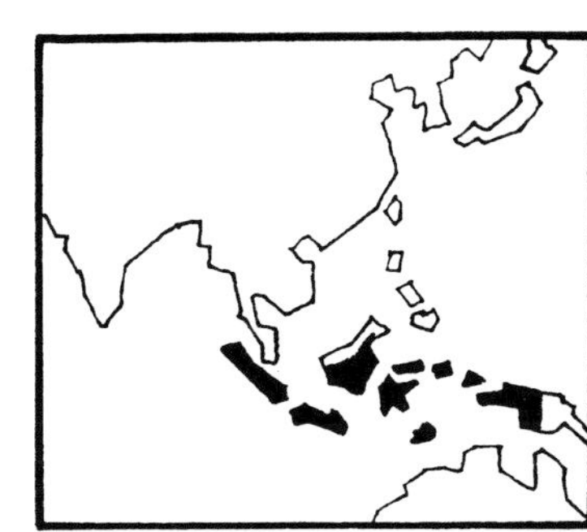

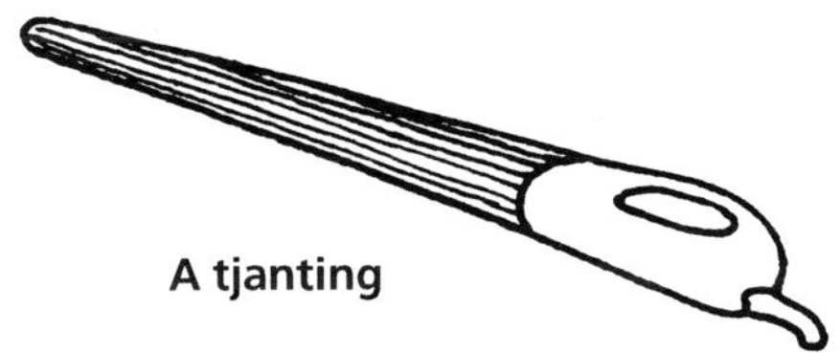

A tjanting

1. Clean and press a handkerchief or piece of natural fiber cloth. Lay the cloth on old newspaper.
2. Drip wax from a lighted white candle onto the cloth in a pattern such as the circle and lines of the diagram *(Step 2)*. Where wax drips, the dye will not take and the cloth remains white.
3. When the wax has hardened, prepare a light colored fabric dye, such as yellow, pink, or light blue. A special batik dye is available from hobby shops. Less expensive ordinary dye is suitable, as long as it dyes cloth in cool water. Hotter water will melt the wax.
4. Dip the cloth in the dye for the length of time indicated in the dye instructions. Then hang the cloth to dry.

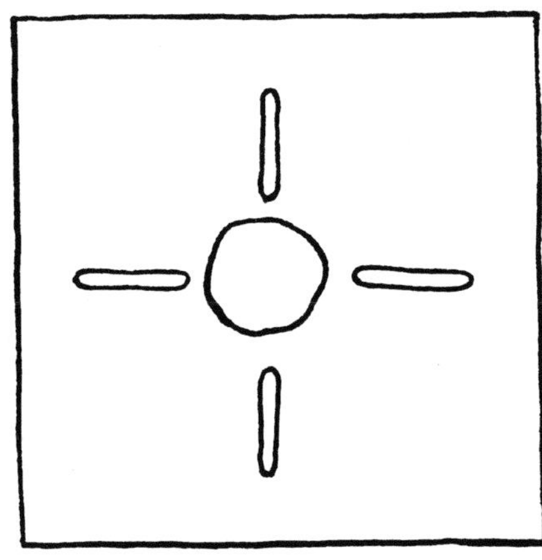

Step 2

(continued)

Name ____________________ Date ____________________

Project 49: Indonesia: Batik *(continued)*

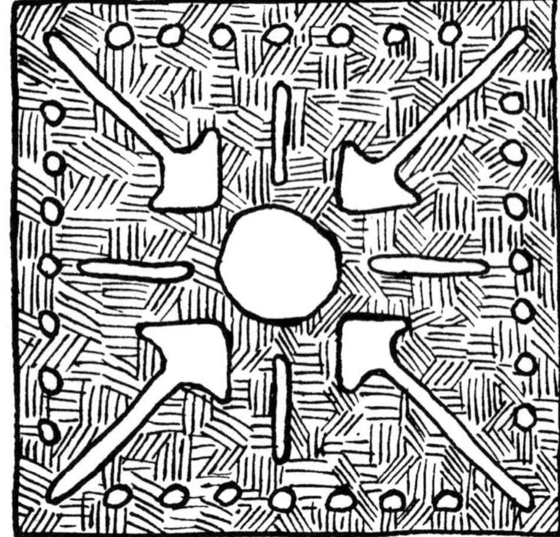

Step 5

5. Once the cloth is dry, lay it on newspaper again. Leave the first wax as it is. Drip another pattern of candle wax on the cloth *(Step 5)*.
6. Prepare the second dye bath. This color should be darker than the first but of a similar hue. Use dark brown or red if the first was yellow, orange, or pink. Use dark blue if the first was light blue or green.
7. Dye the cloth again and allow it to dry.
8. When the dyed cloth has dried, place it between newspapers. Use old ones so that the ink does not stain the cloth. Run a hot iron over the newspaper to melt the wax. The melted wax will be absorbed by the newspaper. Any oily wax remaining can be washed out by a laundry detergent.
9. The batik dyeing is complete. The shapes covered by the first waxing will appear white, by the second a light color, and the rest of the cloth will be of the final dark color *(Step 9)*.

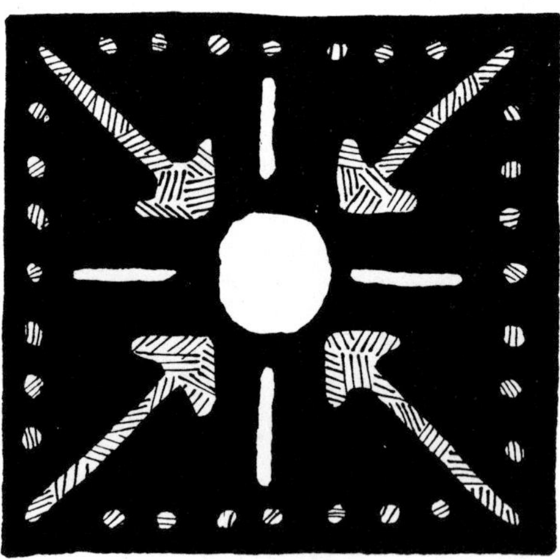

Step 9

Name ______________________________ Date ______________

Project 50: Indonesia: Wayang Puppet

Materials	
For this activity you will need: • one balsa wood block, 6" × 5" × 3" • one balsa wood block, 6" × 3" × 3" • four rods, 3/4" × 5" • one pencil-thick rod, 6" long • two pencil-thick rods, 12" long	• cloth • string • gold paint • enamel paint • hand drill • hobby knife

The *Wayang* puppet show was probably in existence in Indonesia as long ago as the first century. Traditionally meant to hold off evil spirits, Wayang performances were held whenever wars, storms, or famine threatened. Originally telling stories of native heroes, they changed to show Hindu epics when that religion arrived. They modified again with the arrival of Buddhism.

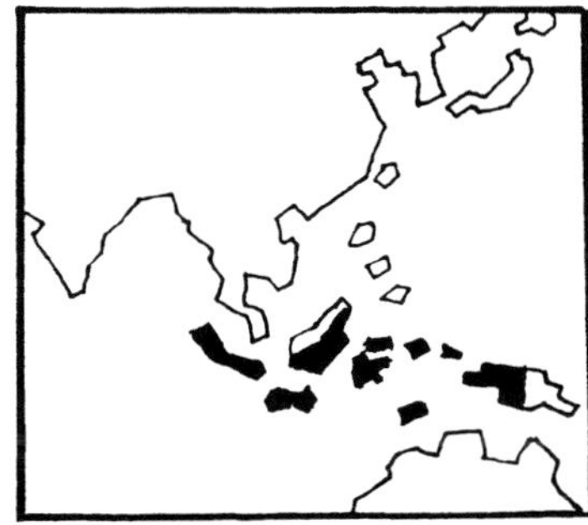

1. From the larger block, carve the head. Drill a hole in the base into which will fit the six-inch rod as illustrated on the following page. Paint the crown with gold and color. Paint fine details for the face.

2. From the smaller block, carve the body as shown on the next page. Cut a hole at the top for the head to fit into. Drill a hole for the pencil-thick rod to fit up through the body. Drill a hole to run string from one shoulder through to the other. Paint the body gold.

3. Cut two 1½" pieces from the thicker rods. Carve them into hands as illustrated. Drill a narrow hole in each hand.

4. Carve the two forearms as shown and glue the hands to them. Paint the arms and hands gold. Color the bracelet.

5. Carve upper arms as shown. Paint arms gold and color the band.

6. Join forearms to upper arms by uniting with strings pushed through holes at the joints as illustrated.

7. Join the arms to the shoulders by running a string from one arm through the shoulders to the other arm as shown.

(continued)

Name ______________________________ Date ______________

Project 50: Indonesia: Wayang Puppet *(continued)*

8. Run the six-inch rod through the body to the neck hole at top as shown at right. Push the hole at the base of the neck onto the end of the rod.

9. Make a twelve-inch-long cloth skirt for the puppet. Tie it above the wider body base. Make other costume details.

10. Tie a three-inch string to the ends of the two narrow rods. Run the other string end through the hand holes and tie as illustrated.

11. To perform, one person holds the puppet body under the skirt with one hand and turns the rod connected to the head with the other hand. Another person operates the two hand rods.

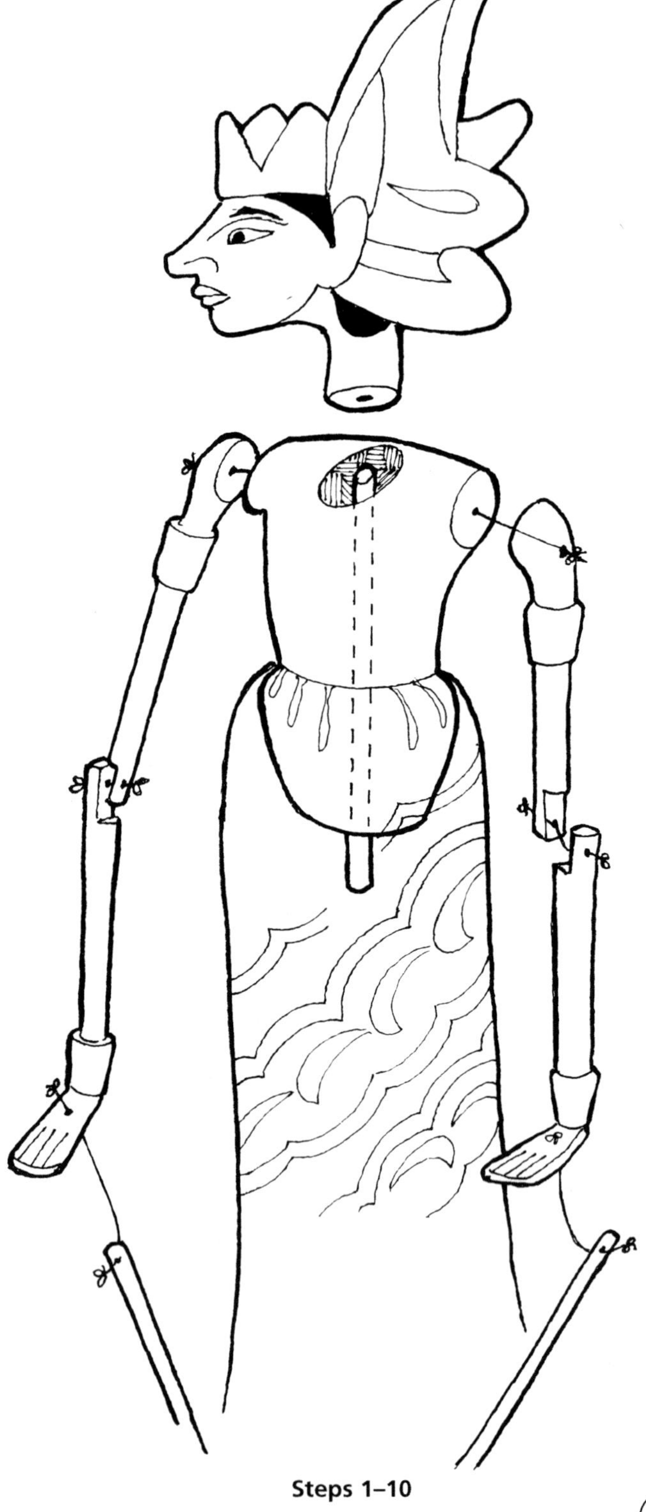

Steps 1–10

Name ______________________ Date ______________

Project 51: Indonesia: Wayang Kulit Shadow Puppets

Materials	
For this activity you will need:	• string
• poster board	• tempera color
• thin wooden rods	• paper fasteners
• bamboo rod	• hobby knife
• flexible cable	• tape

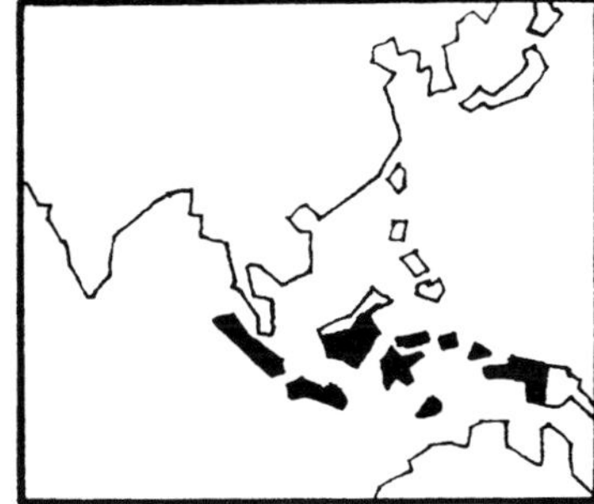

A popular variation of the puppet theater is the *Wayang Kulit,* the shadow puppet plays. Fine lines and holes are cut in these puppets made of water-buffalo leather. Even though it is solely their lacy shadows that are cast on the viewing screen, the puppets are painted symbolic colors. Movement is limited, since they are only jointed at the elbow and shoulder. Rods attached to the wrists move the arms in stiff, formal postures to resemble the classic dancers of Indonesia.

1. Design your puppet. Its silhouetted profile must convey expression. The interior cut-out pattern should be elaborate.
2. Lay out the design on poster board. Each puppet has five parts: the combined head, body, and legs; two upper arms; and two forearms with hands.
3. Paint it before cutting so the paper will not curl.
4. Using a hobby knife, cut out the puppet and then make the interior cuts.
5. Tape a bamboo or wood rod to the back of the puppet for support. Run it as high as possible without interfering with the design perforations. Above that, support it with a flexible cable, taped to the rod end and the puppet's back *(Step 5).*
6. Attach the arm parts to the puppet with paper fasteners *(Step 6).*

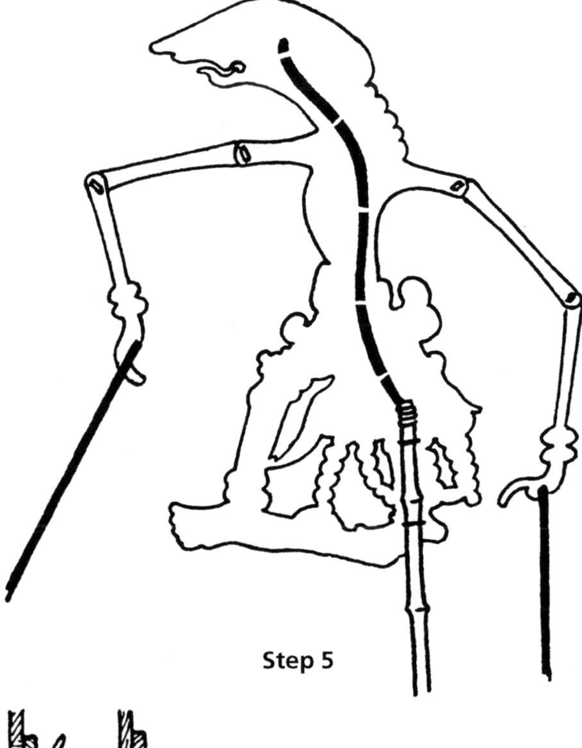

Step 5

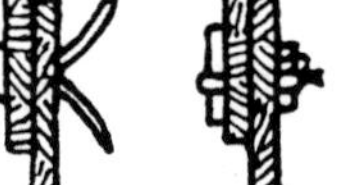

Step 6

(continued)

Name ______________________________ Date ______________

Project 51: Indonesia: Wayang Kulit Shadow Puppets *(continued)*

7. Cut a slit in one end of two 12-inch-long wooden rods.
8. Make a small circle of string. Slip it in the slot at the rod end and glue *(Step 8)*. Sew the string to the puppet's hands. Moving the rod moves the puppet's hands.
9. Display your puppet. If you plan a performance, stretch a large sheet of paper on a wooden frame. Shine light from behind to cast the shadows of the puppets on the paper screen.

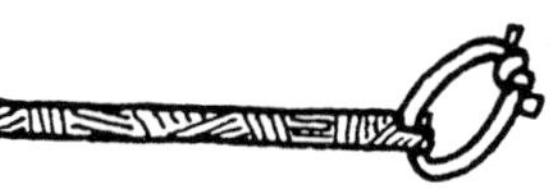

Step 8

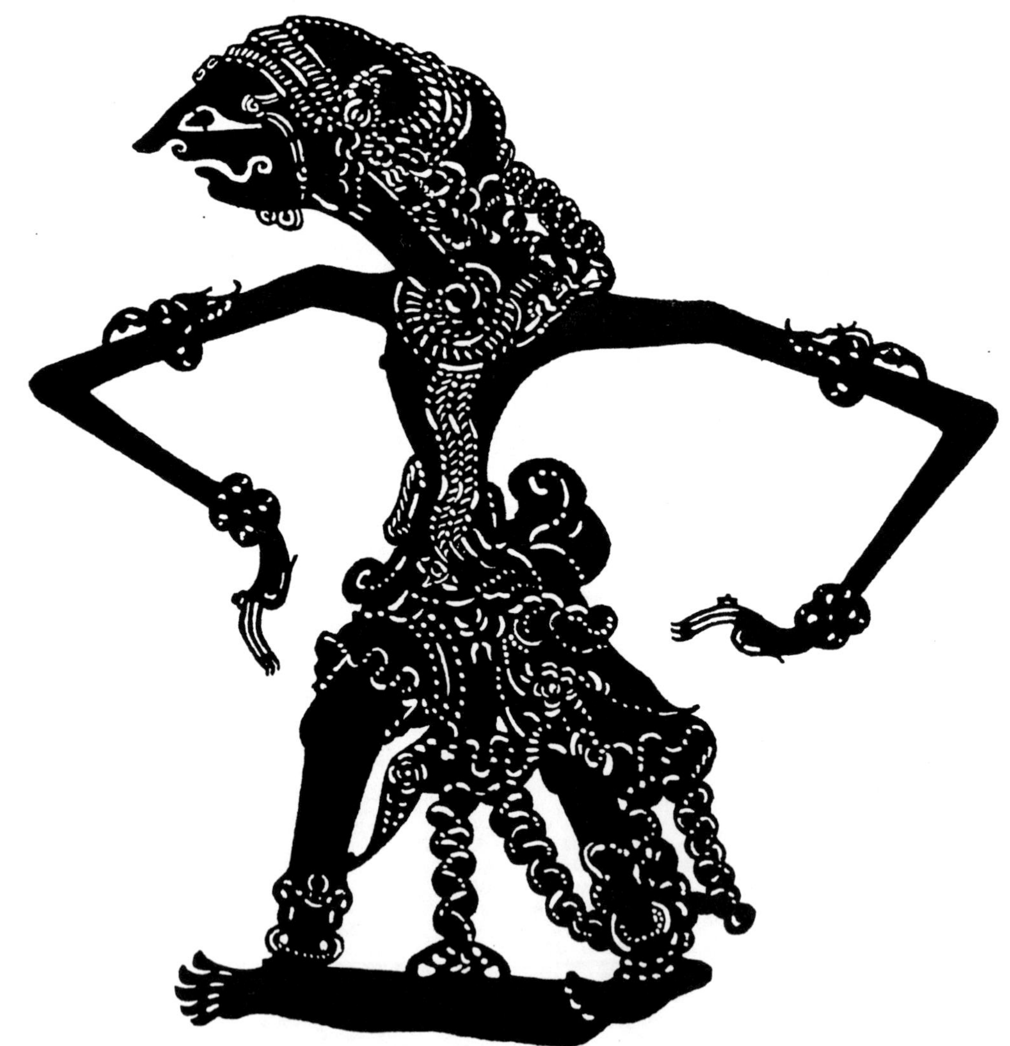

Wayang Kulit shadow puppet

Name ______________________________ Date ______________

Project 52: Polynesia: Tapa Printing

Materials
For this activity you will need: • flat objects to be used for printing • woodcut printing ink or acrylic paint • cloth to print

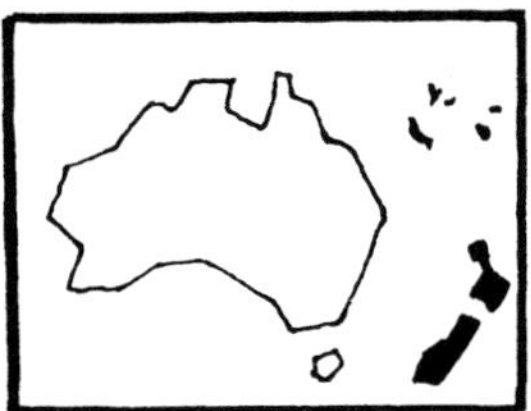

The name *Polynesia* combines two Greek words that mean "many islands," an apt description of the geography of the South Pacific. Scattered over miles of sea, the Polynesians still maintain cultural similarities. One is tapa printing. Tapa is cloth made by crushing, cleaning, then pounding the inside fibers of certain plants or the bark of the textile screw-pine. In the Fiji Islands, tapa cloth is painted freely. On other islands, it is printed by dipping pieces of wood and other objects into coloring and then pressing them on the tapa cloth. These two designs were painted in the Samoan islands.

1. Collect flat objects that can be used to print, such as coins, pieces of wood, bottle and jar lids, pencil ends, etc.
2. Let the collected items inspire a design idea to decorate a piece of cloth with a repeated pattern. Feel free to cut the items into other shapes to develop the design. Draw the final pattern.
3. Lay newspaper on a drawing board and pin the cloth flat to it.
4. Brush the object with which you will print with woodcut printing ink or acrylic paint.
5. Press the object to the cloth. Repeat the printing until the design is complete.

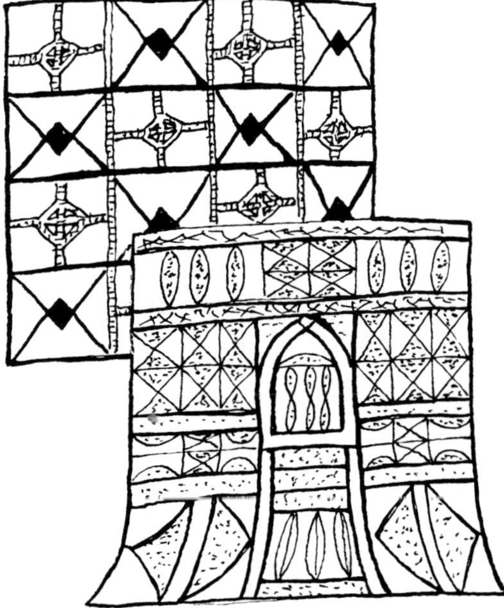

Tapa designs from Samoa

Name ______________________________ Date ______________

Project 53: New Zealand: Maori Wood Carving

Materials	
For this activity you will need: • flat piece of pine wood or balsa wood	• woodcut knives • varnish stain

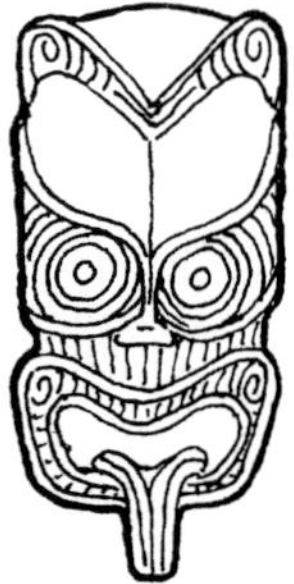

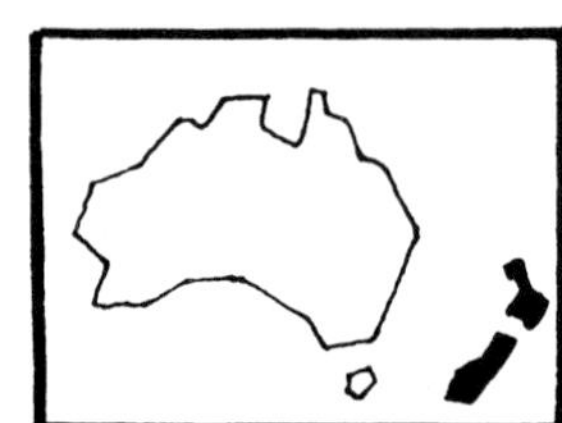

Tattooing might have once been considered a Maori craft, for, until the modern era, men tattooed their bodies and faces with elaborate spiraling decorations. These tattooed decorations were also carved on wooden figures representing ancestors which stood in front of community meeting houses. Heads were carved large in the belief that it is the most sacred part of a figure. Wood carving belongs to the Maori past. Today, there is an attempt to renew interest in wood carving, if not tattooing. Most Maori carving is relief work, although traditional motifs are sometimes painted on flat wooden planks. Carve or paint on wood the spiraling art of the Maori.

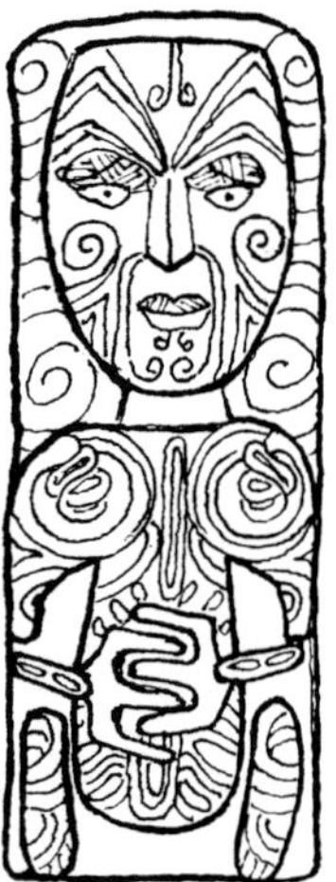

1. Draw a Maori-inspired design on a slab of wood (take care to avoid knots).
2. Use a U-shaped woodcut knife to shape your relief.
3. Use other woodcut knives to finish shaping.
4. 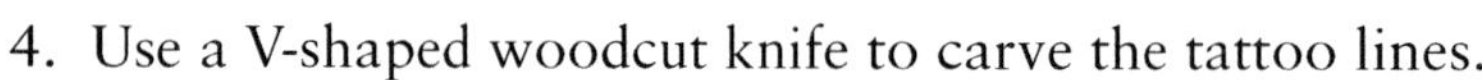Use a V-shaped woodcut knife to carve the tattoo lines.
5. 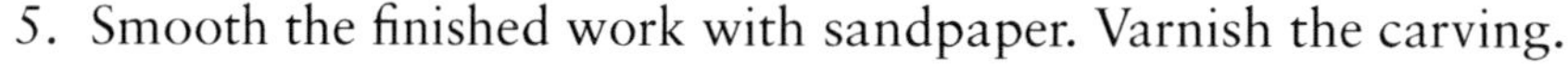Smooth the finished work with sandpaper. Varnish the carving.

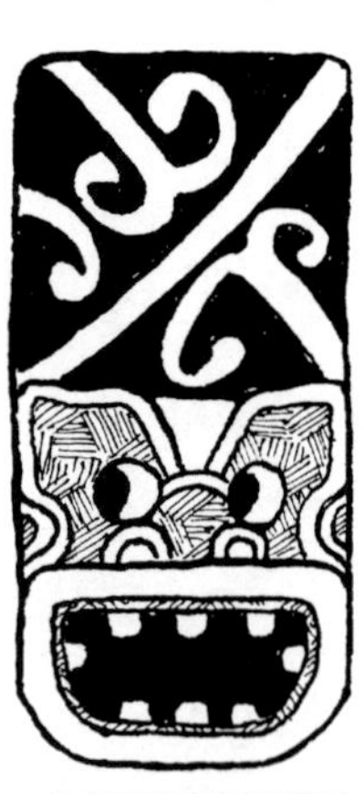

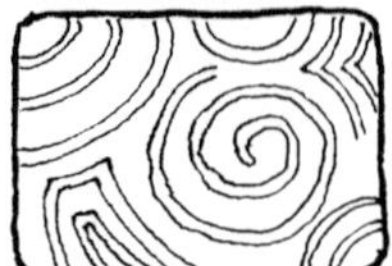

Selection of Maori designs, both carved and painted

Name ______________________________ Date ______________

Project 54: Australia: Aborigine Boomerang

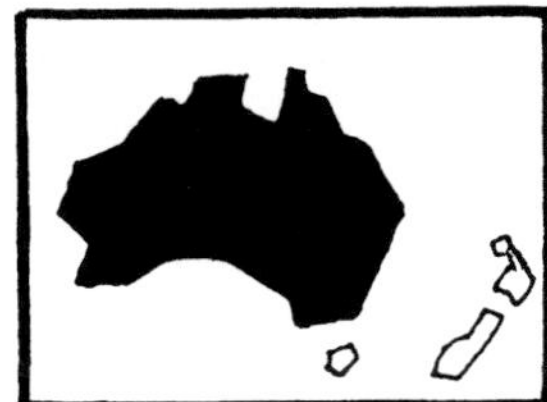

South of the scattered islands of Polynesia lies the largest island in the world, Australia. When most think of the country, cities like Sydney and Melbourne come to mind. Art practiced there is of European origin, brought by the country's immigrants. The native art and craft tradition survives in the interior where the aborigines have lived for thousands of years. You have probably heard of one craft and may know its name, the boomerang. Here are instructions for making a real boomerang and a simple one.

Real Boomerang

Materials	
For this activity you will need:	
• one-foot-square piece of $^{1}/_{4}$"-thick wood	• hobby knife
• jigsaw	• sandpaper

1. Draw the illustrated pattern (see next page) of a boomerang arm on the piece of wood. Turn the pattern over and draw the other arm *(Step 1)*.

2. Cut out the boomerang with a jigsaw.

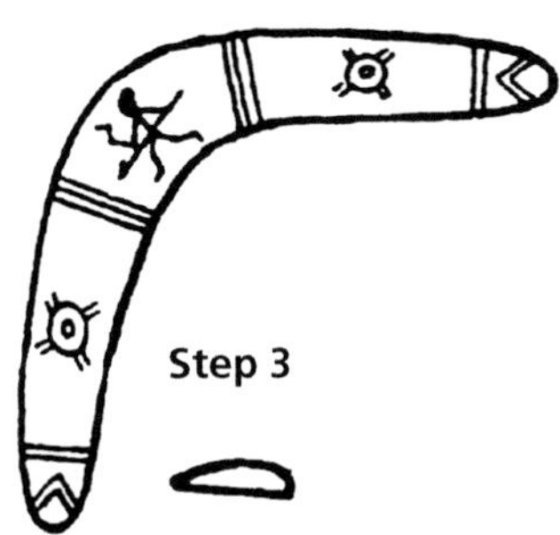

Step 3

3. Boomerang shaping is critical. One side remains flat. The other side is curved like the cross section of an airplane wing. The thicker edge of the curve lies toward the inside of the angle as in the illustrated cross section *(Step 3)*. The tips taper down to an edge. Carve with a hobby knife. Sand smooth.

4. With sandpaper, taper one end of the undersurface, the shaded area in the illustration (also shown in cross section *(Step 4)*).

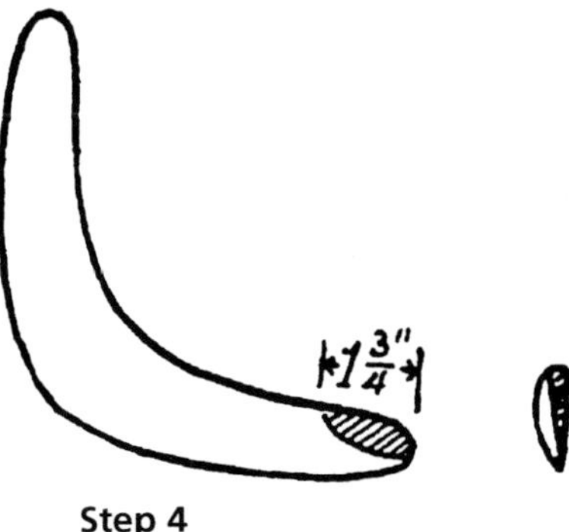

Step 4

5. Decorate by wood burning, shallow carving, or painting. The printed pattern is decorated with a typical design. Only use wood burning under adult supervision.

(continued)

Name ______________________________ Date ______________

Project 54: Australia: Aborigine Boomerang *(continued)*

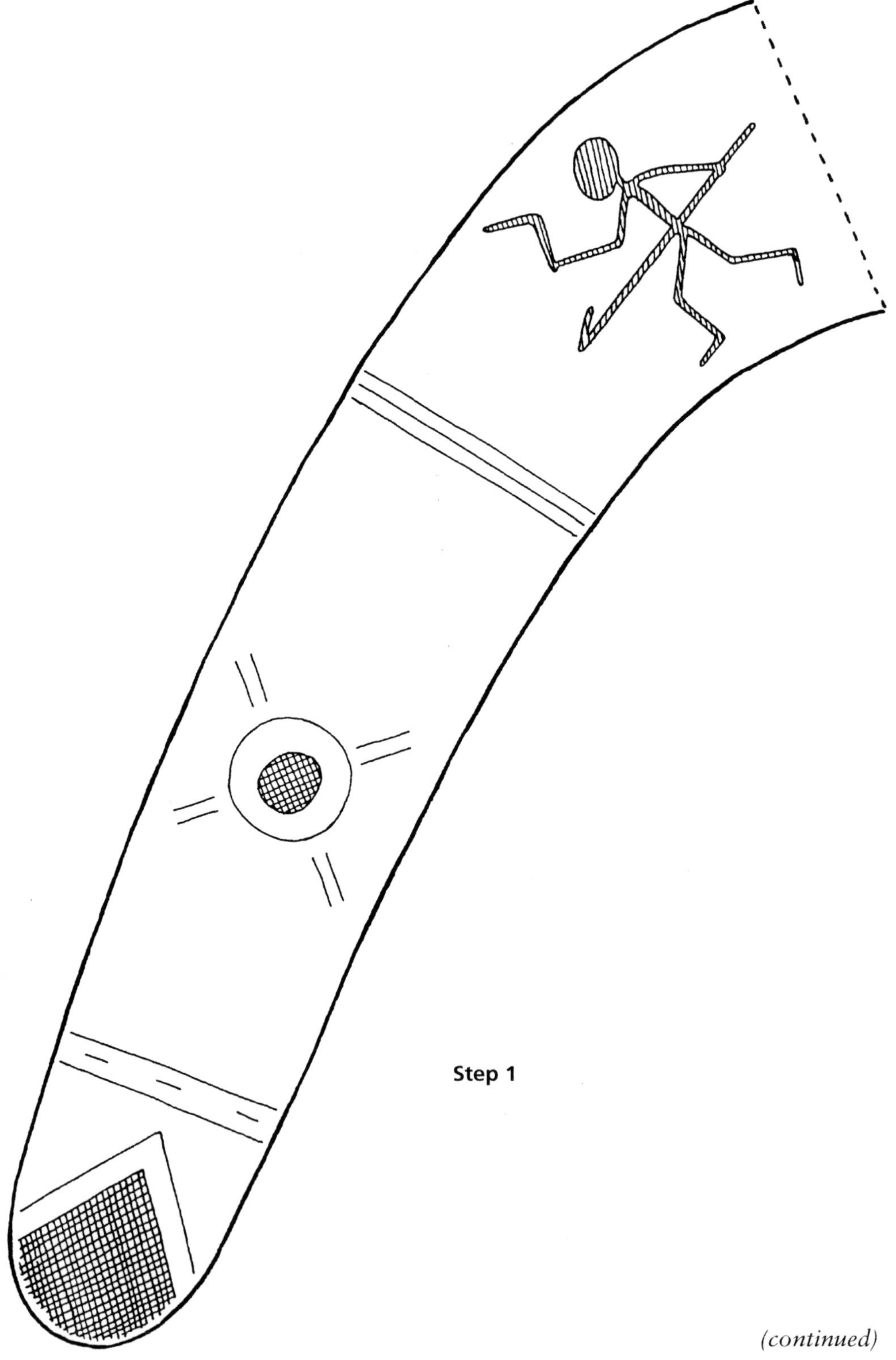

(continued)

Name ________________________________ Date ____________________

Project 54: Australia: Aborigine Boomerang *(continued)*

Throwing the Boomerang

1. Choose a large field for throwing to avoid accidents.

2. If there is wind, face into it at a 45-degree angle *(Step 2)*.

3. Hold one end of the boomerang so that the flat side faces to your right and the curved side to your left, regardless if you are right- or left-handed.

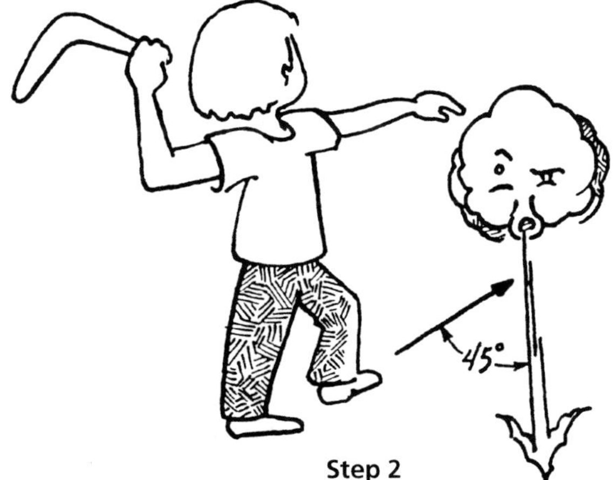

Step 2

4. Holding it vertically, point the angle of the boomerang just above the horizon. Cock your arm, holding it beside your ear.

5. Then throw, bringing your arm forward and down as a football is thrown, releasing the boomerang with a snap so that it spins vertically like a wheel. The faster it spins, the more successful the throw.

6. Throwing requires practice. With small adjustments in its vertical position at the time of release, the aim above the horizon, and its spin rate, you will soon have it returning to you.

NOTE: Practice safely, allowing much open space for throwing. Never take your eye off the boomerang and be sure spectators are as alert.

(continued)

Name ______________________ Date ______________

Project 54: Australia: Aborigine Boomerang *(continued)*

Simple Boomerang

Materials
For this activity you will need: • heavy poster board • hobby knife

1. Cut this boomerang shape from heavy poster board *(Step 1)*.
2. Decorate the boomerang with an aborigine design.
3. Practice throwing using the previous instructions. More simply, lay the boomerang on a piece of wood, letting one arm of the boomerang stick out. Strike the projecting arm with a stick. This sends it spinning to fly off and then return.

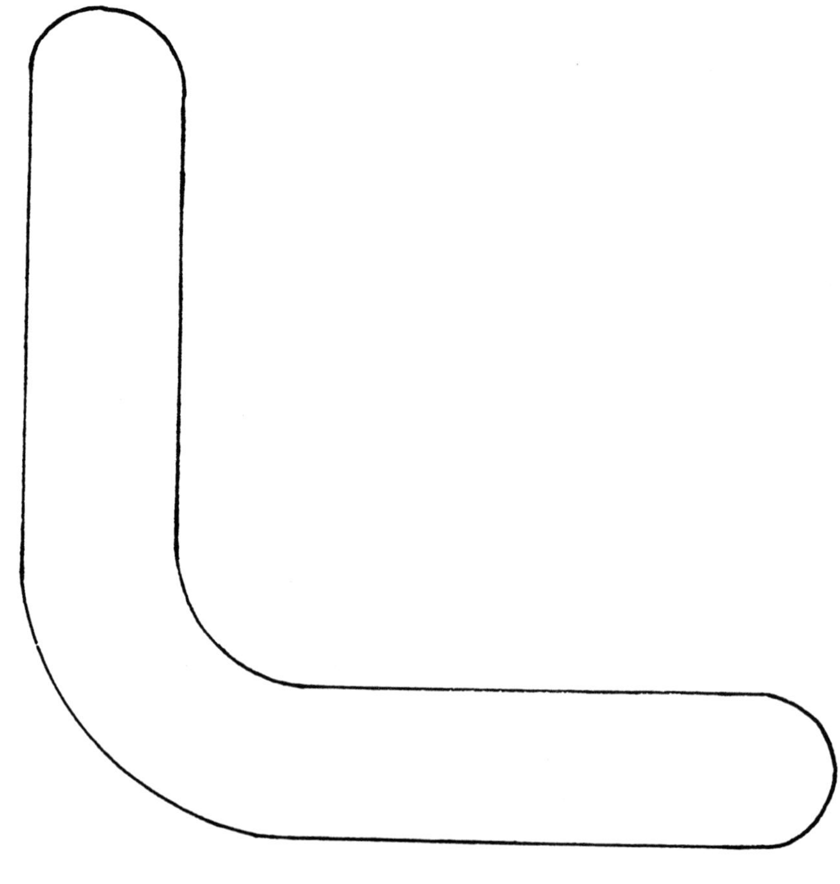

Step 1

Name ______________________ Date ______________

Project 55: Australia: Bark Painting

Materials
For this activity you will need: • paper-thin bark or brown wrapping paper • acrylic paint

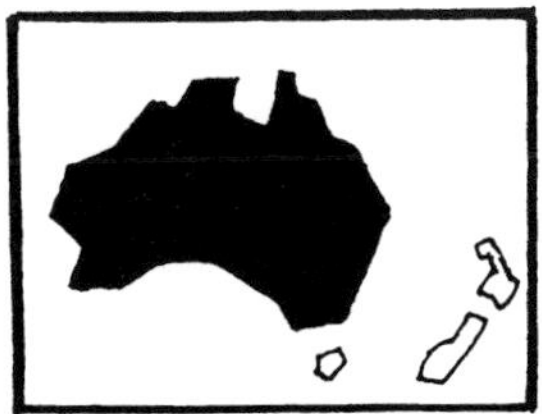

Kangaroo is an aborigine word for one of Australia's unique animals. The one illustrated here was painted some five thousand years ago on a cliff face in Australia. The ancient artist painted with reddish-brown and yellow ocher clay and black charcoal. Australian aborigines still use such natural materials to paint animal and plant designs on thin sheets stripped from the bark of eucalyptus trees.

We realize today that stripping bark away from a live tree damages it. If you do not have dead birch or eucalyptus trees in your area, we recommend using brown wrapping paper instead.

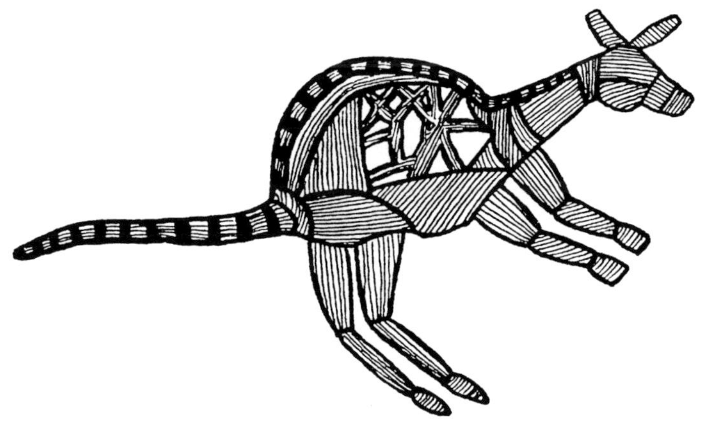

Kangaroo painting about 3000 B.C.

1. Select sheets of reasonable size of bark or paper. Hammer flat any bumps.
2. Dampen the sheet and then press it between boards to dry.
3. When the sheet has dried, paint it with an animal, bird, or plant motif *(Step 3)*. Paint in a flat, two-dimensional style with black, yellow ocher, and reddish-brown colors.
4. The bark painting can be hung without framing. Or make a frame from rough, dark-stained pieces of wood.

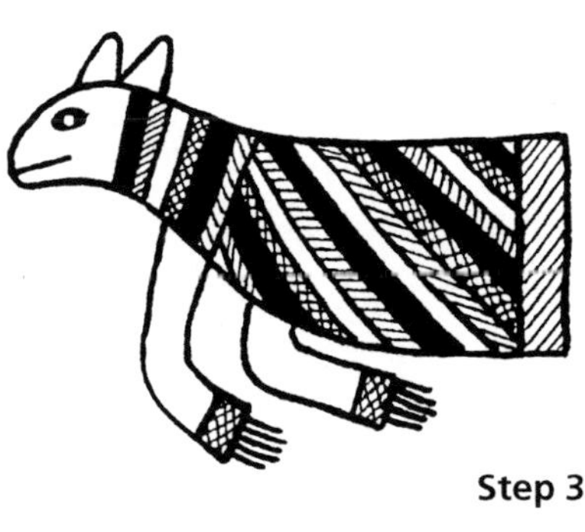

Step 3

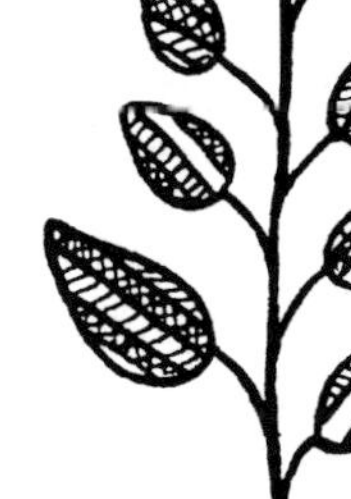

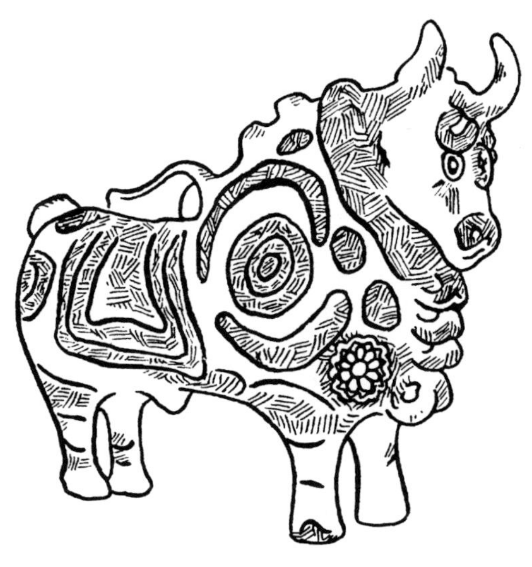

Part VIII:

Central and South America

VIII. The Arts and Crafts of Central and South America

"Latin" America sweeps over a continent and a half, from the hot, dry river bed of the Rio Grande to the icy waters of the Strait of Magellan. With few exceptions, the language of the region is Spanish. However, the cultures are not, and each country has its own traditions. What the Spanish introduced mixed with the native cultures that were in place when the conquistadors arrived, and diversified according to environment and geography. Central and South American cultures may be more Indian than Spanish. In Spain, the word *tortilla* means "omelet." In Latin America, it means the familiar flat cornmeal bread. Similarly, Native American features stand out in Latin American crafts.

Most of Mexico is geographically part of North America, though it has much in common culturally with Central America as well as the American Southwest. Crafts of Mexico are included in Part IX, North America.

Name ______________________________ Date ____________________

Project 56: Latin America: God's Eye

Materials	
For this activity you will need: • two or more sticks	• colored yarn • glue

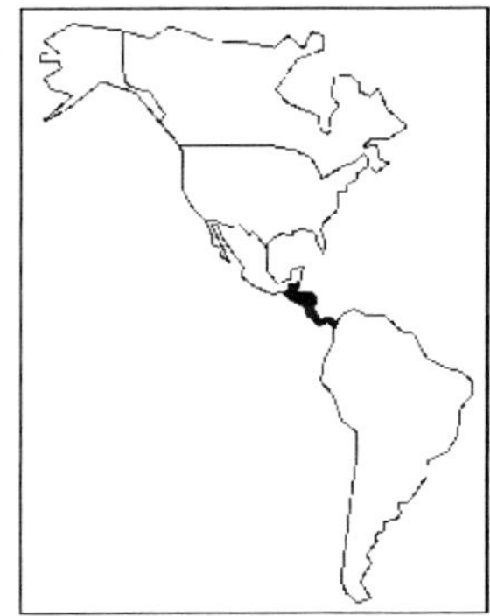

God's eyes—*ojos de dios*—are made throughout Latin America. When given as children's birthday gifts, the number of colors used corresponds to the child's age.

1. Glue the sticks into crosses or stars with four, six, or more arms. If the arms are of equal length, glue a loop of yarn to the upper arm for hanging. A longer bottom arm can be stuck into a base *(Step 1)*.

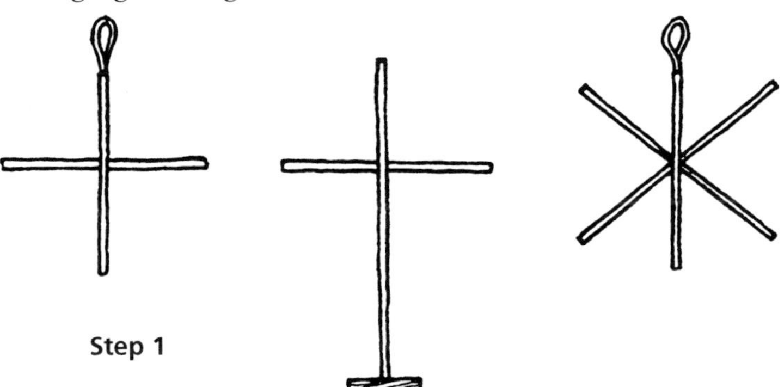

Step 1

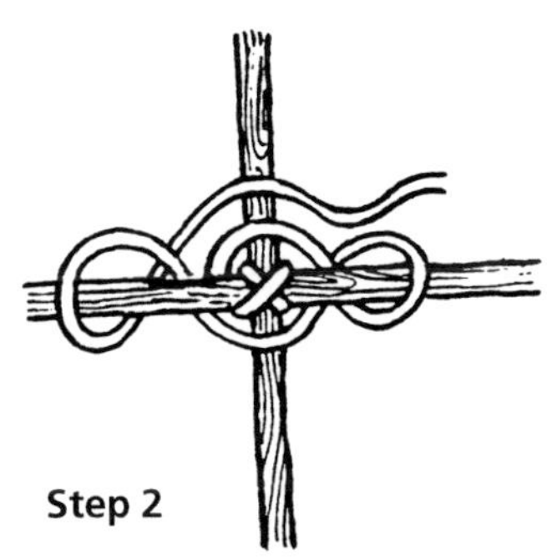

Step 2

2. Tie an end of yarn around the crossing of the sticks. Then wind in a figure eight around the crossing joint *(Step 2)*.
3. Continue weaving the yarn with the figure-eight pattern under and over the arms. Weave from the center outward.
4. When you reach the end of a strand, glue it to the back of a stick. Glue the beginning of the next strand (another color) to that.
5. Continue to cover the sticks, gluing down the last strand end *(Step 5)*.
6. For variety, glue feathers or yarn tassels to the stick ends. Then cover this ornament end with your finished weaving *(Step 6)*.

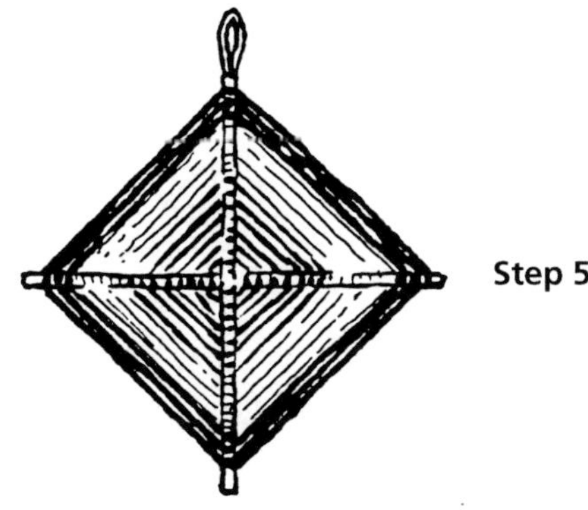

Step 5

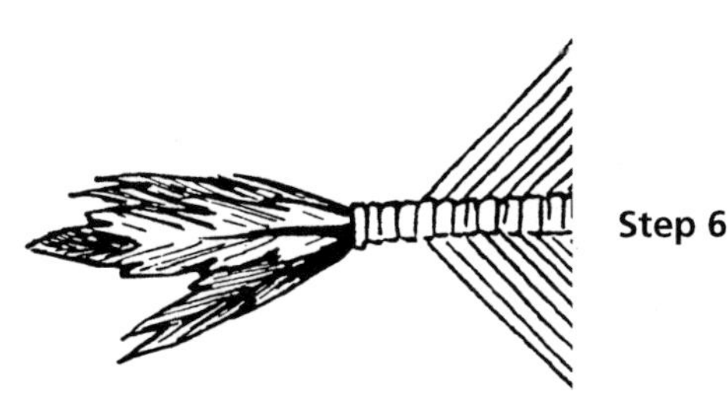

Step 6

Name ______________________________ Date ______________

Project 57: Guatemala: Sawdust Carpet

Materials	
For this activity you will need:	
• bags of sawdust	• plastic bags
• poster paint	• cloth

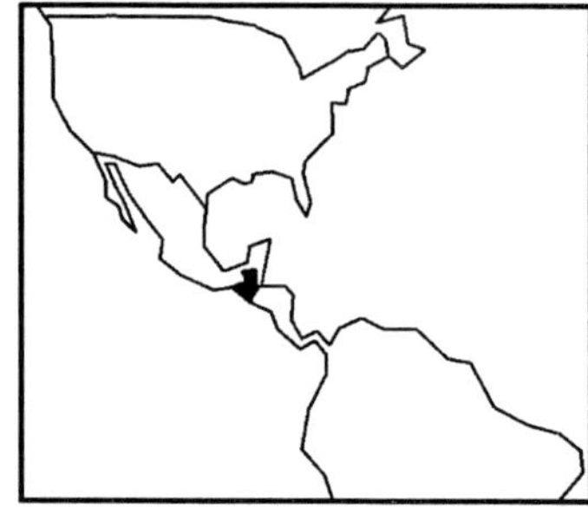

Today half of the people of Guatemala are of native background, many descendents of the ancient Mayan civilization. Many Guatemalans still pray to Mayan gods on church steps before entering for Christian prayers. During religious festivals, colored arches are erected beneath which a vividly colored carpet of sawdust is made (illustrated below). It lasts no longer than it takes the local priests to walk over it on their way to church services.

1. Collect sawdust from a wood supplier or the industrial arts shop.
2. Create a design of floral patterns, scrolls, and contrasting border for the sawdust carpet. Decide on the colors needed.
3. Color the sawdust by pouring thinned poster paint into a plastic bag. Then add a quantity of sawdust and shake well.
4. Once the sawdust is colored, dump each bag's contents into a piece of cloth held over a sink. Let the color run out, leaving the sawdust behind.
5. Open the cloths on a table protected by plastic to dry.
6. Following the design plan, create the ceremonial carpet with the colored sawdust. Photograph it before it is stepped upon.

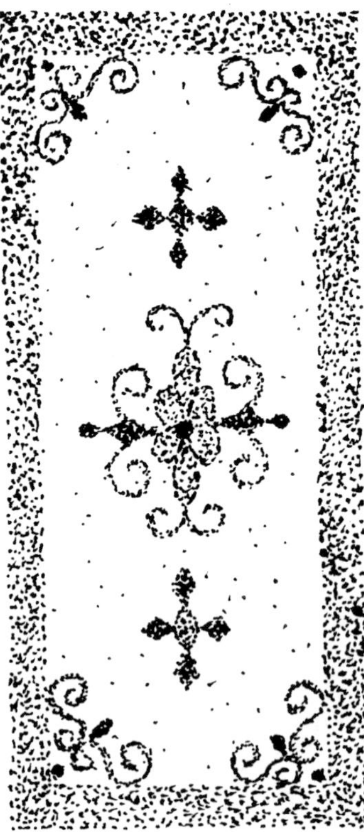

Guatemalan sawdust carpet

Name ________________________ Date ____________

Project 58: Central America: Gourd Containers

For centuries, gourds have been used throughout the Americas for containers. In Central America, round gourds, called *guacales*, are cut into bowls, and elongated ones, called *jicaras*, into drinking cups and jars. Some gourd containers are painted with colored designs. Others are covered with black dye. A workable substitute is a papier-mâché gourd.

Real Gourd

Materials	
For this activity you will need:	
• gourd	• hobby knife
• black enamel paint	• sandpaper

1. Cut away the gourd top. Clean out the inside, scraping away loose skin and removing the seeds.
2. Let the gourd dry in the sunshine. Artificial heat will split it.
3. Follow a plan to cut the gourd. Use a jagged or scalloped top for a bowl as illustrated on the next page, or cut away the bottom for a serving dish.
4. Rub down the inside with fine sandpaper.
5. Paint the gourd with black enamel or a color of your choice. It can also be painted with native designs.

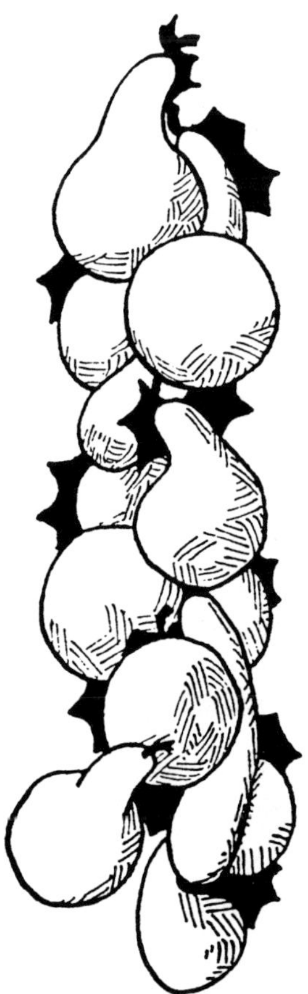

Collection of gourds, both "guacales" and "jicaras"

(continued)

Name ______________________ Date ______________

Project 58: Central America: Gourd Containers *(continued)*

Papier-Mâché Gourd

Materials	
For this activity you will need:	
• wallpaper paste or flour	• newspaper
• collapsible ball or heavy balloon	• petroleum jelly

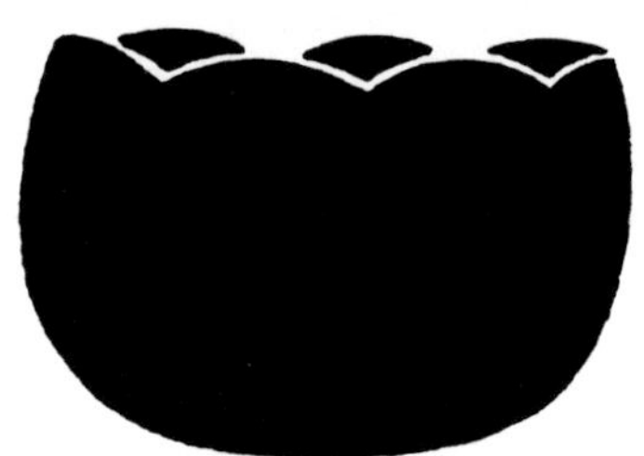

1. First, rip newspaper into long strips.
2. Spread petroleum jelly over the inflated ball or balloon.
3. Prepare wallpaper paste or mix flour with water into a pasty consistency.
4. Holding the ends of a newspaper strip, dip and soak it in the paste. Then, lay it over the ball or balloon.

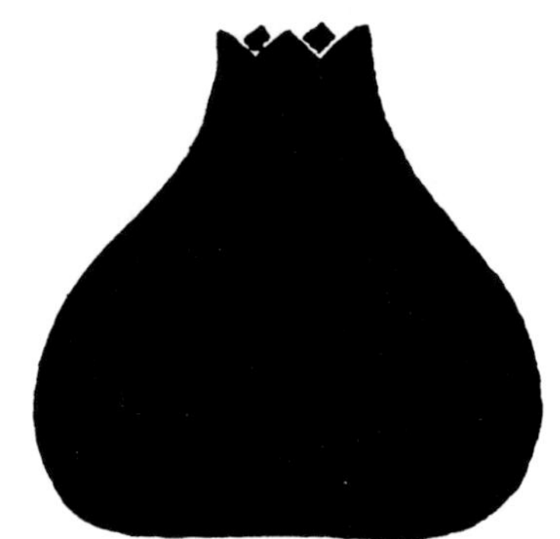

5. Continue applying strips carefully until two or three layers have built up. Be careful to leave the air nozzle of the ball or balloon free. Let dry.
6. When the papier-mâché is dry, apply several more layers of paste-soaked newspaper strips. Let dry again.
7. When the form is completely dry, deflate the ball or balloon and remove it.

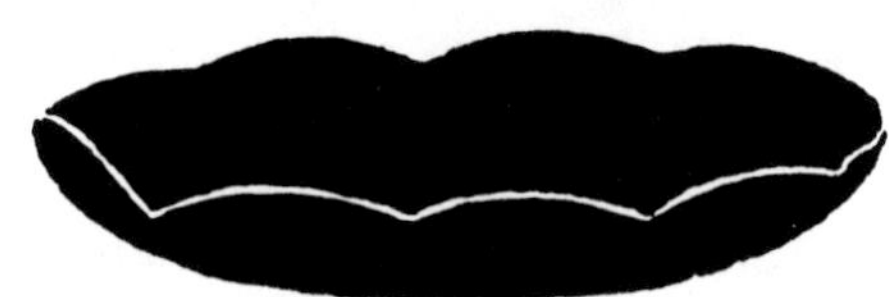

Step 9
Gourds shaped as a bowl, container, and serving dish

8. Paint the papier-mâché ball with varnish to give it a gourd color. Work with it as if it were a real gourd.
9. Use a hobby knife to cut the gourd into the shape of some useful object *(Step 9)*.

Name ______________________________ Date ______________

Project 59: South America: Carved Maté

Materials	
For this activity you will need:	
• gourd	• brown shoe polish
• sandpaper	• hobby knife

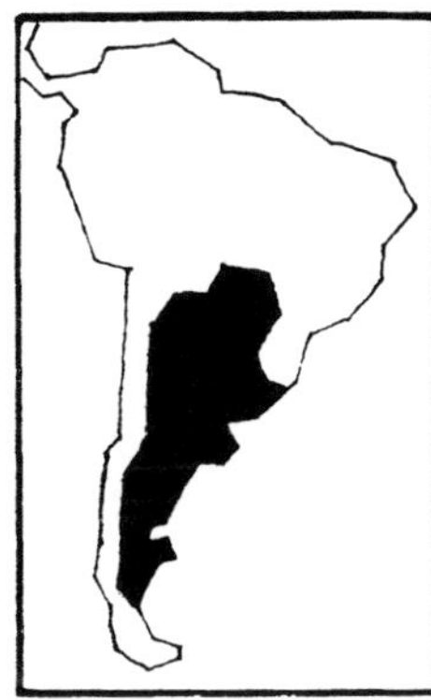

Maté, a tea made from herbs that grow in Paraguay, is drunk in that country as well as in Argentina and Uruguay. Maté is also the name of the cup—made from a gourd—from which the tea is drunk. Folk artists in Uruguay carve scenes in shallow relief on maté gourds such as that illustrated for Step 6. Romantic scenes of gauchos are especially popular. Gauchos were men of mixed Spanish and native blood who worked the large ranches, called *estancias,* of the three countries. You can carve a maté gourd as do the artists of gaucho country.

1. Cut away the gourd top. Clean out the inside, scraping away loose skin and removing the seeds.
2. Let the gourd dry in the sunshine. Artificial heat will split it.
3. Rub down the inside with sandpaper.
4. Darken the gourd by rubbing it with shoe polish. Let the polish dry, then buff it.
5. With a felt-tipped pen, draw a planned design on the gourd.
6. Using a hobby knife, cut away the darker-toned surface of the gourd to reveal the lighter tone beneath. The carving should not be deep *(Step 6).*

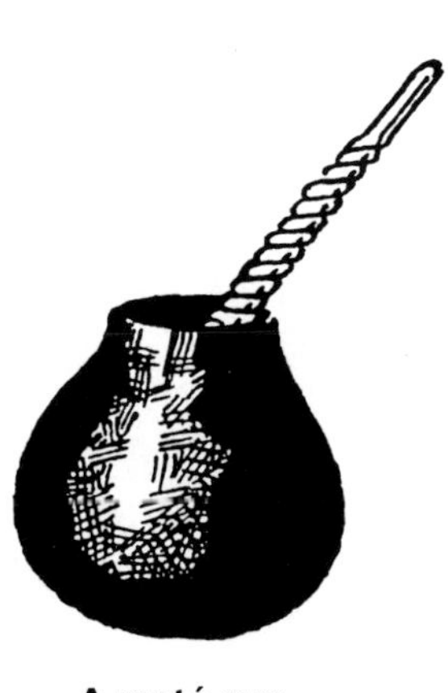

A maté cup

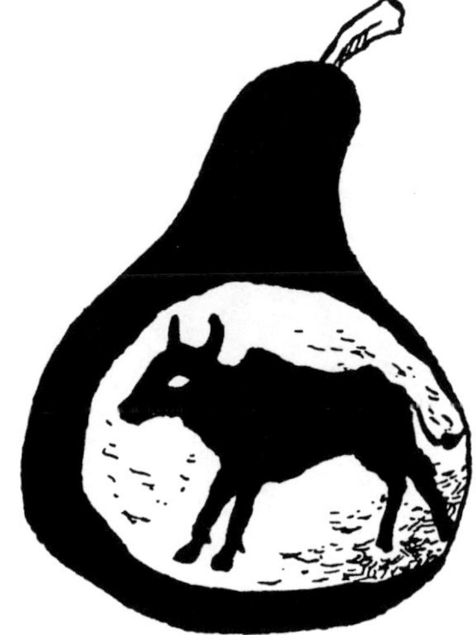

Step 6

Name ______________________ Date ______________

Project 60: Peru: Maté Burilado

Materials	
For this activity you will need: • dried gourd • carbon paper	• India ink • hobby knife • cloth or rag

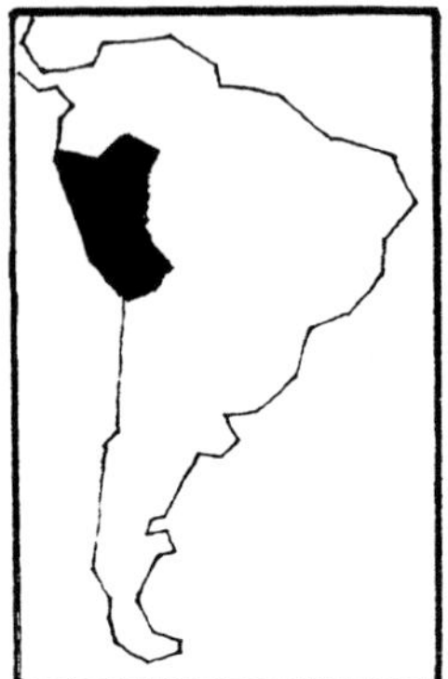

Folk artists in the villages of Huancayo, Ayacuchô, and Lambayeque in Peru create a unique kind of gourd, a maté burilado. This is a gourd engraved with scenes of local life with llamas, peasants, and village buildings such as that illustrated below. For coloring, the engraved gourd is slightly burned. The crowded scenes run in bands around the gourd with many people lined up in profile, similar to the art of the ancient Incas who once ruled much of South America from their Peruvian capital.

1. One part of the gourd is always the same, the lid, which has a zigzag cut with one point flat to locate the proper fit *(Step 1)*. Clean the inside and dry the gourd in the sun. Artificial heat will split the gourd.
2. Around the fattest part of the gourd, plan the main scene. Use a Peruvian village scene or one depicting your own community. For other bands, plan pictures of animals, plants, and abstract designs.
3. Transfer the design to the gourd with carbon paper. Because carbon can rub away, you might prefer working freehand.
4. To engrave your design, use a heavy, sharp needle or small hobby knife.
5. Begin by engraving the borders of the bands. Then decorate within each band.
6. When you have finished the engraved design, spread India ink over the entire gourd surface. Before it dries, wipe the ink off the surface with a cloth, leaving ink within the lines to remain distinct against the lighter color of the gourd.

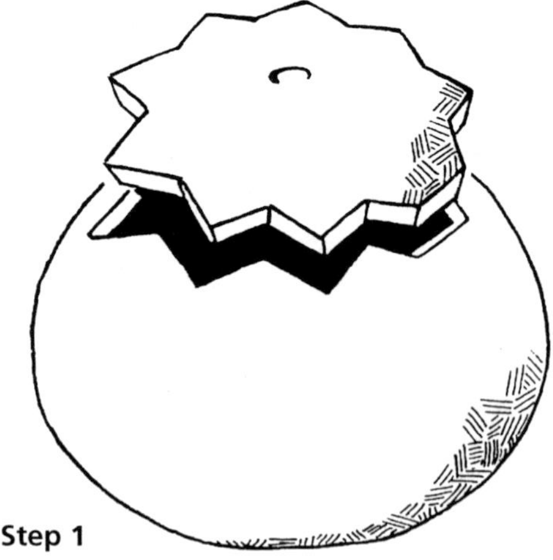

Step 1

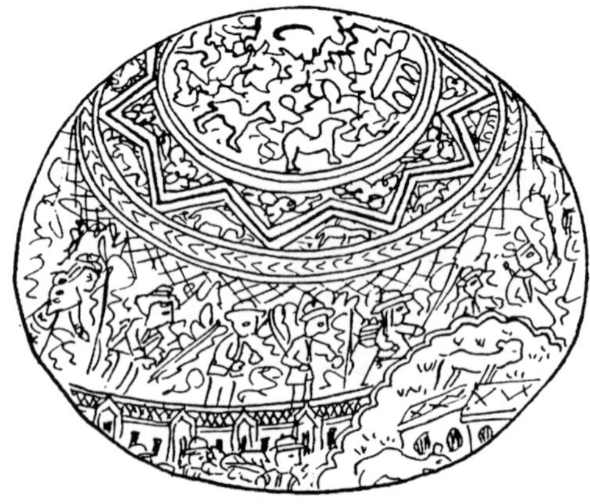

Sketch of the intricate design of a maté burilado

Name ______________________________ Date ______________

Project 61: Peru: Bull of Pucará

Materials
For this activity you will need: • self-hardening clay • tempera paint

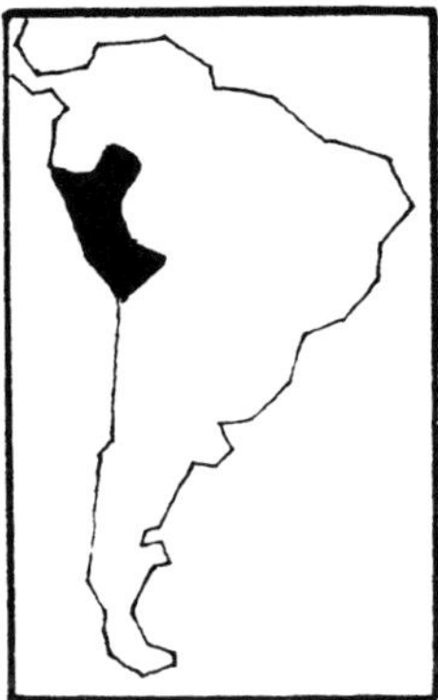

Throughout Latin America, whole villages are devoted to a single traditional craft. Pucará, near Titicaca, the world's highest lake, is one such village. Below is an example of the clay bulls sold in the Pucará railroad station. In ancient Inca legend, bulls brought health and fertility to farm animals, a belief still held by many Peruvian farmers. With holes in their backs, the clay bulls of Pucará held candles for use in ceremonies.

Make a decorative Pucará bull or, inspired by the idea, make a clay figure of some other symbolic animal. Decorate it with clay rosettes and flowers. Peruvian artists do not use bright colors but prefer light and dark brown with touches of white.

1. Model your animal in clay. It should be small enough to hold in your hand. Make legs short and heavy to support the animal.
2. Scoop a hole out of the back of the animal large enough to hold an ordinary candle. Reaching through the hole, scoop more clay away to let the inside clay dry at the same rate as the outside to prevent cracking.
3. Add clay decorations of rosettes, loops, snakes, etc.
4. When the animal is thoroughly dry, use tempera paint to decorate it with two tones of brown and white.

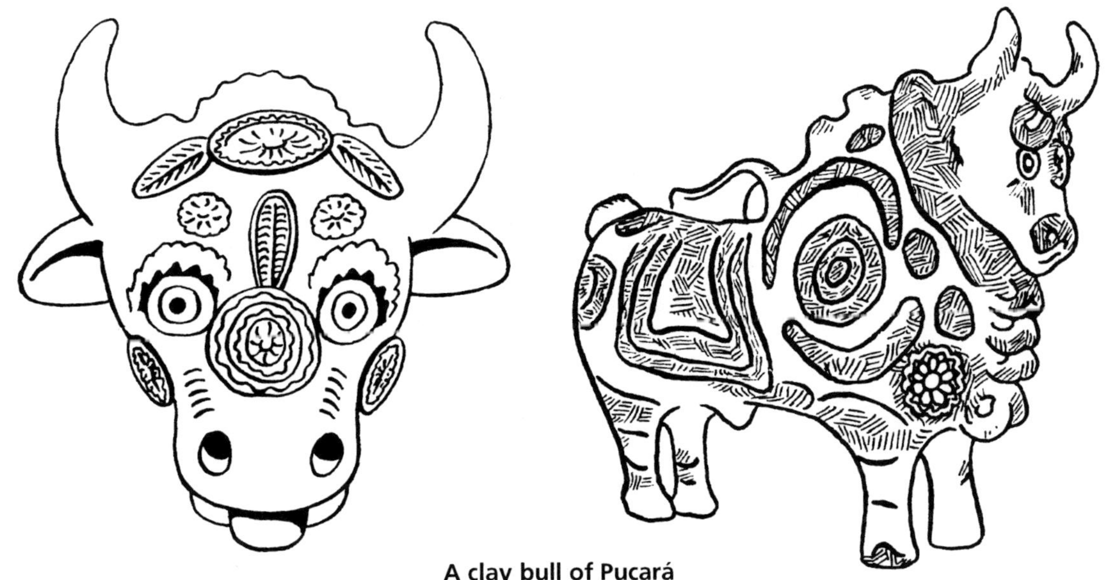

A clay bull of Pucará

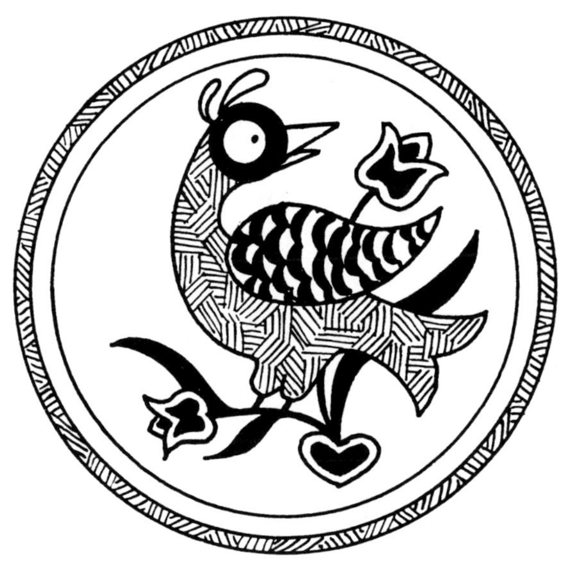

PART IX:

North America

IX. The Arts and Crafts of North America

The traditional crafts of North America tell something of the origins of the people who settled the continent and the life they made for themselves in the New World. For example, signs hanging above colonial stores looked much the same as those swinging in front of European shops. The Germans of Pennsylvania decorated their barns as they had done in Germany. In the same way, folk art of the American Southwest and Mexico has a Spanish flavor and that of Hawaii reflects the Polynesian cultures of the Pacific islands.

The American environment has had its effect on these ethnic traditions. In their new homes, settler women had to do without the shops of European towns and cities. They had to make do with homespun material, rags, and patches. So were born American patchwork and rag rugs. It is that "make-do" aspect that distinguishes many American crafts.

One branch of folk art is pure American—that of the continent's native peoples. Their crafts are unique to their regions. So, too, are the materials, as they worked with clam shells from Atlantic beaches or porcupine quills around the Great Lakes. As with all craft objects, the environment, needs, and desires of Americans are reflected in their arts and crafts. Today many enjoy the traditional crafts first practiced generations ago, even as technologies inspire new types of crafts.

The Tree of Life activity is best handled as a group project with each student making one or several of the tree trimmings to wire to the tree structure. The Flowered Skull project uses papier-mâché; you might want to refer to the papier-mâché techniques of Part I. This book avoids most metal crafts, but tin-can art plays such a significant part in Mexican folk art that it is introduced in the Tin-Can Art project. Because of the possibility of sharp metal edges, a class must be responsible enough to handle this project. Aluminum beverage cans, which are easily cut with shears, can be used instead of heavier produce cans.

Name ______________________ Date ______________

Project 62: Native North America: Beaded Wampum Belt

Materials	
For this activity you will need:	
• purchased beads	• hammer
• 2 yardsticks or strips of wood	• cotton thread
• 2 wood pieces, 2" × 1" × $\frac{1}{2}$"	• needle
• headless nails	• graph paper

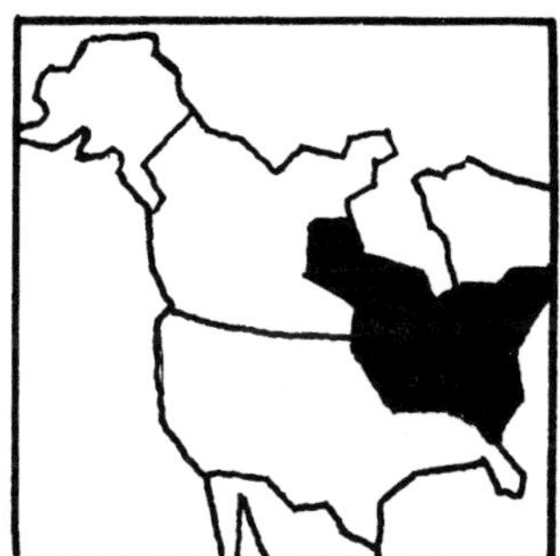

Wampum, stringed shells used as a medium of trade or cultural exchange, originated among the Iroquois people of the Northeast. Wampum soon became widely used throughout the eastern region of North America. With the arrival of Europeans, beads replaced shells for making wampum.

We might wonder at the idea of using beads for money. Yet, we use slips of paper as money and shares of huge companies are exchanged on Wall Street for mere sheets of paper. Not only was wampum sometimes used for money, it sealed treaty agreements and trade guarantees, and was used for recording tribal records. Wampum strands were also woven into belts to be used in religious ceremonies. The illustration shows a Huron wampum belt exhibited in the Smithsonian Institution in Washington, D.C. Using a handmade bead loom and purchased beads, you can weave a beaded belt of your own design.

Huron tribe wampum belt

1. Purchase a collection of beads, not too small and all the same size.
2. The bead loom must be as long as the belt you will make. Therefore, two yardsticks will make a 36-inch belt, long enough for most people. Long strips of wood serve the same purpose. Nail the two small wood pieces between the longer pieces *(Step 2)*.

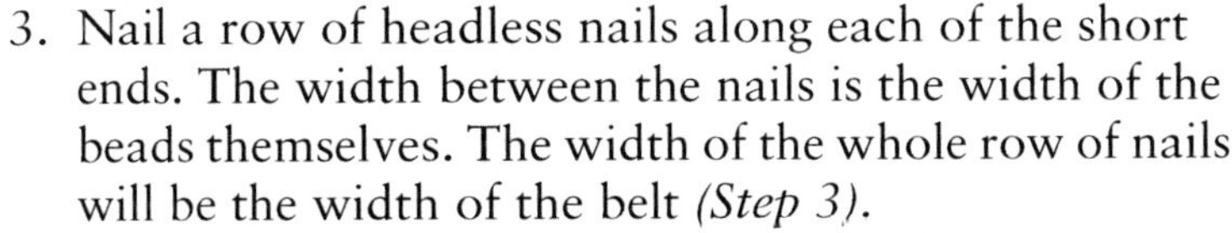

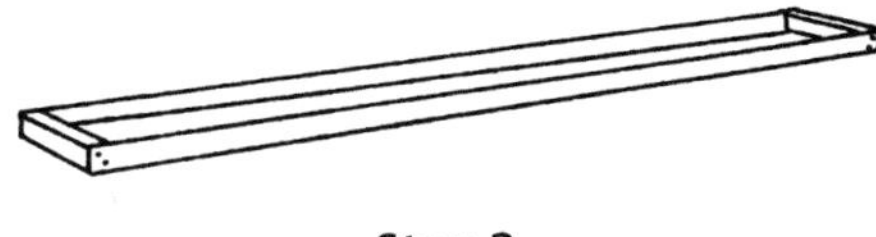

Step 2

3. Nail a row of headless nails along each of the short ends. The width between the nails is the width of the beads themselves. The width of the whole row of nails will be the width of the belt *(Step 3)*.
4. Tie one end of a cotton thread to a nail and the other end to the nail opposite the first. Tie long threads to the rest of the nails, so you have threads running between the nails stretched lengthwise over the frame. Leave a short length of string beyond the nail to hang as fringe *(Step 4)*.

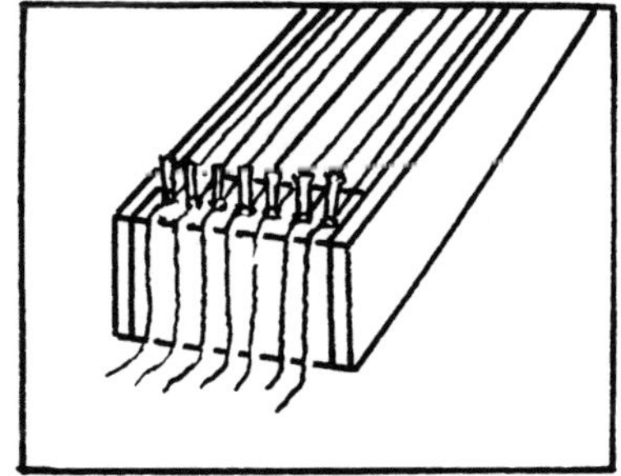

Steps 3 and 4

(continued)

Name ______________________________ Date ____________________

Project 62: Native North America: Beaded Wampum Belt *(continued)*

5. Create a bead design on graph paper, a single dark color against a light background or one of several colors. The squares of the graph paper represent the beads. There will be as many squares across the graph paper design as there are spaces between the string *(Step 5)*.
6. Tie the end of another thread near the upper end of the loom thread farthest to the left. Use a needle to string beads on this thread, according to the number and color of beads of your graph plan *(Steps 6 and 7)*.
7. Pass the beaded thread under all the loom threads *(Steps 6 and 7)*.
8. Push each bead up between the loom threads.
9. Using the needle, thread the bead thread back through the beads, but this time thread over the loom threads, holding the beads in place *(Step 9)*.
10. Thread a second row of beads according to your graph plan under the loom threads next to the first row. Push the beads up between the loom threads and thread the bead threads back through the beads, but over the loom threads, as before.
11. Continue weaving the belt with row after row of beads until the entire belt has been woven. Anytime the beading thread comes to an end, tie another length of thread onto it somewhere in the middle of a row of beads *(Step 11)*.
12. When the beading has reached the far end of the loom frame, tie the beading thread tightly to the last strand. Untie two adjacent thread ends from the nail and tie securely together. Do this for each pair of thread ends, letting the thread ends dangle as fringe *(Step 12)*.
13. The completed beaded piece can be worn as a belt. Wrap one end of it over the other. If you do not wish to make a band of beads long enough for a belt, you can produce a shorter loom and make beaded bracelets or headbands.

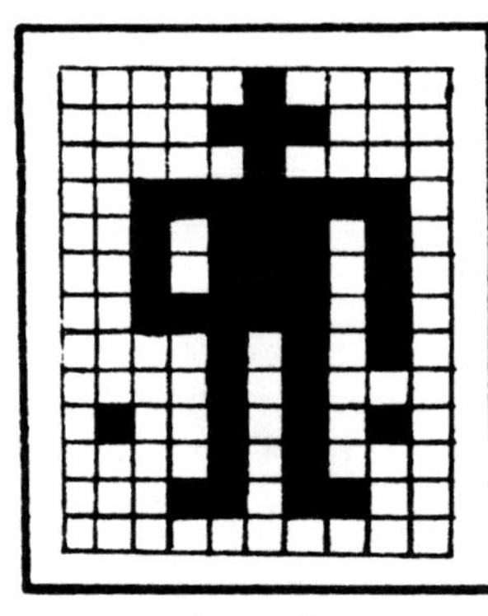

Step 5

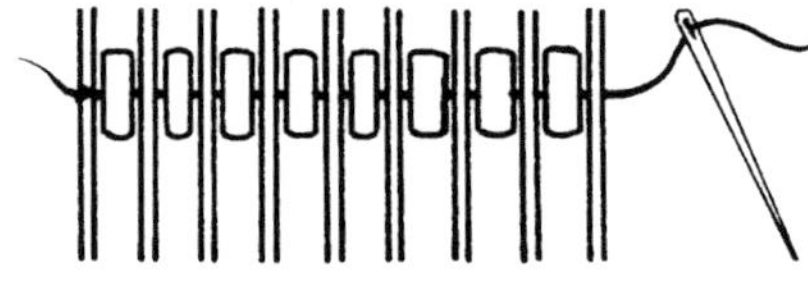

Steps 6 and 7

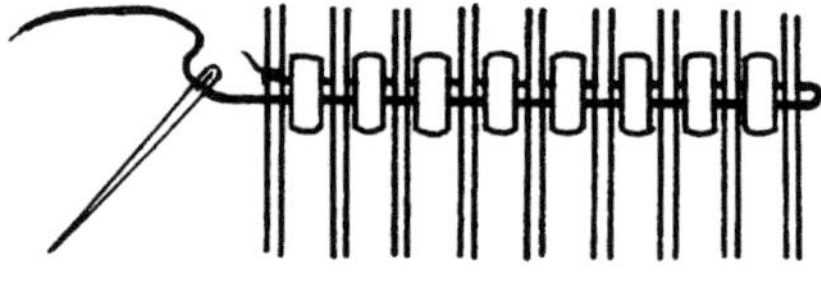

Step 9

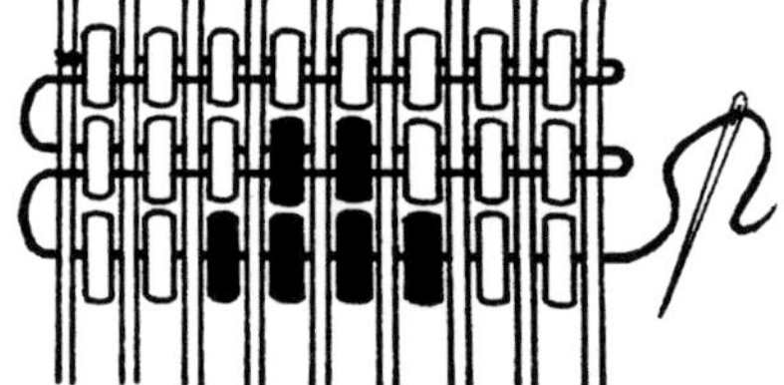

Step 11

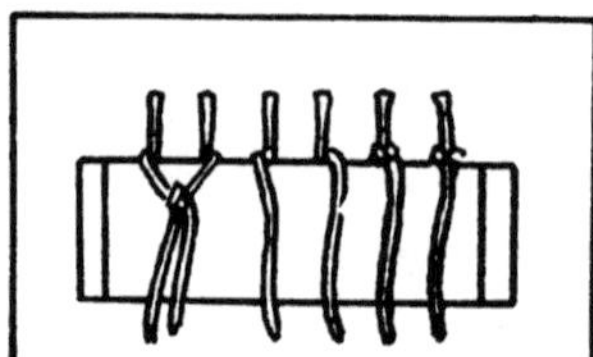

Step 12

Name ______________________ Date ______________

Project 63: Native North America: Hopi Rain Sash

Materials	
For this activity you will need:	
• cotton string of various colors	• pencil or ruler
• 2 wooden rods, 6" or longer	• melted candle wax

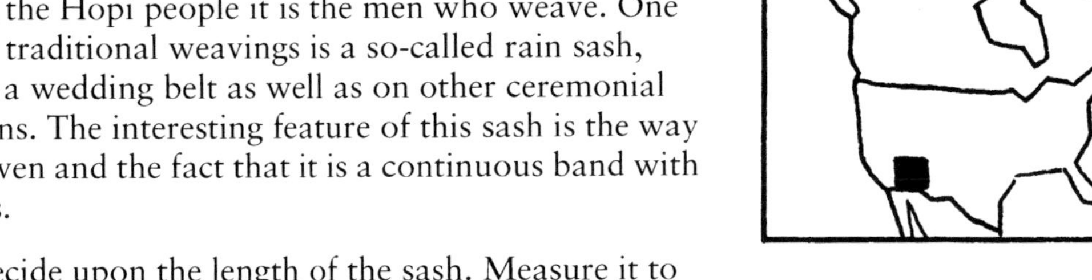
Weaving has long been an important craft in the American Southwest, where Navaho women have woven blankets prized in collections around the world. Among the Hopi people it is the men who weave. One of their traditional weavings is a so-called rain sash, used as a wedding belt as well as on other ceremonial occasions. The interesting feature of this sash is the way it is woven and the fact that it is a continuous band with no ends.

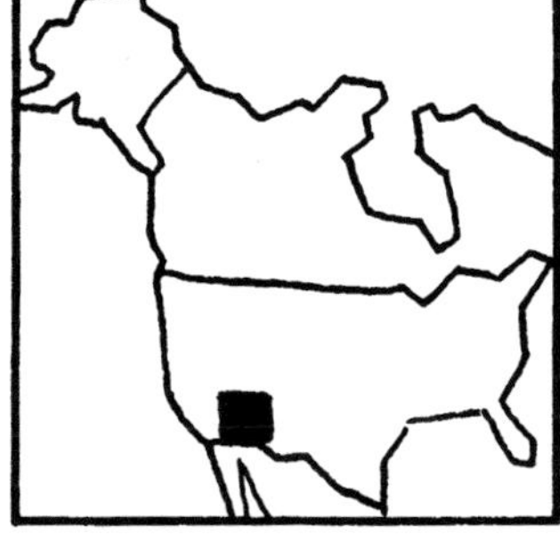

1. Decide upon the length of the sash. Measure it to fit the width of a skirt bottom or to be slightly larger than your waist size.

2. Fix two wooden rods securely to something so that they project horizontally. They can be tightened between two vises or nailed to the top of a workbench or wooden box. The distance between the two should be half the circular length of the sash you will make *(Steps 2 and 3)*.

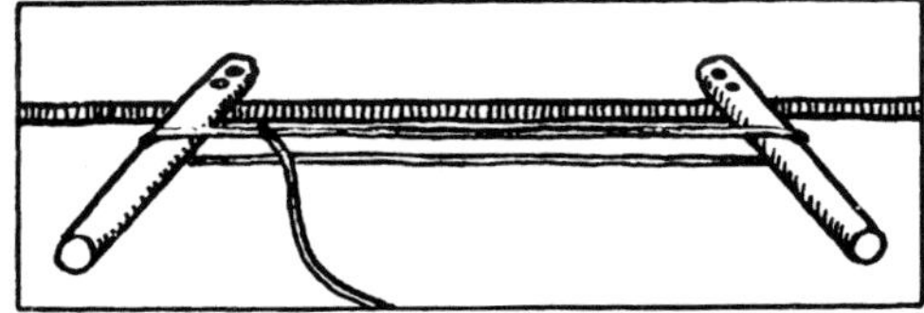

Steps 2 and 3

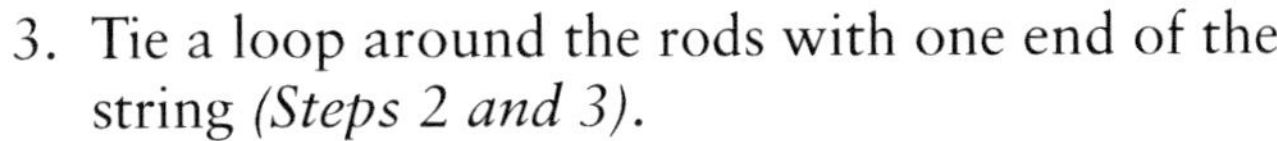

3. Tie a loop around the rods with one end of the string *(Steps 2 and 3)*.

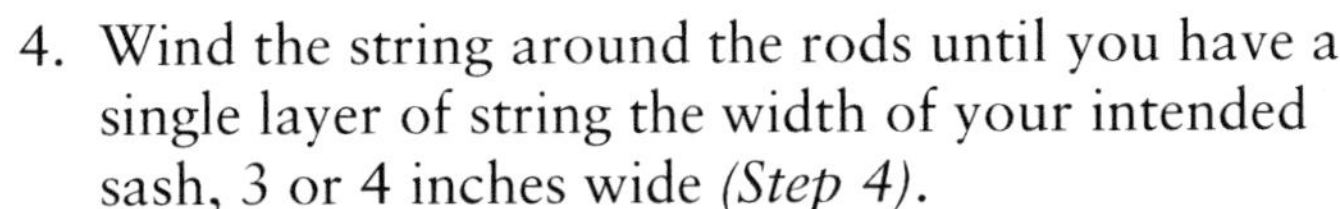

4. Wind the string around the rods until you have a single layer of string the width of your intended sash, 3 or 4 inches wide *(Step 4)*.

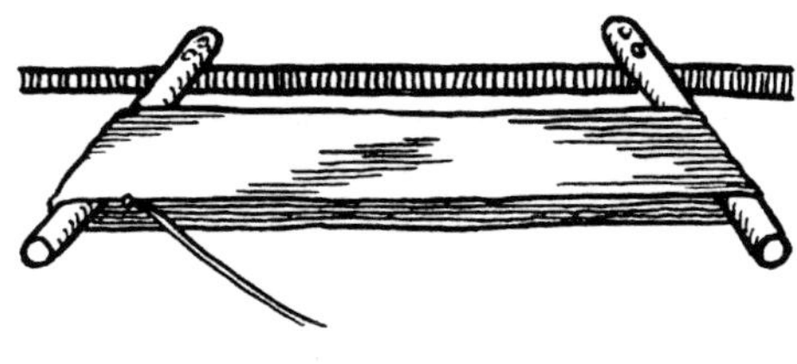

Step 4

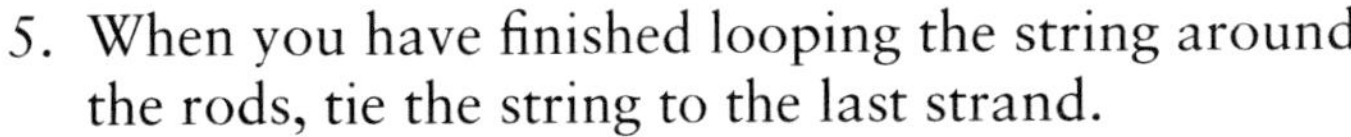

5. When you have finished looping the string around the rods, tie the string to the last strand.

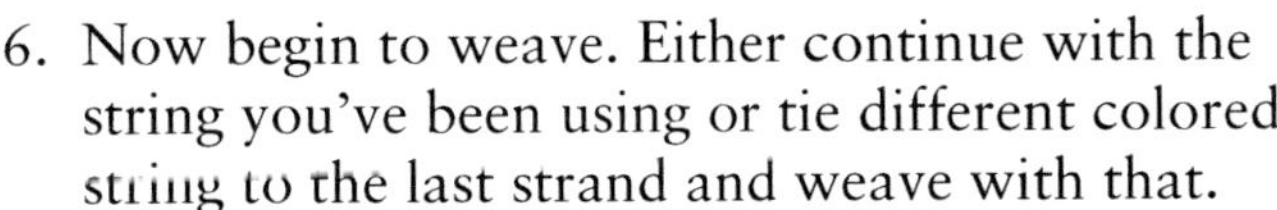

6. Now begin to weave. Either continue with the string you've been using or tie different colored string to the last strand and weave with that.

7. Decide on a weaving pattern—under one string, over one, under one, over one, or over three, under two, and so on for another pattern.

(continued)

Name ______________________________ Date ______________

Project 63: Native North America: Hopi Rain Sash *(continued)*

8. Use a pencil or ruler to lift the strands of the first row in the correct sequence of your pattern. This means poking the pencil through the strands, under one, over one, under one or whatever your pattern indicates *(Step 8)*.

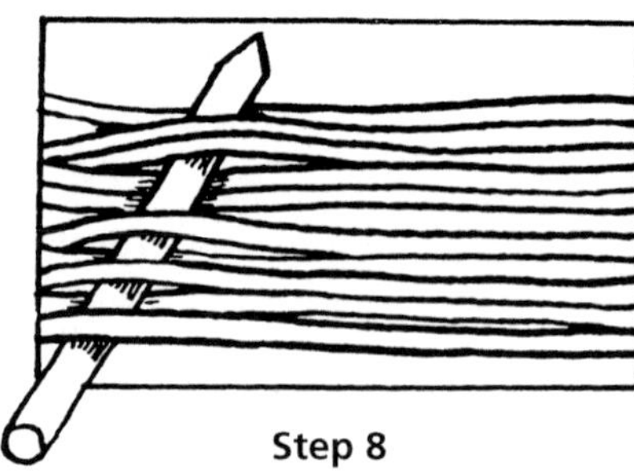

Step 8

9. Dip the string end into melted candle wax to stiffen the end. When it is hardened, poke it through the strand network made by the pencil. Pull the string the whole way through, then remove the pencil.
10. Use the pencil to arrange the strands for the next row. Weave the waxed string tip back though the strands.
11. Continue this weaving for row after row of your weaving plan *(Step 11)*.

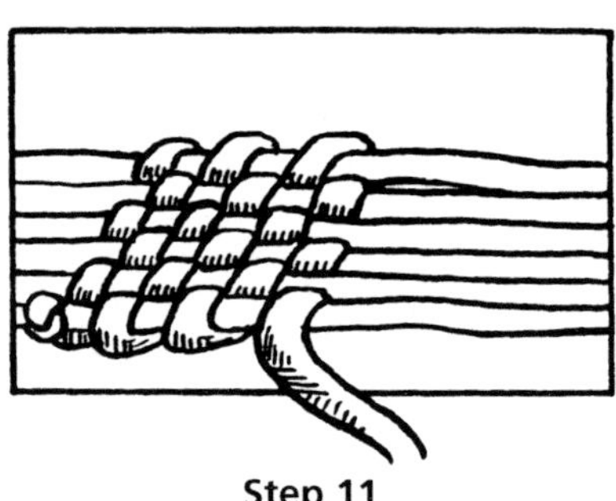

Step 11

12. When you reach either of the rods holding the string, simply slide the weaving away from the rod in order to continue your weaving.
13. As you weave, keep pushing the weaving string tightly against the previous row so that the weaving will not be too loose. You can use a wide-toothed comb to push the weaving strands tight against one another. You will also have to occasionally rewax the string end.
14. When you have woven the complete sash, tie the string end securely to the last strand.
15. Remove the sash from the rods. You can sew it to the bottom of a skirt for decoration. Or you can wear it as a decorative belt, hanging loosely around your waist *(Step 15)*.

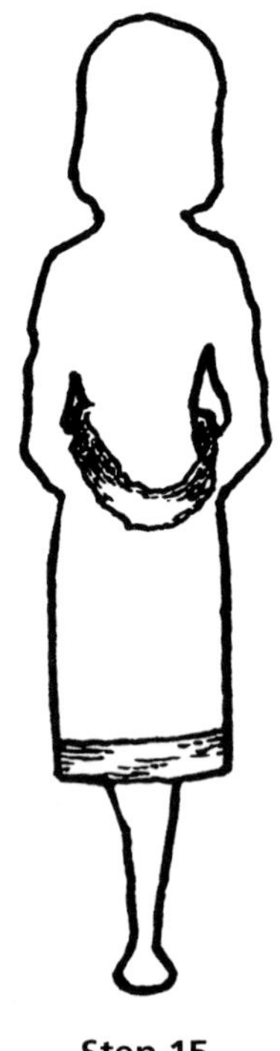

Step 15

Name ______________________________ Date ______________

Project 64: Native North America: Quillwork

Materials	
For this activity you will need: • plastic drinking straws of different colors • small cardboard box with lid to decorate	• sheet of heavy paper • razor blade or hobby knife • glue

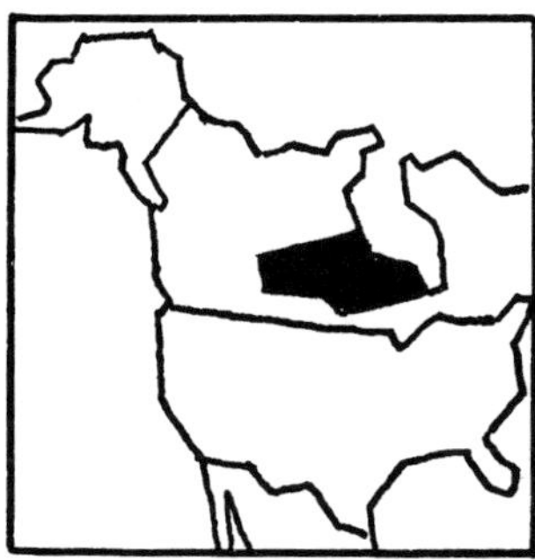

Until Europeans introduced glass beads, porcupine quills were a decorating material for many native tribes. The best quillwork was that created by the Chippewa and Cree of sub-arctic Canada.

Porcupine quills are smooth and shiny. First soaking them in water, the quill workers pulled them through their teeth to flatten them. The quill strips were twisted, braided, or folded around string to be sewn as applied decoration to cloth or leather.

Instead of porcupine quills, this project simulates one quillwork technique by using plastic drinking straws. Use different-colored straws to create a colorful box lid decoration.

1. Cut plastic straws into four strips each with a hobby knife or razor blade *(Step 1)*.
2. Plan a design for the quillwork to the size of the box lid to be decorated. The quills (straw strips) lie parallel to one another *(Step 2)*.

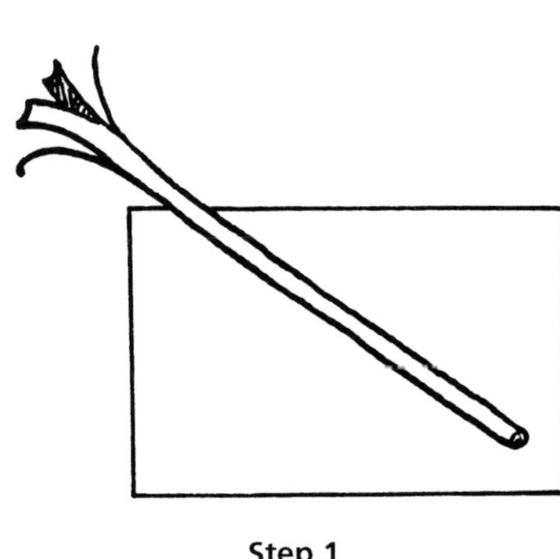

Step 1

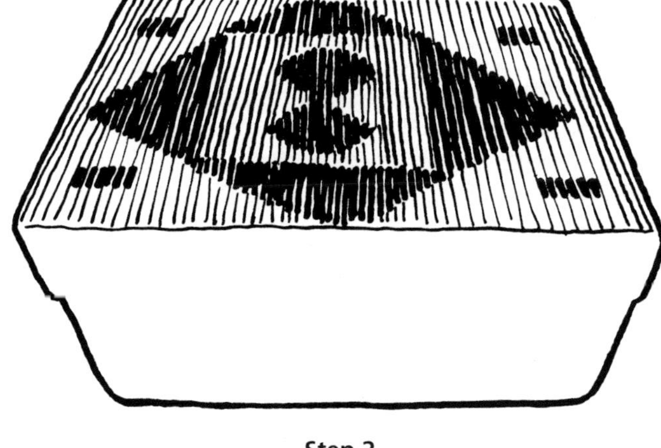

Step 2

(continued)

Project 64: Native North America: Quillwork *(continued)*

3. Draw slot lines on the lid according to your plan and into which the quill (straw) ends will be pushed. (Dark lines of *step 3* diagram) Avoid making slot lines too long. Instead, plan a staggered slot line such as with the bottom and top lines of this plan.

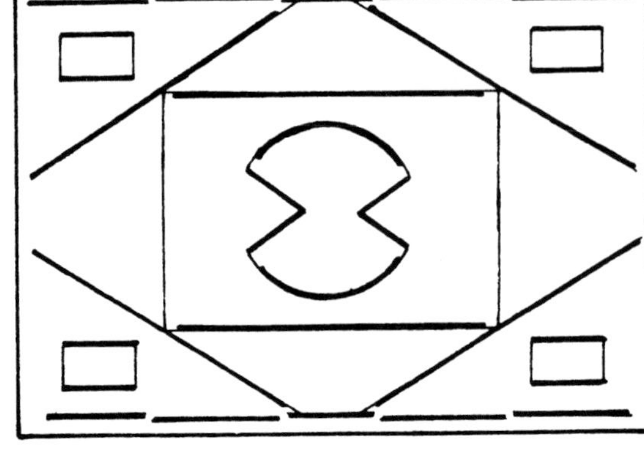

Step 3

4. Draw the plan on the box lid.

5. Cut the slot lines with a razor blade or hobby knife.

6. Bend the ends of each quill (straw strip) and stick through the slot, holding them in place. Cover the entire lid with quills (straw strips) according to the colors of your design plan.

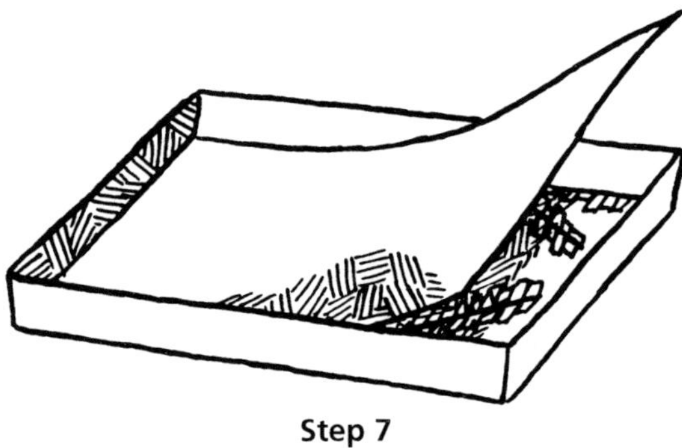

Step 7

7. When the lid has been covered, cut a piece of heavy paper the size of the inside of the lid. Spread glue on this paper and fix it inside the lid covering the protruding quill (straw) ends. Weight down the paper until the glue dries to hold it in place *(Step 7)*.

Name ______________________________ Date ______________

Project 65: Colonial North America: Braided Rug

Materials
For this activity you will need: • cloth scraps • needle and thread

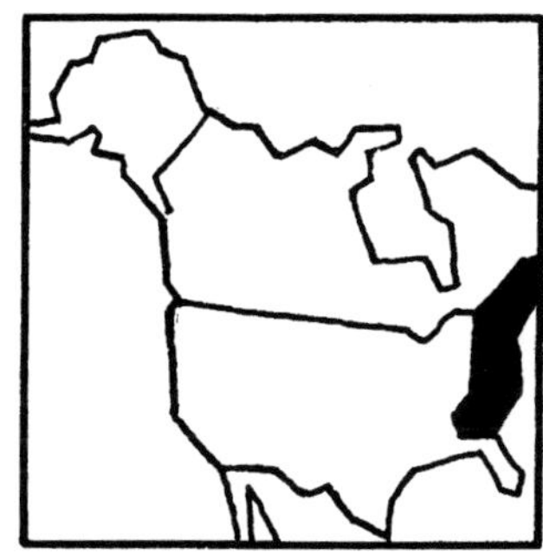

In the earliest settler houses floors were bare, often just packed earth. Even after floor boards were laid, cold drafts entered between gaps in the planks. Animal skins first served as rugs to protect against damp and cold, but it was not long before colonial women began making floor coverings to brighten their homes and make them warmer underfoot. Settlers saved scraps of cloth left over from making clothes or cut up worn-out clothing to make needed rugs. Of the various kind of rag rugs, the braided rug remains as popular as ever. Collect rags to make your own braided rug.

1. Collect a large number of cloth pieces. Cut these scraps into narrow strips.
2. Divide the rag collection into three equal piles.
3. Sew the rag pieces within each pile end-to-end to make three rag ropes. Try to control the pattern of the finished rug by letting colors in each of the rag ropes match those in the same position in the other two ropes *(Step 3)*.

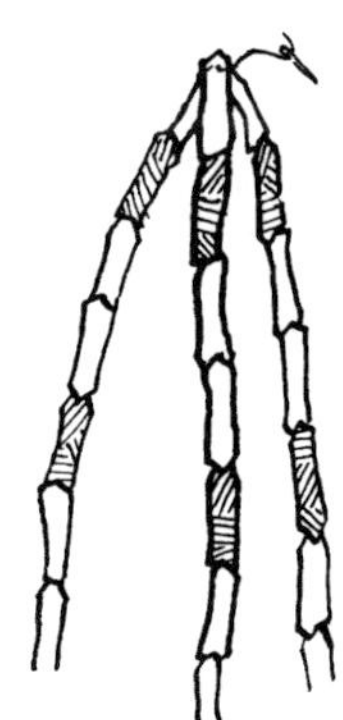

Steps 3 and 4

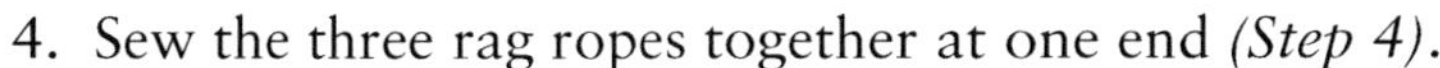

4. Sew the three rag ropes together at one end *(Step 4)*.
5. Braid the three rag ropes together as one braids hair. Bring the left-hand strand over the one next to it to become the middle strand. Then bring the right-hand strand over that to become the middle strand. Next the left-hand strand is brought to the middle, then the right-hand, the left-hand, and so on, until the complete rope has been braided. Twist the ropes as you braid. One rope in the illustration appears black to more clearly show the braiding process *(Step 5)*.

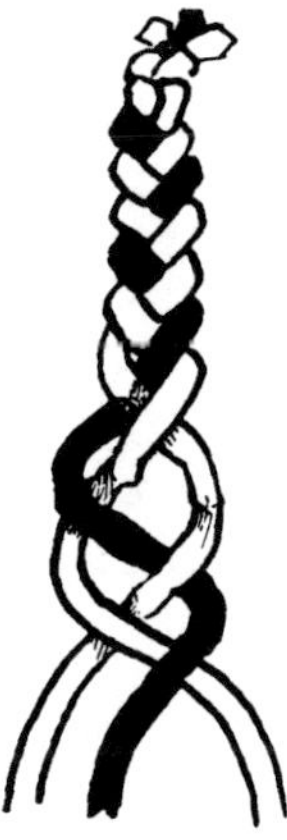

Step 5

(continued)

Name ______________________________ Date ______________

Project 65: Colonial North America: Braided Rug *(continued)*

6. Coil the braided rag rope. As you coil the braid, sew the edges of the rope together so that the coil shape holds *(Step 6)*.

7. You can also coil an oval rug, the more usual shape for a braided rug. Leave five inches of the beginning-end of the rope straight and coil around this, sewing the rope edges together as you coil *(Step 7)*.

8. Coil until you reach the end of your braided rag rope. Sew the end tightly into the rug. The braided rug is complete *(Step 8)*.

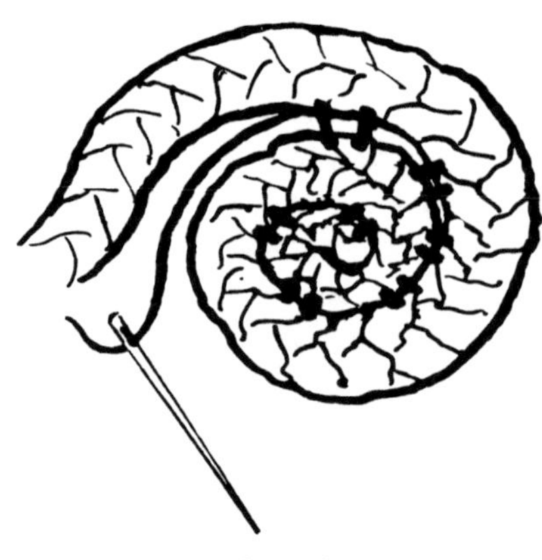

Step 6

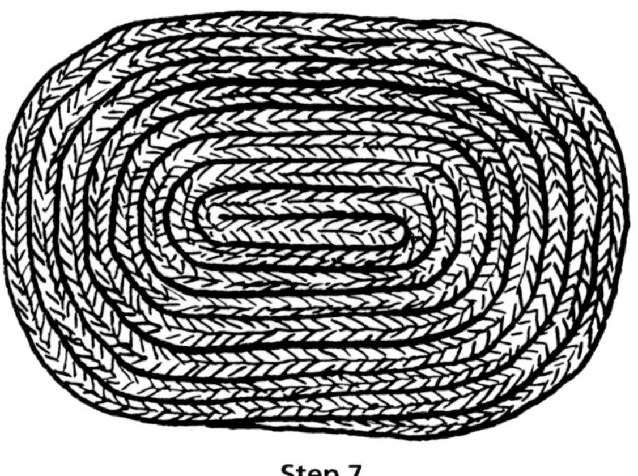

Step 7

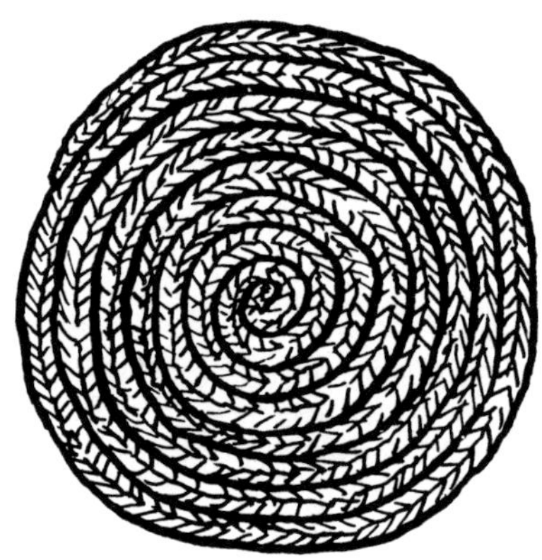

Step 8

Name ______________________________ Date ______________

Project 66: Colonial North America: A Penny Wooden

Materials		
For this activity you will need: • soft pine or balsa wood block, 1" × 1" × 3"	• eight $1\frac{1}{2}$"-long wooden rods • four wood screws • hobby knife	• drill • four $1\frac{1}{2}$" lengths of wire or matchsticks

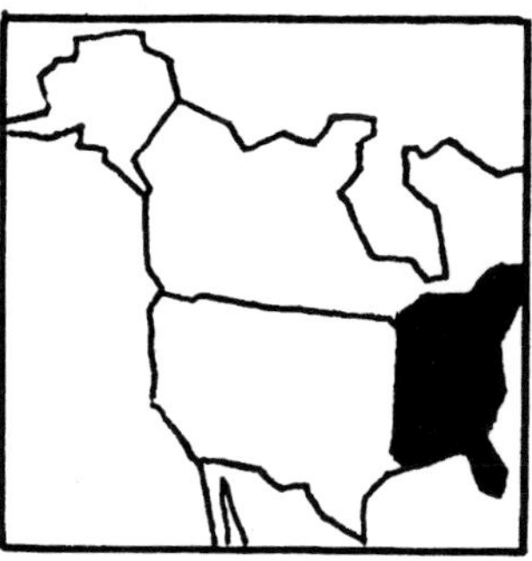

By the eighteenth century in North America many early colonial villages had grown into towns with shops, including toy stores. A popular toy was a penny wooden. Costing little, the doll came without features or clothes so that a child would paint the face and fashion a costume for it. Because of its movable arms and legs, the penny wooden remained popular long after colonial times and could still be purchased at a local store well into the nineteenth century.

1. Carve the head and torso of the doll from the block of wood. As in the illustration, keep the shape simple *(Step 1)*.
2. With a small drill bit, drill a hole through each of the wooden rods $\frac{1}{4}$-inch from one end *(Step 2)*.
3. At the hole end cut a $\frac{1}{2}$-inch notch in four of the rods. Carve a projection, $\frac{1}{2}$-inch long at the hole end of the other four wooden rods *(Step 3)*.
4. Join the upper and lower parts of the arms and legs with short pieces of wire, twisting the ends to make them secure. The joints of original penny woodens were joined with wooden pegs. Instead of wire, you can use matchstick ends for wooden pegs *(Step 4)*.
5. Use wood screws to attach the arms to the shoulders and the legs to the bottom of the torso. Drill a screw hole in the rod ends first in order not to split them when screwing the arms and legs in place. Do not screw so tightly that the arms and legs cannot be moved *(Step 5)*.
6. Like a youngster of several centuries ago, paint features on the face of the penny wooden and dress it in a colonial costume.

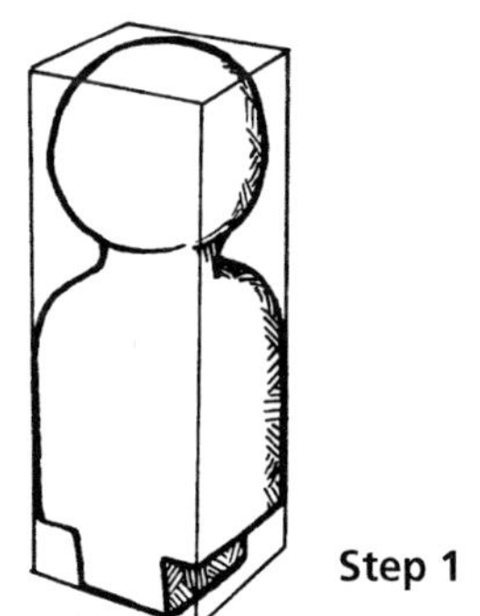

Step 1

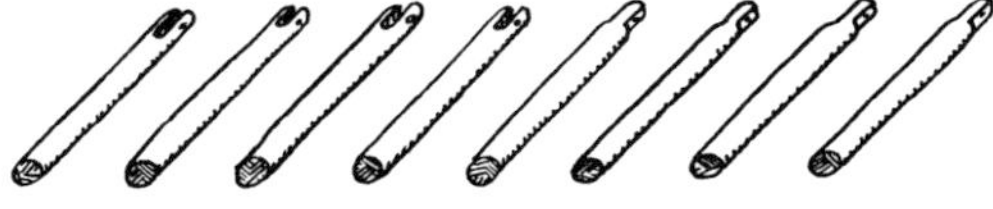

Steps 2 and 3

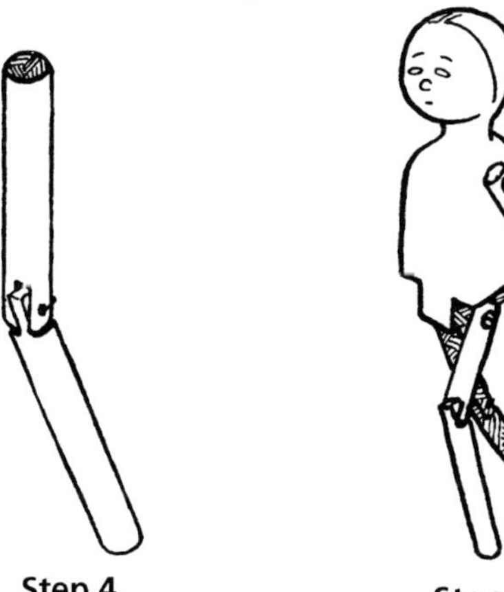

Step 4 **Step 5**

Name ______________________________ Date ______________

Project 67: Pennsylvania Dutch: Hex Signs

Materials	
For this activity you will need: • poster board • tempera or poster paints • pencil	• 6" length of string • thumbtack • scissors • black felt-tipped pen

If you travel through southeastern Pennsylvania, you may hear words that make no sense to you. They are Pennsylvania "Dutch" dialect words derived from the German language these people brought from Europe centuries ago. Another surprise of your Pennsylvania trip would be discovering large designs painted on the sides of barns. They are hex signs, symbols of Germanic origin. Though the German word "Hex" means a witch and her curse, the Pennsylvania Dutch consider their hex signs a kind of charm. Here are some typical hex signs and their meanings.

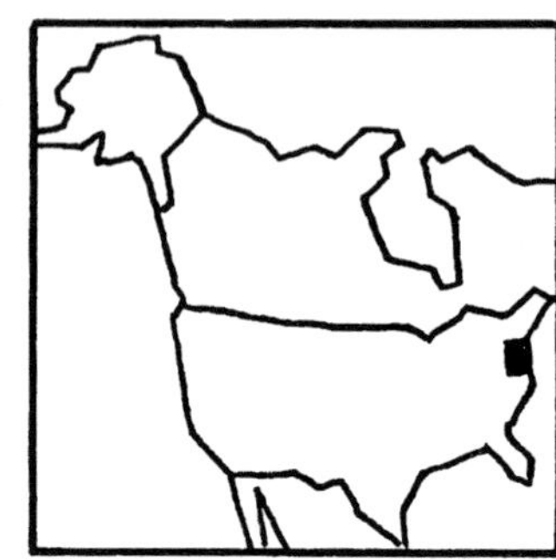

Distlefink: This is a finch which feeds on thistles. The distelfink is a symbol for good luck. The tulip stands for faithfulness.

Raindrops: The raindrop hex sign encourages rainfall, necessary in farming country. It is frequently combined with other symbols.

Rosette: A six-petaled rosette can subdue evil. The hearts nestled within the rosette of this hex sign symbolize love.

Tulip: The tulip stands for faithfulness, here combined with the hearts of love. The border shape symbolizes the sea of life, which will remain calm as long as love and faithfulness are practiced.

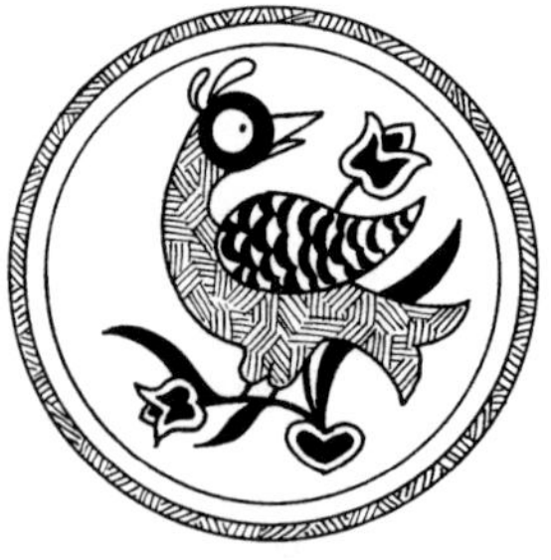

Distlefink

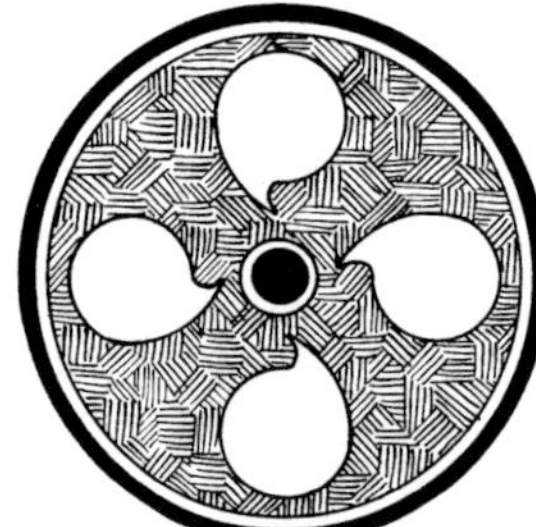

Raindrops

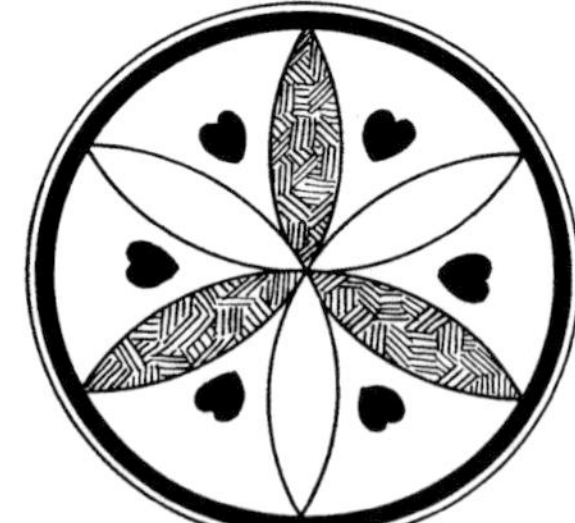

Rosette

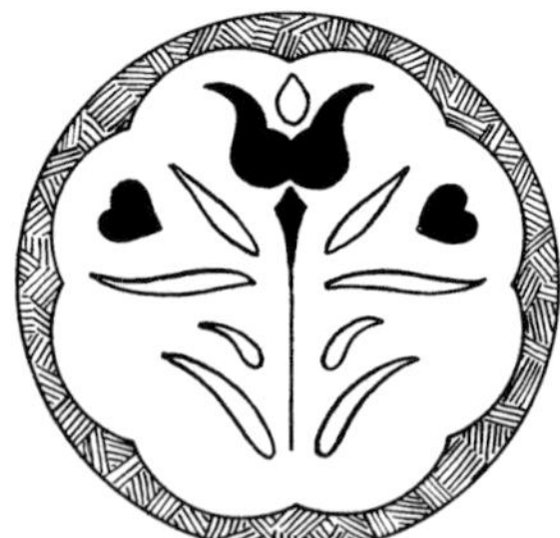

Tulip

(continued)

Name ______________________________ Date ______________

Project 67: Pennsylvania Dutch: Hex Signs *(continued)*

Hex sign colors also have meanings.

red: action, freedom, life, love

yellow: children, divinity, gentility, the sun

blue: heaven, holiness, protection, truth

green: abundance, good luck, spring, vegetation

brown: business, humility, death, worldliness

white: innocence, joy, purity, protection

black: darker forces of nature

Now that you know some of the symbolism of hex signs, design one of your own.

1. Draw a 12-inch circle on a sheet of white poster board by thumbtacking one end of a 6-inch-long string in the middle of the poster board. Make a loop at the free end and insert a pencil point through the loop. Swing the pencil in a circle by pulling the string tight with the pencil point held through the loop to draw on the poster board *(Step 1)*.

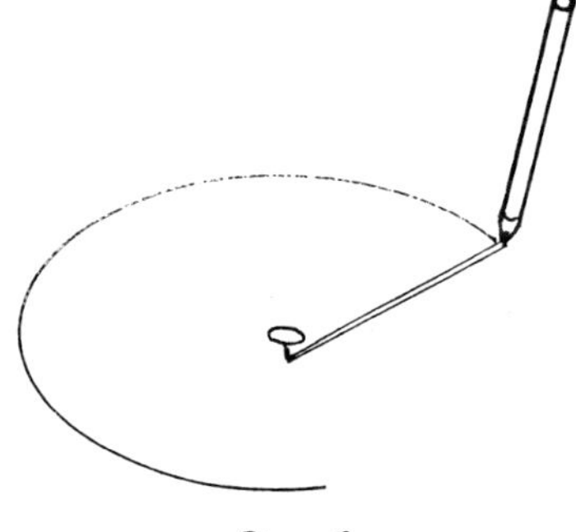

Step 1

2. Use the hex signs shown in this chapter to inspire your own design. Do not copy the illustrations exactly, but design one to suit yourself. Combine proper symbols and colors to visualize your symbolic message. Draw your hex design in pencil within the circle on the poster board.

3. Darken the penciled lines with a black felt-tipped pen.

4. Color the hex sign with the proper symbolic colors.

5. Cut out the circular hex sign and hang as decoration.

Name ______________________________ Date ______________

Project 68: Nineteenth-Century North America: Gilt Frame

Materials	
For this activity you will need:	• gold spray paint
• wooden picture frame	• dark green or brown acrylic paint
• plaster of paris or window glass putty	• felt-tipped pen
• $\frac{1}{2}$" nails	• hammer

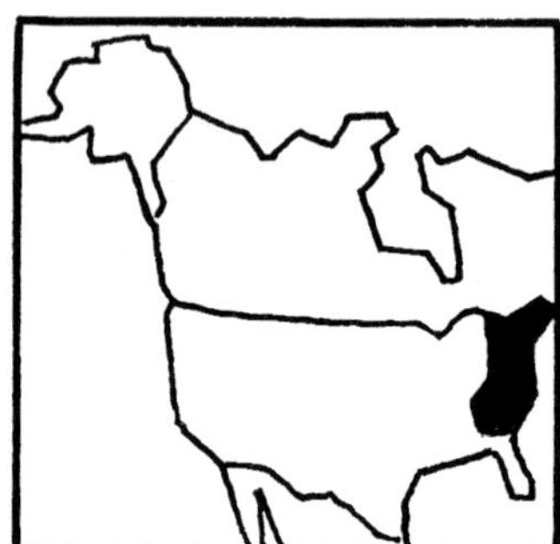

Called "looking glasses" by early Americans, the first mirrors on the continent came from Europe. By 1700 they were being made in the colonies. The frames of early mirrors were wood elaborately carved and gilded. After the American Revolution, two kinds of framed mirrors were very popular. One was the constitution mirror shown below left. Next to it is the girandole. It held a round, convex mirror that reflected a room interior like the wide-angle lens of a camera. An eagle was usually perched atop its intricately carved frame.

In time frames became even more ornate as plaster of paris decoration was applied to a simple wood frame. You can adopt this method to produce a frame of the early American style.

1. Begin with an ordinary wooden frame. The broader the frame surface, the better.
2. Plan a design for the frame. It can have flowers, leaves, an eagle, scrolls, and the like. Let the object that the frame will display inspire your design. It might hold a mirror or a reproduction of an eighteenth- or nineteenth-century painting.
3. Lay out your design on the wooden frame with a felt-tipped pen.

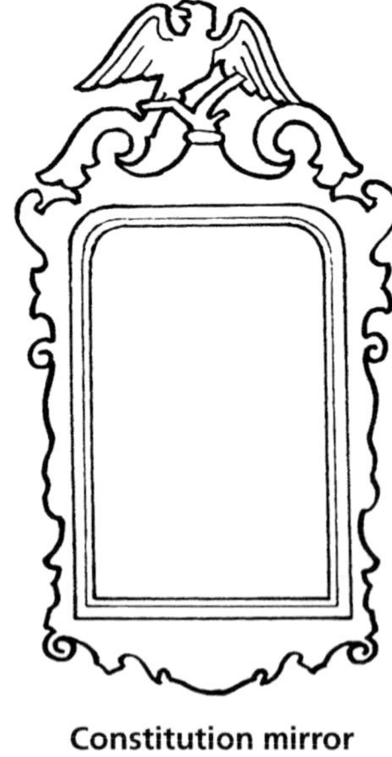

Constitution mirror

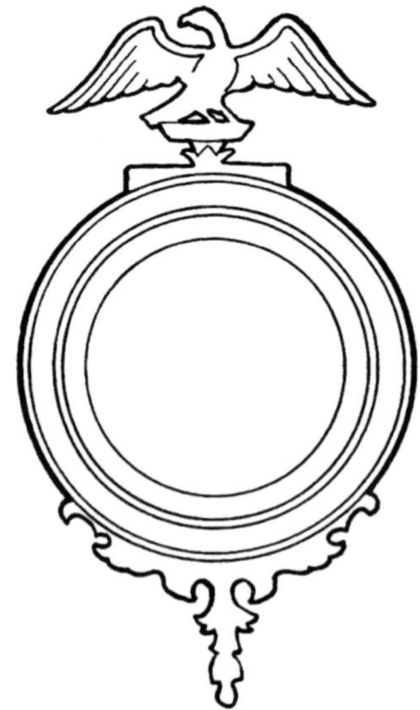

Girandole mirror

(continued)

Name ______________________ Date ______________________

Project 68: Nineteenth-Century North America: Gilt Frame *(continued)*

4. Nail small nails partway into the wood in areas that will hold the heaviest part of the decoration *(Step 4)*.

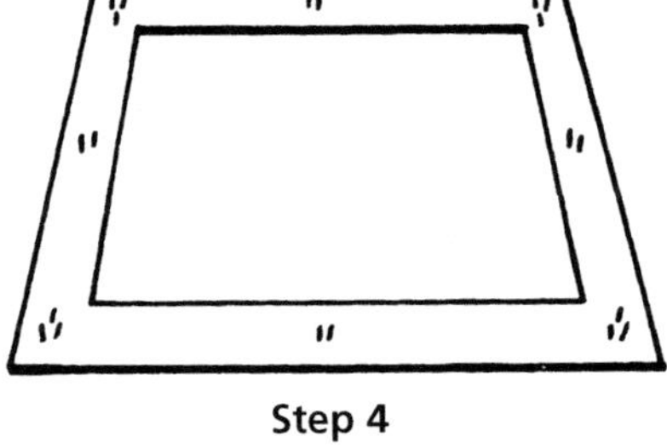

Step 4

5. If using plaster of paris, mix with a small amount of water so that it can be easily managed.

6. Use the moist plaster of paris or more easily managed window glass putty to develop your three-dimensional design. Model flowers, leaves, and bird shapes at the corners and middle parts of the frame *(Step 6)*.

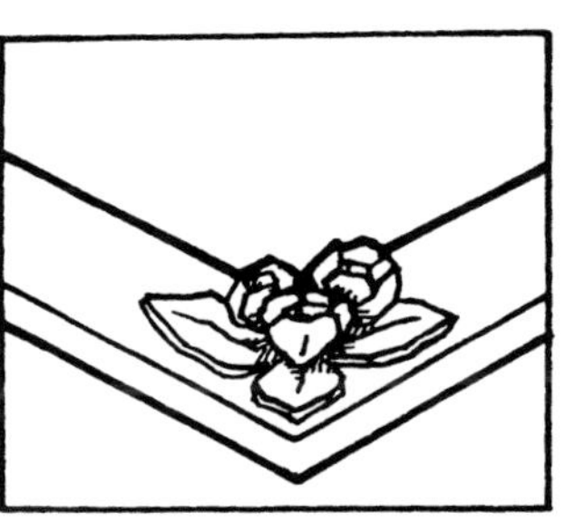

Step 6

7. When you have finished modeling the decoration on the frame, let it dry. Plaster can take minutes. Putty can require days.

8. Once the decoration has dried, paint some of the recesses of the modeling a dark green or brown color with acrylic paint. Make only touches or single strokes of the paint. This will create an antique appearance and cut down the brightness of the gold.

9. When the acrylic paint has dried, spray the frame with gold paint. Spray it more thinly into the recesses so that some of the shaded acrylic color shows through.

Name ______________________________ Date ______________

Project 69: Nineteenth-Century North America: Whirligig

Materials	
For this activity you will need:	
• 2" × 2" × 12" piece of wood	• 9"-long piece of hanger wire
• 2 tongue depressors	• colored plastic tape
• hobby knife	• poster paint

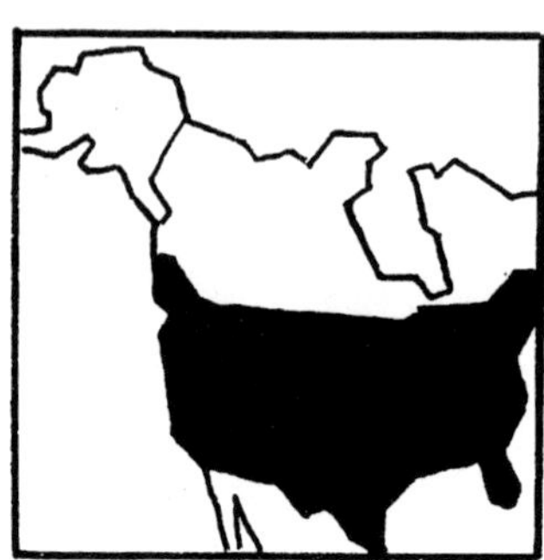

A whirligig was a weather instrument that showed if the wind was blowing and how strong it blew. Poked in the grass of yards or nailed on a porch railing, whirligigs merrily fanned their arms in the breeze of nineteenth-century afternoons.

The heads and bodies of whirligigs were all of one piece. The arms, held to the figure with a narrow rod, became the paddles that spun in the wind. You can make a whirligig in the fashion of a nineteenth-century gentleman, such as the copies shown here.

1. If you wish, carve the wood piece to give it some shape. Or else simply paint it to appear as a person.
2. Cut a piece of wire from a clothes hanger, or wire of similar thickness, to 9 inches in length.

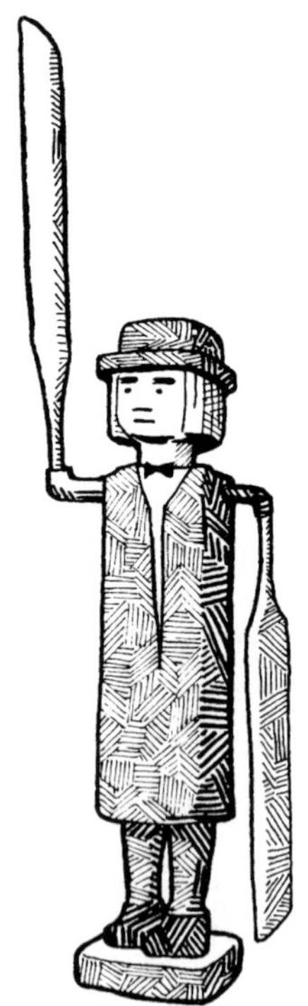

Nineteenth-century whirligigs

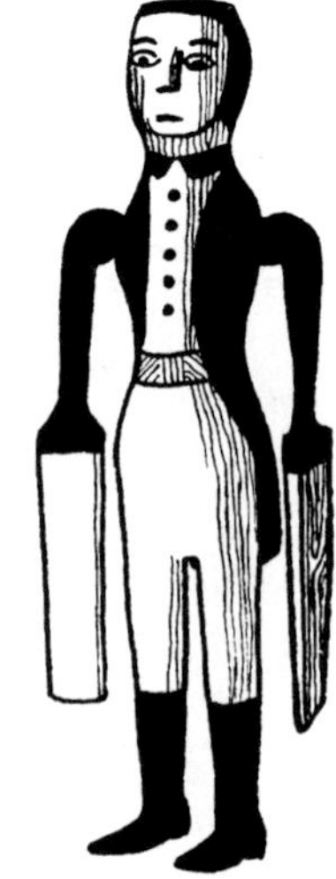

(continued)

Name ______________________ Date ______________

Project 69: Nineteenth-Century North America: Whirligig *(continued)*

3. Drill a hole through the wood at the shoulder, wide enough for the wire to loosely fit through.

4. Pass the wire through the hole and then bend one end up and the other down. Make the bend $\frac{1}{2}$-inch away from the side of the wood block *(Step 4)*.

5. Select plastic tape that is the same color as the figure's clothing. With the tape wrap one tongue depressor to one wire length so that it is parallel to the face of the whirligig. Let the depressor end protrude below the tape to serve as the whirligig's hand *(Step 5)*.

6. Wrap the second depressor tightly to the other wire perpendicular to the face of the whirligig. Let the end of the depressor protrude to be the hand *(Step 6)*.

7. When the whirligig is placed in the wind, the paddle arms will turn. If you wish to leave the whirligig outside, paint it with two coats of clear varnish to weatherproof it. Glue a rod in a hole drilled in the base or nail the whirligig to a porch railing to make it a permanent fixture.

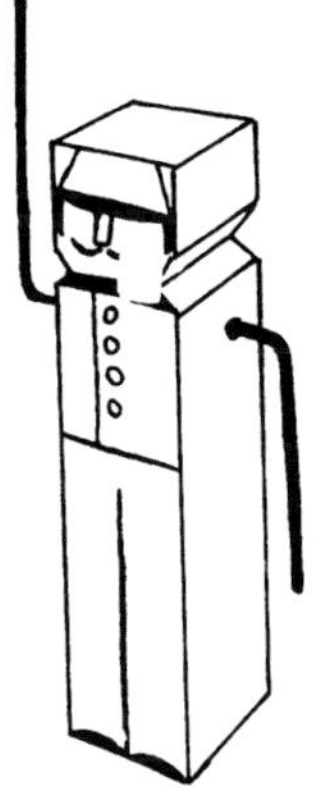

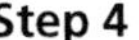

Step 4

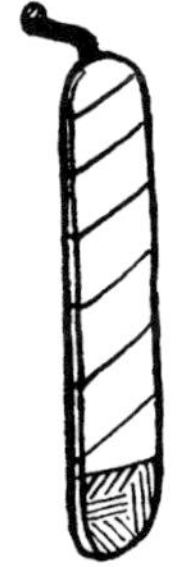

Step 5

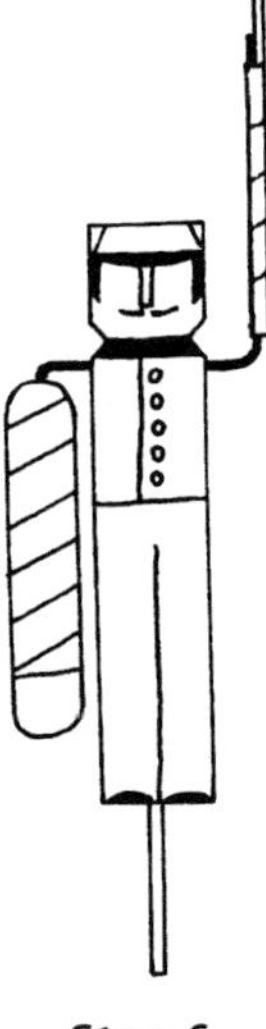

Step 6

Name ________________________ Date ________________

Project 70: Nineteenth-Century North America: Ship in a Bottle

Materials		
For this activity you will need: • bottle of clear glass • block of soft wood • piece of white cloth	• white thread • photocopy paper • putty • wood staples	• pins • screwdriver • hobby knife • spoon

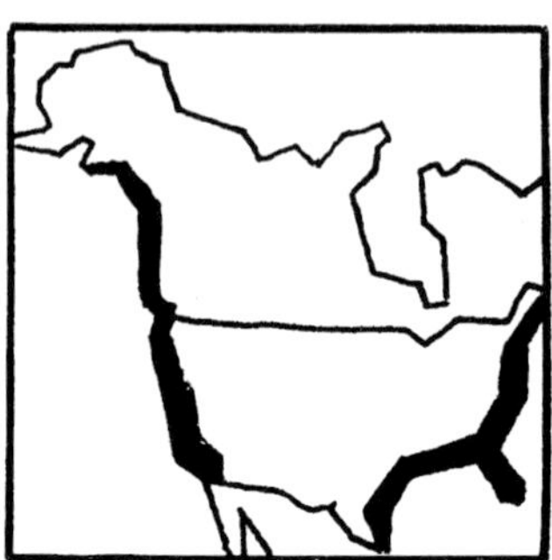

The excitement of flying we feel today was experienced in the nineteenth century by going to sea in handsome sailing ships. Young imaginations were fascinated with models of those ships with their slick shapes and the intricate rigging of their sails. More magical than the finely detailed models of famous ships are models built in bottles, like that illustrated here. How do these fully rigged, tall-masted schooners get inside? Here you perform the magic yourself with a simple ship model. Having learned the trick, you can make more elaborate models of your design.

1. Select a bottle of clear glass. Avoid a neck which is too narrow. The dimensions of your boat will depend upon the size of the bottle and its neck width.

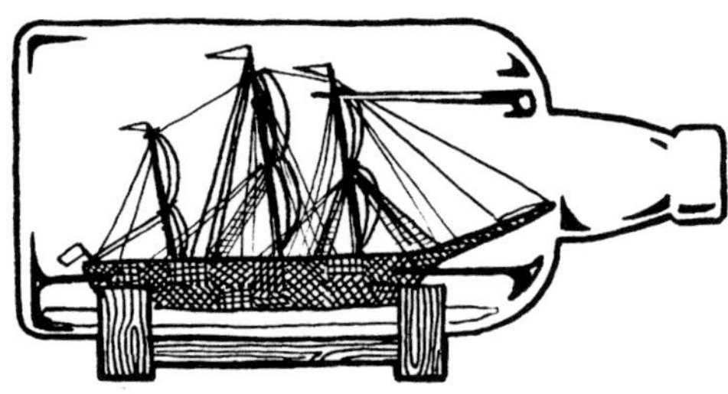

Model ship in a bottle

2. Carve the piece of wood into the shape of a ship's hull. The piece must be small enough to slip through the neck of the bottle *(Step 2)*.
3. Tightly roll a piece of photocopy paper into a pencil-thick tube and glue to keep the shape. This will be the ship's mast. It must be short enough to stand upright on the ship's hull inside the body of the bottle.

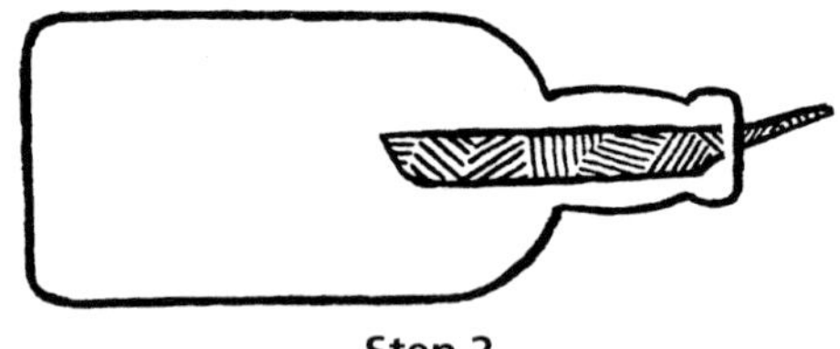

Step 2

4. Tack a wood staple onto the deck of the ship's hull as base for the mast. Tack another staple at the front of the hull *(Step 4)*.
5. Cut a notch at the bottom of the paper mast and set the notch over the mast staple on the deck. The paper mast should be able to be raised and lowered while set on the staple.
6. Make two more tight paper rolls, not wider than the ship's hull, for the yardarms of the mast. Glue each to hold the rolled shape. They must be short enough to fit across the body of the bottle when the mast is upright.

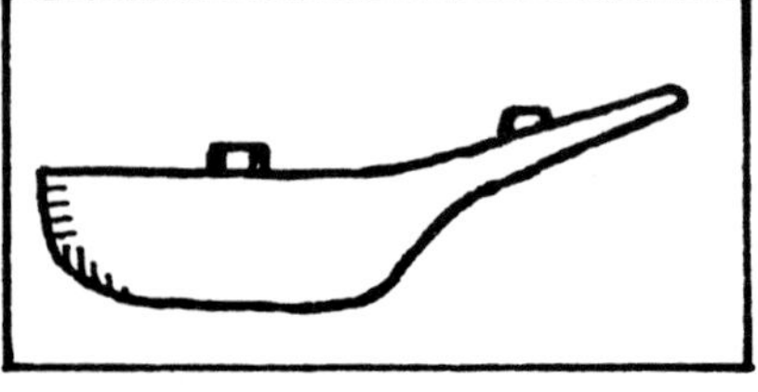

Step 4

(continued)

Name ______________________________ Date ____________________

Project 70: Nineteenth-Century North America: Ship in a Bottle *(continued)*

7. Pin the yardarms to the mast so that they can be turned. Bend the point of each pin upward after it has passed through the yardarm mast *(Steps 7 and 8).*

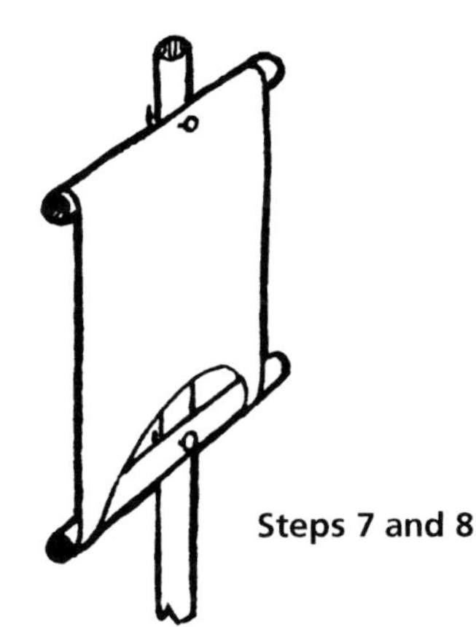

Steps 7 and 8

8. Cut a piece of cloth to fit on the yardarms then glue it to the yardarms as shown *(Steps 7 and 8).*

9. Stand the mast upright on the mast staple. Glue a piece of thread from the top of the mast down to the back of the boat *(Steps 9, 10, and 11).*

10. Glue a second thread to the top of the mast, then poke through the staple tacked to the boat front. Let the thread hang long through the staple *(Steps 9, 10, and 11).*

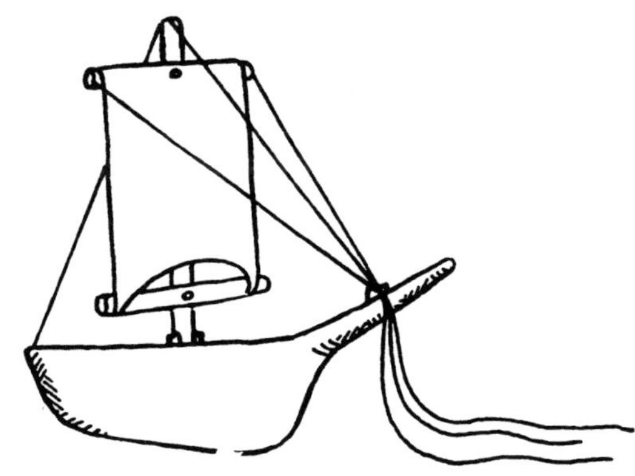

Steps 9, 10, and 11

11. Glue threads to each end of the top yardarm, then thread them through the staple tacked to the deck front, letting the long ends hang through *(Steps 9, 10, and 11).*

12. Paint the hull of the boat, the mast, and the yardarms brown. When the color has dried, decorate with details in color as you wish.

13. When the model has been decorated with colored paint, lower the mast to the deck. Turn the yardarms so that they lie parallel to the mast.

14. Spoon putty into the bottle so that the putty lies in a layer along the bottom of the bottle as it lies on its side. Pat the putty flat inside the bottle with the spoon.

(continued)

Name ______________________________ Date ______________

Project 70: Nineteenth-Century North America: Ship in a Bottle *(continued)*

15. With the mast lying down and the yardarms lying parallel to it, insert the boat into the bottle through the neck. Make sure to keep the ends of the rigging threads outside of the bottle. Using a long screwdriver, or something similar, tap the boat into the putty until it is safely stuck in place *(Step 15)*.

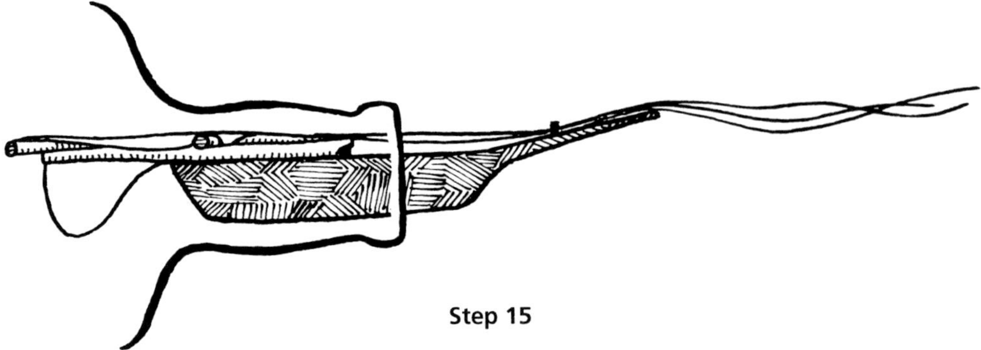

Step 15

16. The rigging threads lie through the staple of the boat bow and out the neck of the bottle. Gently pull them, raising the mast upright. Manipulate the threads of the yardarms, mast, and sail to fix them in position.
17. Put a drop of glue on the end of a stick or pencil. Reach it through the bottle neck to glue down the threads just in front of the bow staple.
18. When the glue has dried and the threads are secure, reach through the bottle neck with a hobby knife and cut off the loose thread ends. Your ship model now stands upright in the bottle.
19. When the putty has dried, after a week's time, you can paint it blue with a long-handled brush and poster color. If you wish, you can make a stand for your bottle to keep it from rolling and knocking the ship off its moorings *(Step 19)*.

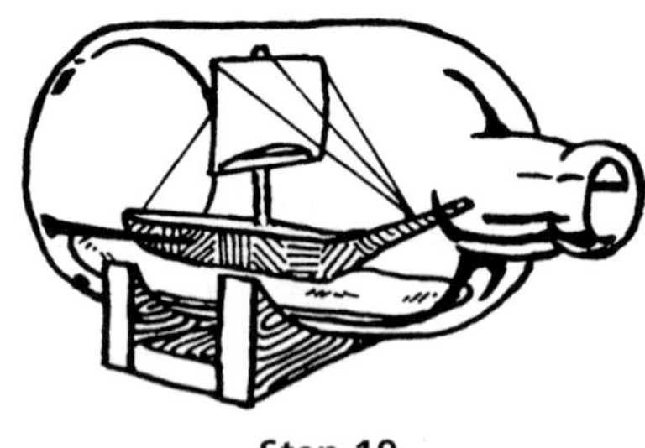

Step 19

Name ________________________________ Date ________________

Project 71: Mexico: Tree of Life

Materials	
For this activity you will need:	• wire
• self-hardening clay	• varnish
• $^1/_2$-inch-thick wooden rods	• poster paint
• 1-inch-thick wooden rod	• hand drill

The Tree of Life is said to have stood in the Garden of Eden. So Adam and Eve, angels, and the serpent are nestled among its flowers and leaves in the illustration on the next page. Above rises a figure of God with stars bobbing about. Like the Maya and Aztec artists of ancient Mexico, modern folk artists use bright colors to give life to their art. Orange (a favorite Mexican color), red, and yellow dominate the vivid hues of the Tree of Life.

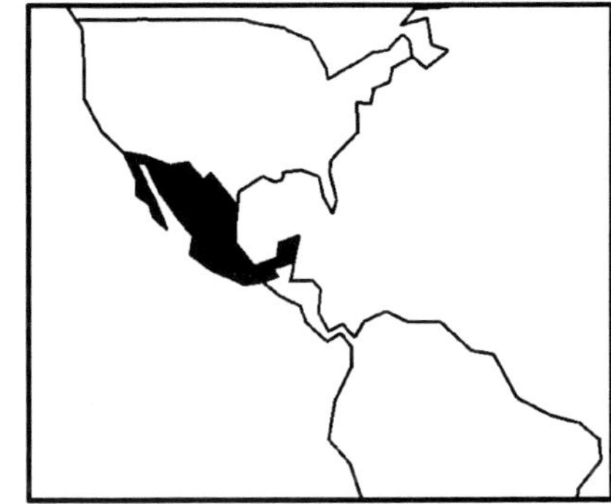

1. Begin by making a wire frame, or armature, for each object to be attached to the tree. Twist wire into the approximate shape of the intended object—an angel, star, flower, etc. Leave at least ten inches for fastening the finished piece to the tree *(Step 1)*.

2. Use clay to fashion the figure around the wire support. The long end of the wire projects from the piece *(Step 2)*.

3. When the clay has dried, paint the piece with bright colors.

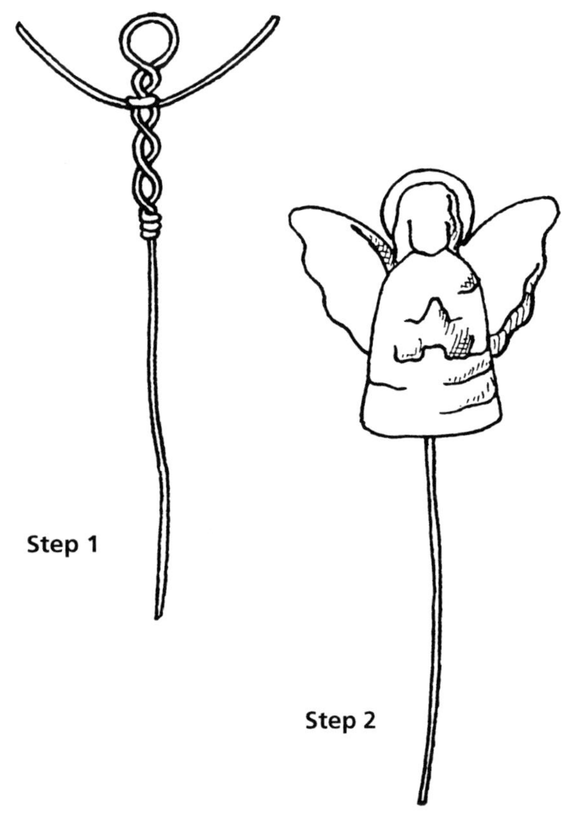

(continued)

Name ______________________________ Date ______________

Project 71: Mexico: Tree of Life *(continued)*

4. The tree structure is made by poking the small wooden rods through holes drilled in the thicker rod. This structure can be mounted in the hole of a wooden base. The size of the tree should depend on the number of people making figures for it *(Step 4)*.

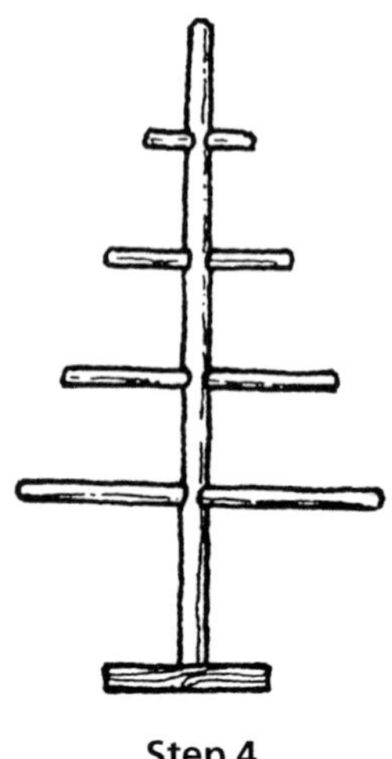

Step 4

5. Varnish the tree structure with a dark wood stain.

6. Wire the pieces to the tree, wrapping the wire ends around the rod branches. Work from the trunk outward, letting the outer angels, stars, and flowers bob on their long wire ends.

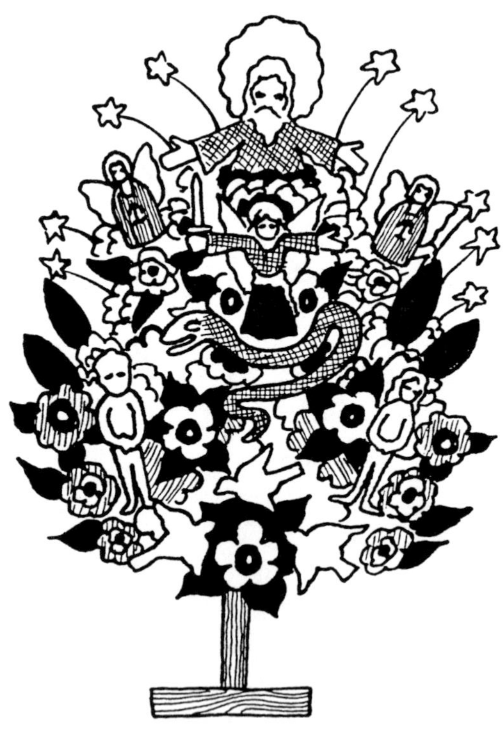

Tree of Life

Name ____________________ Date ____________

Project 72: Mexico: Flowered Skull

Materials	
For this activity you will need: • wallpaper paste or flour • collapsible ball or heavy balloon	• newspaper • petroleum jelly • enamel paint

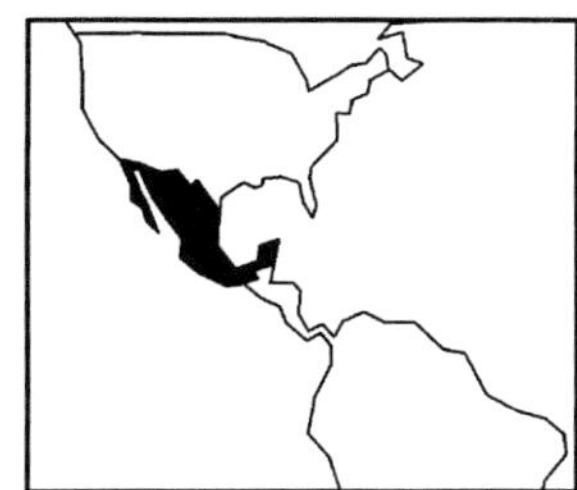

The appearance of skeletons in Mexican art continues a tradition as old as Aztec art. They show up especially on November 2, the Day of the Dead in Mexico. Skulls grin with a difference in Mexico, as folk artists paint them with bright colors and flowers. For your Halloween, or just for the fun of it, create such a flowered papier-mâché skull.

1. Papier-mâché, cheap, easy to use, and durable, is a favorite folk art material. First, rip newspaper into long strips.
2. Use a collapsible ball or heavy balloon for a model support. Spread petroleum jelly over the inflated ball or balloon.
3. Prepare wallpaper paste or mix flour with water into a pasty consistency. Holding the ends of a newspaper strip, dip and soak it in the paste. Then lay it over the ball or balloon support *(Step 3)*.

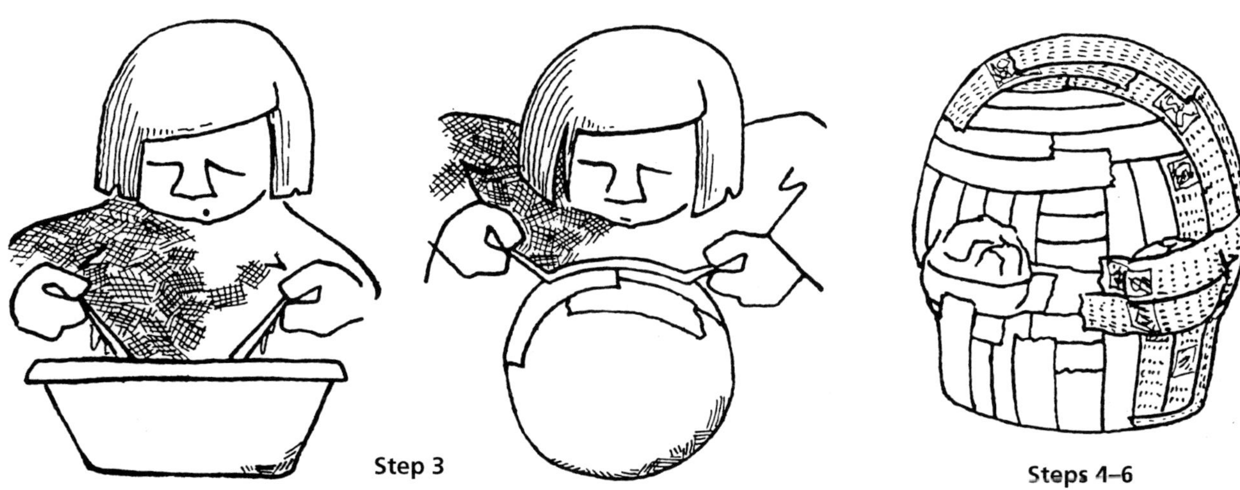

Step 3 **Steps 4–6**

4. Continue applying the paste-soaked strips, being careful to leave free the air nozzle of the ball or balloon *(Steps 4–6)*.
5. Build up two to three layers of pasty newspaper strips *(Steps 4–6)*.
6. Stick wadded paste-soaked newspaper in place for the cheeks. Build up the chin in the same way *(Steps 4–6)*.

(continued)

Name ______________________________ Date ____________________

Project 72: Mexico: Flowered Skull *(continued)*

7. When the first few layers are dry, apply several more layers of paste-soaked newspaper. Give a smooth finish to these last layers.

8. When the skull has thoroughly dried, release the air from the ball or balloon and remove it. Cover the opening with paste-soaked strips.

9. Paint the skull with enamel paint.

10. Paint flowers and other decorations to complete the skull.

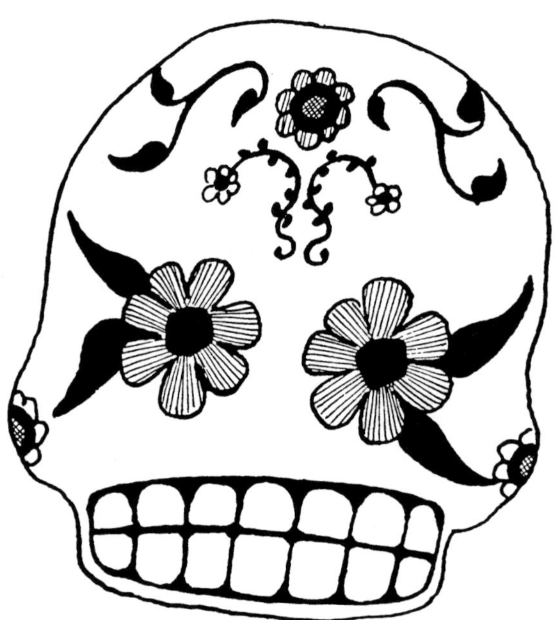

Mexican flowered skull

Name ______________________________ Date ______________

Project 73: Mexico: Tin-Can Art

Materials	
For this activity you will need:	
• tin can	• nails
• hardware-store enamel paint	• hammer

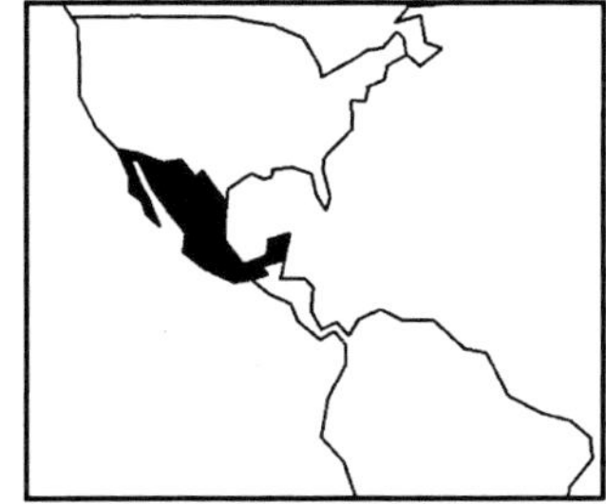

Mexican artisans have long recognized the source of working material that tin cans offer. Now, as petroleum and industrialization lead Mexico's economic development, tin-can art survives as a folk tradition. If your imagination is as rich as that of Mexican artisans, you will be able to create much from tin cans. Aluminum beverage cans are even easier to cut. Here is a suggestion.

1. Clean away any food residue inside the can. Remove the top and bottom (if necessary) with a can opener, making a clean cut. Remove the label and wash away its glue. Use steel wool to remove the painted labeling of aluminum cans. Rims can be cut away (if necessary) using tin shears.

2. Make a Mexican-style candle holder (illustrated below) by puncturing designs in the side of the can with nails or punches. Support the inside with a wood block or styrofoam to avoid flattening the can when pounding the puncturing point with a hammer.

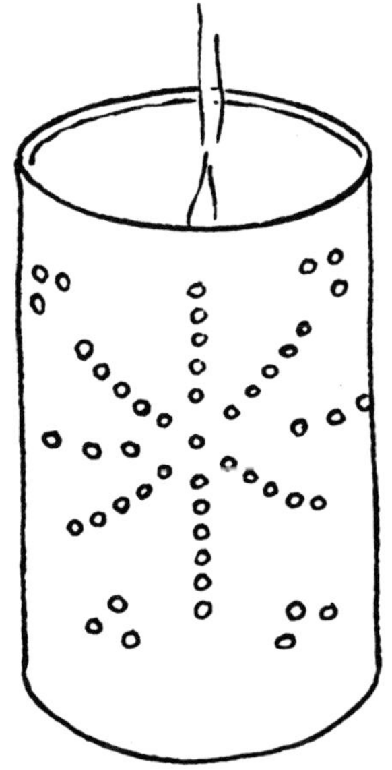

Mexican-style candle holder

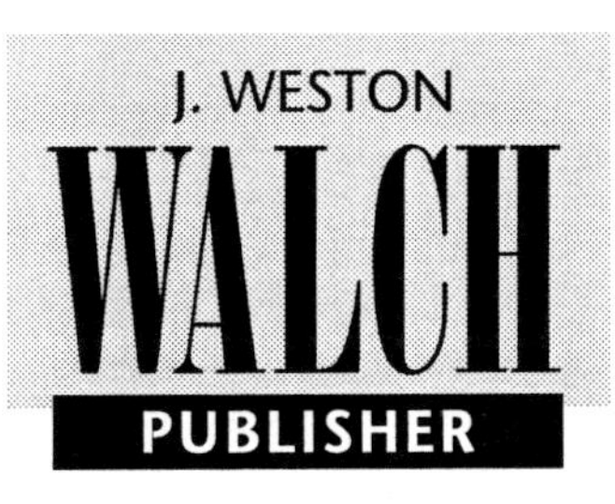

Share Your Bright Ideas with Us!

We want to hear from you! Your valuable comments and suggestions will help us meet your current and future classroom needs.

Your name____Date__________________

School name______________________________Phone________________________

School address____

Grade level taught_______Subject area(s) taught______________________Average class size_____

Where did you purchase this publication?______________________________________

Was your salesperson knowledgeable about this product? Yes_____ No_____

What monies were used to purchase this product?

___School supplemental budget ___Federal/state funding ___Personal

Please "grade" this Walch publication according to the following criteria:

Quality of service you received when purchasing	A	B	C	D	F
Ease of use	A	B	C	D	F
Quality of content	A	B	C	D	F
Page layout	A	B	C	D	F
Organization of material	A	B	C	D	F
Suitability for grade level	A	B	C	D	F
Instructional value	A	B	C	D	F

COMMENTS:____

____

What specific supplemental materials would help you meet your current—or future—instructional needs?

____

Have you used other Walch publications? If so, which ones?______________________

May we use your comments in upcoming communications? ___Yes ___No

Please **FAX** this completed form to **207-772-3105**, or mail it to:

Product Development, J.Weston Walch, Publisher, P.O. Box 658, Portland, ME 04104-0658

We will send you a **FREE GIFT** as our way of thanking you for your feedback. **THANK YOU!**